John Boyle

BLOOD RANSOM

STORIES FROM THE FRONT
LINE IN THE WAR AGAINST
SOMALI PIRACY

BLOOMSBURY
LONDON · OXFORD · NEW YORK · NEW DELHI · SYDNEY

KU-769-976

Adlard Coles Nautical
An imprint of Bloomsbury Publishing Plc

50 Bedford Square
London
WC1B 3DP
UK

1385 Broadway
New York
NY 10018
USA

www.bloomsbury.com

BLOOMSBURY, ADLARD COLES and the Diana logo are
trademarks of Bloomsbury Publishing Plc

First published 2015
This edition published 2016

British Library Cataloguing-in-Publication Data
A catalogue record for this book is available from the British Library.

Library of Congress Cataloguing-in-Publication data has been applied for.

ISBN: PB: 978-1-4729-2768-2
ePDF: 978-1-4729-1269-5
ePub: 978-1-4729-1268-8

2 4 6 8 10 9 7 5 3 1

Typeset in 11.25pt Haarlemmer MT Std by Deanta Global Publishing Services,
Chennai, India

Printed and bound in Great Britain by CPI Group (UK) Ltd, Croydon CR0 4YY

To find out more about our authors and books visit www.bloomsbury.com. Here you
will find extracts, author interviews, details of forthcoming events and the option to
sign up for our newsletters.

CONTENTS

01

A FAILED STATE

Imagine a country that has had no government for more than a generation. No law, no education, no health care. Nothing.

This country is for the most part a hostile desert of rock, scrub and thorn. Ravaged by drought and some of the planet's worst famines, one quarter of a million people dying here in just one year barely merits a mention on world news channels.

In the south, there has been a vicious civil war between brutal Muslim extremists whose favoured form of punishment is beheading, fighting an often unpaid militia loyal to the various attempts at establishing a government. At times, outside armed forces have intervened but usually withdrawn soon after having sustained unacceptable casualties. The country's capital, once a stylish Italian colonial city, is now reduced to a rubble that in places resembles Second World War Stalingrad. The rest of the country is fought over by clan chiefs and armed warlords. It's a place where the AK-47 rules. It's the place that you call home.

In the absence of any government, what were once rich fishing grounds that fed your family and village have been plundered – the reefs that your father and his before him fished have been torn up and destroyed by huge foreign fishing boats that you watched helplessly from the shore. The breeding grounds for what fish have not been sucked up by those monsters are gone, and there are no longer fish or lobster to catch.

Unnoticed by the rest of the world, the 2004 tsunami that devastated South-east Asia also wiped out your country's coastal villages and killed your friends and family. Its aftermath brought sickness to many and deformities in newborn babies, as toxic waste illegally dumped in contravention of all international law by unscrupulous European and Asian profiteers was washed ashore.

You are in your teens, your twenties, even your thirties, and have grown up to know nothing other than this. You are young, but your life has no hope and no prospects. Your family die early of hunger and illness. There is only one way you can ever make a difference in your life.

You become a pirate.

02

PIRATES IN PARADISE

The prison governor showed us through the razor-wire-topped gate, locked it and left. The Somali pirate work gang slowly put down their tools and stood watching us silently. Two white guys with cameras was something different in their day, a change from lugging blocks and mixing concrete to extend the hilltop prison that between the six of them was destined to be their home for a combined period of over 100 years.

The guard in the watchtower, automatic rifle on his shoulder, lit a cigarette and watched with detached interest.

I felt I should do something, anything to break the impasse, maybe start filming, though footage of a group of prisoners standing motionless, staring at me, was hardly going to win awards.

Then the tallest, clearly the captain as he was older than the rest, broke into a smile. 'You BBC?' Thumbs up, smile to the camera. 'Cigarette?' With no interpreter to assist, those seemed to be the only words we had in common.

Apart from the captain, none appeared over 20 years old. In their blue prison fatigues, they looked exactly what they were – impoverished young Africans who had seen a way out of poverty and taken it. Except for one who looked angry that we were there and repeatedly made slashing motions with his finger across his neck, face-to-face they didn't fit my image of ferocious marauders of the sea. I might have had a different impression if they were pointing AK-47s at me, ripping through my possessions, and steering my boat towards the Somali coast to face months of captivity as a hostage.

A month before, I'd had no idea of the complex story surrounding piracy in the Indian Ocean, beyond occasional BBC news headlines about pirates taking a vessel or themselves being captured. Then, on Facebook of all places, I'd seen an album of photos taken by a friend of mine – Ronny Jumeau, Seychelles Ambassador to the UN – shot on a day he went out with the Seychelles Coastguard. I'd put together a loose proposal for a documentary, *Pirates in Paradise*, to *National Geographic*, and when they gave me the green light, I'd headed to Seychelles to track down the story.

And with Ronny's help, the story had just unfolded for us. If only journalism were always this easy!

On aerial patrol with the Seychelles Defence Force, I witnessed the incredible surveillance power of the on-board cameras – a capability that has helped secure the prosecution of many alleged pirates who, realising capture was inevitable, threw their weapons overboard so they could claim just to be innocent sailors blown off course. Little did they realise that their every action had been caught in detail by the plane circling several kilometres away.

There was an uncanny similarity between the aircrew and the pirate crew – apart from the South African pilot, all were young men in their early twenties, passionate in the defence of their ocean. I wondered if the tables had been turned – the pirates being born in Seychelles, and the aircrew in Somalia – how many of the aircrew would also have ended up as pirates trying for a better life for themselves, and how many of the pirates would have ended up guarding their seas.

Later, filming outside Victoria's Central Court, it was hard to think that the dozen men – many just boys – sitting smoking in the sunshine were among those who had brought world shipping to its knees. Dressed now in clean casual clothing supplied by the prison, well fed and with the sores of weeks at sea healed, they looked little different to passing Seychellois. Only the fact that they were handcuffed in pairs gave them away as being some of the most wanted men on the planet – each looking at sentences exceeding 20 years for piracy.

Judge Duncan Gaswaga had given us special permission to film in his court. In the tiny court room, paint peeling from its walls, the pirates sat disinterestedly as the lawyers haggled over legal issues. Many of the defendants were in their teens – one claimed to be just 12 years old and certainly looked no older than that – but of course none had any documents. Every now and then, when a point was raised that needed their attention, they would huddle round the single interpreter as he explained to them what was happening.

These pirates were running the defence of being simple fishermen, blown off course. The fact that when they were captured there was not a single fishing line, hook or net on board, and no means of freezing or salting their catch, didn't seem to them a problem.

While the court progressed and the lawyers debated legal technicalities, I focused my camera on the Somali defendants. The hearing seemed of no interest to them. Occasionally they chatted quietly among themselves; some seemed to glaze over and be close to sleep. The 12-year-old seemed confused and a little scared by all that was happening around him. These were the first alleged pirates that I had encountered in the flesh, and they were as far away from the demonised image I had expected as could be imagined. I started wondering about their back stories.

Who were these pirates who were costing the international economy an estimated US$12 billion every year, and who were making the seas off the Somali coast the world's most dangerous stretch of ocean? Were they just young men driven to piracy by desperation, or were they part of a far wider criminal conspiracy?

Prosecutor Michael Mulkerrins had at that time jailed more Somali pirates than anyone else on the planet, and saw them just as small players in a bigger picture. 'The foot soldiers have got nothing to lose. We've heard stories about them being paid 500 US dollars, or the first one on the bridge gets a Mercedes. If they are successful, they earn money and respect back home. If they are not successful, they are expendable.'

Defence lawyer Tony Juliette was in daily contact with his pirate clients. To him, they seemed accepting of their situation – maybe the food and treatment they received in a Seychelles prison was preferable to the hardships they had undergone. 'I've found them to be very, very simple folks and very indifferent to the circumstances that they were facing. Despite having advised them of the severity of the charges, they did not appear too overly concerned about the potential personal consequences to them.'

Like hyenas of the sea, Somali pirates range over a thousand kilometres from their home shores seeking their prey. Most, when arrested, have open sores from exposure to sun and salt, and many are suffering from malnutrition. No one knows how many are simply lost at sea, dying of starvation after running out of fuel, or drowning when their boat sinks. They have to take on the worst that the Indian Ocean can throw at them.

On board the European Union Naval Force (EUNAVFOR) flagship SPS *Patiño*, Commander Enrique Cubeiro told me how even that huge vessel had been attacked by pirates. In rough 3- to 4-metre seas, about 45 minutes before dawn, pirates on a small skiff approached and tried to board, firing AK-47s at the ship – the bullet holes were still visible. This experienced naval commander expressed his views on the pirates as seamen: 'For me, it's impressive that they stay in these conditions all this time at sea.'

One-third of all the planet's oil passes through the Gulf of Aden: rich pickings for the pirates, and they have had some spectacular successes. In 2009, the fully laden Saudi tanker MV *Sirius Star*, with ship and cargo together valued at around US$150 million, was released after payment of a US$3 million ransom. Within a year, that ransom was way surpassed by the US$9 million paid in 2010 for the Greek-owned MV *Maran Centaurus*. The world was equally shocked when pirates captured the Ukrainian ship MV *Faina*, carrying a cargo of tanks and weapons. After a ransom in excess of US$3 million was paid, the pirate leader was quoted as saying '... no huge amount has been paid, but something to cover our expenses.'

The Somali pirates have also had outstanding failures, such as the container ship MV *Maersk Alabama*, captured by four pirates in April 2009.

When it became clear that the *Alabama* was being boarded, Captain Phillips sent his crew to a safe room deep below decks from where the ship's engines could be controlled. When Phillips was captured on the bridge by the pirates the crew shut down the engines and power, leaving the ship dead in the water. While searching for the secure room, the pirate leader Muse was captured by the Chief Engineer Mike Perry in a struggle that resulted in Muse receiving a stab wound to the hand. Meanwhile, American warships USS *Bainbridge* and *Halyburton* were closing on the scene.

The pirates realised that their best course was to abandon the *Alabama* in the ship's lifeboat, which could get them back to Somalia. The crew agreed a hostage exchange – Muse for

Phillips – but at the last minute the pirates forced Phillips to accompany them.

During the stand-off between the American warships and the pirates in the lifeboat, Navy SEALS were parachuted to the scene, and the pirate leader Muse was lured on board one of the ships, purportedly to negotiate their safe passage to Somalia. In an impressive display of marksmanship, the SEALS succeeded in simultaneously shooting all three remaining pirates still on board the lifeboat and rescuing Captain Phillips. The fourth pirate, Abduwali Muse, who features more than once in this book, is presently serving a 33-year sentence in a US prison.

Three years after the *Maersk Alabama* incident, on the bridge of another container ship of the Maersk fleet operating in the same region, the Filipino captain showed me his chart, on which he recorded pirate encounters with a pencilled cross. There were a surprising number of crosses on his chart – though so far the ship had managed to evade being boarded.

'Every night we pray for safety here, because this is our life – pirates any time. We don't know what will happen to us.'

On board the Basque purse-seiner MV *Alakrana*, I watched the catch of huge silver tuna being unloaded. This boat had already been captured once by pirates in October 2009, the ship and its crew of 36 released after 47 days, after payment of a ransom said to be US$4 million. Two pirates captured once the ransom was paid were tried in Madrid, and received sentences totalling 439 years each. The vessel continues to fish the rich fishing grounds of the western Indian Ocean and has already been subject to another pirate attack, this one fought off by the armed on-board security.

No boat is safe – but it's the smaller vessels and their crews whose stories nobody knows.

Few will have heard of Gilbert Victor, a simple boat-delivery skipper, but he was the first Seychellois to be taken by Somali pirates. He didn't want to talk in any detail about the seven months held hostage at the point of AK-47s, but a tear trickled down his cheek as our conversation reopened the memories. He told me that ours was the last interview he would give. He just wants to be left alone and to forget.

Gilbert thinks 'pirates' too kindly a word. 'They are hijackers. It's just like they hijack a plane. Will you call them Somali hijackers – that's what these people are – kidnappers.'

Nor will many have come across Rolly Tambara, a 70-year-old grandfather whose tiny fishing boat was seized, and who was subjected to mistreatment and brutality during the 12 months he was held hostage.

And then there are the forgotten hostages – poor seafarers from Third World countries, who are still being held, abandoned by their shipowners.

There is another side to the Somali pirates' story.

The root cause of piracy is that the world has left Somalia to its own devices for over 20 years, which has resulted in a state of anarchy and lawlessness. To put it in the most basic terms, Somalia has become a state in free fall.

With no functioning government to protect their waters, the seas off Somalia fell victim to twin evils – the pillage of fish stocks by foreign fleets fishing illegally in their waters, and uncontrolled dumping of toxic waste.

Calling themselves the Somali Coastguard, small bands of Somali fishermen, who saw their livelihood being taken from them, started approaching the foreign vessels and hijacking them to extract compensation.

That's how it started. But things have moved on. Piracy has become big business.

I met with Seychelles government minister Joel Morgan, who leads the country's battle against piracy. He was uncompromising. 'Piracy is organised crime. It involves international financing. It involves a number of people who are implicated in terrorism. It involves a number of people who are in it just for the money, and it involves also people from within Somalia who see it as an investment – a very lucrative but risky business.'

While the pirates have had financial successes – and this is reflected in visible improvements in the standard of living in pirate-inhabited areas of Somalia – the annual cost of piracy to the world economy has been estimated by the World Bank at a staggering US$18 billion.

With vessel insurance rates rocketing, a whole new security industry has grown around the pirate threat and for the first time in our planet's history, the navies of every superpower have united in battle against a common enemy – a couple of thousand ragtag, barefoot Somalis in small boats. These massive international efforts seemed to be having results: the problem is contained by a steel ring of warships and aerial surveillance. Contained, but by no means eradicated.

Minister Joel Morgan's prognosis was pessimistic: 'Piracy is definitely increasing in its range and evolving in its nature. And it will continue to do so as long as there is a possibility of capturing ships and human beings and holding them to ransom, and as long as the state of Somalia remains a failed state. Basically, the problem of piracy lies on land in Somalia.'

As the story evolved for our film, I found myself wondering. If the seas off my coastal village home had been ravaged by overfishing, if I had watched my family go hungry and my children suffer from ailments caused by the dumping of toxic waste, would I too have turned in desperation to piracy?

The documentary was delivered and aired around the world, but the story of Somali piracy and its victims continued to progress. Usually when a film is finished, I move on to the next project, but the tragic story of Somalia and the strange phenomenon of its

21st-century pirates had hooked me. I wanted to learn more; I wanted to be able to talk with the convicted pirates whom I had filmed in the prison to discover what desperation had driven them to risk their lives in small boats at sea.

I had to go back...

03

THE LEGENDARY LAND OF PUNT

The legendary Land of Punt, sometimes known as the land of the god, was an Egyptian trading partner known for producing and exporting the goods most treasured by ancient civilisations; the exotic, such as wild creatures and ivory; the essential slaves; the aromatic resins favoured most by the wealthy, such as myrrh and frankincense; and of course the greatest treasure of all, gold.

The exact location of Punt is still debated by historians but it is quite possible that this rich and fabled land could have been what is today called Somalia. The Bible's three wise men may well have started their journey in what is now Somalia's pirate region of Puntland.

Throughout the 19th and 20th century, Somalia was shaped as a result of British, French and Italian colonialism. In 1936, Italy created Italian East Africa, encompassing much of central Somalia and regions of Ethiopia, while British Somaliland in the north was considered vital to Britain's strategic influence in the Gulf of Aden. During the Second World War, both nations fought over their interests, but in 1950 the boundaries of what would eventually become today's Somalia were defined – the UN Trust Territory of Italian Somaliland, together with British Somaliland.

Independence granted by Italy and Britain in 1960 created a united Somalia – a poor, underdeveloped, divided fledgling country with little real chance of success.

None of this meant much to the Somali people, whose existence had always been based not on nationhood but on two basic tenets – their family and clan history and allegiances, together with a nomadic lifestyle. While the average Somali was unable to read or write, they could recite their family history back up to 20 generations. Due to the hostile nature of the country, their lifestyle was a nomadic one, herding their animals and following water and grazing wherever it might be found.

As in so many places in the world, the boundaries drawn by former colonial powers had little bearing on the true situation. To this day, so many of the planet's war zones have been created by jolly nice chaps in a government office thousands of kilometres away, drawing a line on a map to create a jolly nice new country: Palestine; Cyprus; India and Pakistan; Northern Ireland ... Somalia was no different. The borders of the new country did not take into account that Somalis dominated areas of Kenya, Djibouti, and Ethiopia. The nomadic existence of many Somali herders and the ill-defined frontiers worsened the problem. Somalia as a country never existed – it was another product of Western colonialism leaving lines on a map and saying, 'Here you are, you are now a country under one government. Good luck!' It never was a genuine nation state – and despite best efforts probably never will be.

Instead of focusing on building the country internally, within four years of independence Somalia was involved in border conflicts with both Ethiopia and Kenya.

In 1969, within two years of his election, Somalia's second democratically elected President, Abdirashid Ali Sharmarke, was assassinated by his own bodyguard – not the first attempt on his life. Shortly afterwards, Mohamed Siad Barre assumed power in a military coup. Barre declared Somalia a socialist state, nationalised most of the economy and developed strong ties with the Soviet Union. His was a brutal Marxist dictatorship, insisting upon the supremacy of party and nation, as opposed to the local clan loyalties that are such a strong feature of Somali culture.

Despite widespread starvation caused by a severe drought in 1974–1975, Barre embarked on an invasion of the Somali-inhabited Ogaden region of Ethiopia in 1977. It was a war that the impoverished country, already on its knees, just could not afford nor hope to win. The Soviets sided with Ethiopia, and with the help of Soviet advisers and Cuban troops, the Ethiopians repelled the Somali army. In addition to the loss of much of the Somali army's tanks and planes, the war had another impact – the mass exodus of hundreds of thousands of displaced Somali refugees from Ethiopia over the borders into Somalia, a country totally unable to deal with the human tragedy of the influx.

Although he clung to power for a total of 20 years, this disastrous campaign was the start of a long slide into political decline for Barre. Clan- and regional-based guerrilla groups proliferated, all with the aim of overthrowing this disastrous totalitarian government. In response, and ignoring the traditional importance of the clan system, Barre increasingly centred his government and all investment in the capital Mogadishu, with members of his own clan awarded almost all positions of influence. In 1988, full-scale civil war broke out and by 1991 Barre had fled the country, leaving behind him a nation of feuding warlords.

Somalia descended into anarchy, and the most intense conflict in the south disrupted farming and livestock production, causing widespread famine. Food flown in by international agencies was looted by the warring militias. In December 1992, the UN actively intervened, sending a peacekeeping force of 35,000 troops (including US Marines) in Operation Restore Hope to re-establish order and safeguard relief supplies.

This intervention by the UN between 1992 and 1995 proved a futile attempt to shore up the now fragmented and collapsed nation state. In 1993, 18 US Army Rangers were killed when Somali militias shot down two US helicopters over Mogadishu. Hundreds of Somalis died in the ensuing battle, depicted in the film *Black Hawk Down*. The US involvement formally ended in March 1994, and in March 1995 the remaining UN forces were evacuated, having failed to achieve their mission.

Meanwhile, the nation created on a drawing board by European bureaucrats continued to fall apart. The former British protectorate of Somaliland declared unilateral independence in 1991, while the Puntland region declared autonomy in 1998.

During the rest of the decade, the situation got worse rather than better. From late 1994, the capital Mogadishu was divided between the two most powerful of the warring factions. The only remotely stable region was the breakaway republic of Somaliland in the north-west, which had introduced an interim constitution in 1997, with an elected president. Beyond its territory, the would-be republic did not succeed in winning international recognition.

By 2004, no less than 14 attempts had been made to establish transitional governments, whose range of influence was often just a few city blocks of Mogadishu, well within mortar range of Islamist insurgents. Meanwhile, as often unpaid soldiers engaged in a vicious and bloody struggle over individual streets and houses in the capital, the remainder of the country was ignored and left with no government other than what could be cobbled together locally with zero funding.

During this decade, the Islamic Courts Union (ICU) became for a time Somalia's strongest fighting force, seizing most of the south of the country and also Mogadishu, driving out the Transitional

Federal Government (TFG) and competing warlords who had controlled the capital for almost 15 years and immediately imposing Shari'a law. The TFG, with the assistance of Ethiopian troops and African Union peacekeepers, managed to drive out the ICU and regain control of the capital.

Fighting continued throughout the southern part of the country between Al Shabab (an extremist offshoot of the ICU, now allied with Al Qaeda) and government forces backed by African Union troops. The brutality of Al Shabab is horrific, featuring executions, beheadings and the chopping off of limbs as the norm.

So volatile is Mogadishu, the seat of government, that President Abdullahi Yusuf only entered the city in 2007 for the first time since taking office in 2004. Al Shabab continues to hold large swathes of the country and to launch attacks in Mogadishu.

Contingents from Burundi, Uganda, Ethiopia, Kenya, Djibouti and Sierra Leone, among others, have tried to bring peace, suffering considerable casualties of their own in the process. The West seems to have left it to Africa to sort out its own problem.

Al Shabab's destabilising regime of terror isn't just limited to Somalia; they are active throughout the region. They claimed full responsibility for the attack on the Westgate shopping mall in Nairobi, apparently in response to Kenyan forces being deployed against them inside Somalia. At the end of 48 hours of carnage – a suicide attack that none of the terrorists survived – 67 people were dead and around 175 wounded.

From the outside, Somalia looks like a chaotic mess. Anarchy and warfare reign in the south, surrounding the supposed seat of national government in Mogadishu – a government that at times is only a few city streets away from the front line. The north enjoys a relative degree of stability in Somaliland, and to a lesser degree in Puntland, having some of the features of true government.

But Somalia has a structure of its own. Somalis have a long tradition of fierce wars between clans, and of intense loyalties to family, tribe and clan. The post-imperial vision has already broken down into three clearly independent, self-governing states with the Mogadishu coalition government being irrelevant to the northerly Puntland and Somaliland. Yet the divisions run even greater and deeper – analysts also regard as autonomous to some degree the territories of Northland, Maakhir, Galmudug, Ahlu Sunna Wal Jama'a (itself geographically two regions), and of course the fluctuating areas controlled by Al Shabab and the Hisbul Islami. Even within these geographical zones there are further subdivisions of the clans. How could this ever represent a united nation? It's a unique society and should never have been set up as a single state. But it was...

As if Somalia had not been dealt a bad enough hand, nature continued to conspire against the nation and its people. The ravages of drought and famine struck repeatedly, in a country with no overall infrastructure nor government to deal with it. The UN appealed time and again for food aid for over half a million starving people who had left their homes, headed for the towns and cities seeking survival and found themselves in refugee camps.

One might imagine things couldn't possibly get worse, but they did. In December 2004, tsunami waves generated by an undersea earthquake off Indonesia hit the Somali coast. Hundreds of deaths were reported; tens of thousands of people were displaced.

That decade was a sad litany of continued natural disaster and manmade misery. Droughts in the years 2000, 2001, 2005, 2006, 2008 and 2011 left an estimated three million or more Somalis on the brink of starvation, in a country with a population of just ten million. The 2011 drought was the worst that had struck the country in 60 years. The tales of individual suffering and tragedy were countless. With almost annual crises and droughts, even the relief agencies reported donor fatigue from contributors to aid.

The complexity of the ever-changing political situation, of the ever-shifting front lines of battle, of territory lost and held almost by the city block, of starvation and relief efforts, of international intervention both successful and not, of the involvement of African Union forces and their dead and wounded – this history of Somalia over the last couple of decades would itself fill a book. It has been estimated that over 400,000 have been killed in fighting since 1991; that in the two years alone between 2010 and 2012, 260,000 died of starvation; and that 1.5 million people have fled the country, many only to refugee camps in neighbouring nations.

It is against this background that the phenomenon of Somali piracy was born.

Somalia had never had a well-developed fishing industry; historically, it had been entirely local and on a small scale. Until the second half of the 20th century, few Somalis outside fishing communities consumed fish. One Somali described the attitude of his countrymen to me: 'Why should I eat fish when I can eat goat or mutton...'

This had begun to change in the 1970s with the development of better cold-storage facilities and the creation, with Soviet help, of an industrial fleet. Sadly, for want of spare parts and maintenance, these vessels had fallen into disuse, and fishing again became mainly of importance to coastal villages and towns.

Somalia's coastline is the longest on the African continent, and the Indian Ocean off its shores is – or was – abundant with fish. Massive shoals of tuna and Spanish mackerel roamed the continental shelf, all but fished out in many regions of the planet's seas, but until the collapse of government in Somalia, barely exploited here.

Most of the coastal communities in Somalia had survived from their rich inshore waters, fishing from small open boats within sight of land, where their fathers and grandfathers had fished before them. As with all artisanal fisheries, there had been a natural balance – the manner of fishing and the quantity of fish taken had no impact on fish stocks. As an illustration, many Somalis fished by freediving for lobster, which were so plentiful on the coral reef they could be collected by a man on one lungful of air.

With the collapse of central government to defend the waters, or control and license the fisheries, huge industrial vessels from both Europe and Asia arrived for the pillage – like a modern-day gold rush. The boats came in with giant trawl nets that not only removed the fish but also destroyed the reef. Since their arrival, lobsters have not been seen for many years in certain regions. Furthermore, these high-tech craft, with their spotter helicopters and purse-seine nets, can encircle and destroy a school of tuna within hours.

The neutral wording of a 2005 report by the Food and Agriculture Organization of the UN (UNFAO), simply assessing world fish stocks, and with no ulterior motives, stated:

'The large pelagic species are tuna and big mackerels, mainly yellowfin tuna, longtail tuna, bonito, skipjack tuna and Spanish mackerel. They are usually caught in inshore waters... They also make important contributions to artisanal fishery production. These stocks are lightly exploited by the artisanal fishery sector, but are heavily exploited by the industrial fishery sector, mainly by foreign-flag distant-water fishing fleets, and it is possible that they are overexploited.'

The UNFAO report continued: 'There are also an estimated 700 foreign-owned vessels that are fully engaged in unlicensed fishing in Somali waters. This illegal, unregulated, and unreported fishing, offshore as well as inshore, with the difficulties it causes for legitimate Somali fishermen, causes great problems for monitoring, control and surveillance of the Somali EEZ (Exclusive Economic Zone). It is impossible to monitor their fishery production in general, let alone the state of the fishery resources they are exploiting.'

There was no stopping the illegal fishing: no control on quantities taken; no control over species quotas; no control over net mesh size; no control over use of trawls that damaged the seabed and the reef; totally out-of-control mass destruction of the ocean habitat, whether by the most high-tech Western purse-seiner or by the dirtiest, oldest, rustiest tub from a poor Asian nation. Fleets that had destroyed their own fish stocks in the fishing grounds of their own nations and in the wider ocean – who should have known better, but who scented easy money – despoiled the seas off Somalia as there was no law, government, higher authority, navy or coastguard to prevent them.

High-seas trawlers from countries as far-flung as South Korea, Japan and Spain have operated down the Somali coast, un-policed, unregulated and without licences, for the best part of two decades, according to the UN. They often fly flags of convenience, which aid the ships in skirting international regulations and evading censure from their home countries. There is no doubt at all that this illegal fishing was the catalyst for the piracy problem.

Not only were their fish stocks destroyed, but the Somalis' own nets were swept away by these huge industrial vessels, they complained of being fired on by foreign fishermen with water cannons and firearms, and at times their very boats were crushed by the foreign ships and the crews lost at sea. Again quoting the UNFAO report:

'The foreign vessels compete with the artisanal fishermen, by coming close inshore and inflicting losses, including physical confrontation between the two sides which has led to gear losses and at times to loss of life.'

Another United Nations report in 2006 said that Somali waters had become the site of an 'El Dorado for fishing fleets of many nations', ruthlessly looting Somali stocks and freezing out the region's own rudimentarily equipped fishermen. An estimated US$300 million-worth of seafood was being stolen from the country's coastline each year, and it could well be more, as the foreign fishermen were not exactly furnishing accurate accounts! Impossible to quantify is the cost of the destruction of habitat that once supported Somalia's coastal fisheries.

Uninhibited illegal fishing and the consequent degradation of the marine habitat were not the only issues. The 2005 UNFAO report comments: 'There is also strong suspicion of illegal dumping of industrial and nuclear wastes along the Somali coast.'

Although Somalia's political instability has hampered the collection of conclusive scientific data in support of this, historic dumping of toxic waste in the country seems to be a generally accepted fact. While certain Asian nations stand accused, the principal trail of evidence leads back to Italy, Somalia's former colonial ruler.

As environmental legislation throughout Europe became more rigorous in the 1980s, the costs involved in disposal of contaminated wastes of all types – toxic, nuclear and hazardous – spiralled. Multiple permissions were required, along with transporters with fully licensed specialist vehicles, and a final approved and safe dumping site. Wherever huge profits can be made, organised crime scents an opportunity, and here it lay in circumventing the safe and lawful disposal of such waste products, cutting all the corners, and disposing of waste from questionable sources.

Toxic waste from throughout Europe and the United States was channelled into Italy, where a Mafia syndicate, the 'Ndrangheta, took over. There were allegations of unauthorised and unsafe disposal on land, but many allegations centred around disposal at sea. A supergrass named Francesco Fonti, himself previously a member of 'Ndrangheta, told of the sinking of at least 30 ships laden with toxic waste, much of it radioactive.

The initial dumping ground was the Mediterranean. The Italian environmental NGO Legambiente provided Italian prosecutors with data concerning the suspicious disappearance of around 40 ships in the Mediterranean – vessels that were carrying dubious cargoes, which disappeared in good weather sending out no MAYDAY, and whose crews had then simply vanished.

Fonti also told of Somalia as a preferred location for dumping the waste, citing one specific example of 600 drums of toxic waste from Italy, Switzerland, Germany, France and the USA, whose final destination was the Somali coast.

In the mid-1990s, the Italian press was filled with reports about the scandal. An Italian investigative TV journalist, Ilaria Alpi, and her cameraman were researching the story when they were murdered in Somalia. According to Fonti, they were eliminated because they had witnessed toxic waste actually arriving in the Somali port of Bosaso.

As sensational scandals alleging paybacks to politicians and cover-ups in the highest places rocked Italy, the containers on the Somali seabed lay slowly rotting. In many cases, regulated disposal of toxic waste requires containers with a 1,000-year life. The cheap metal canisters used in this illegal dumping were a rusting time bomb – one that exploded when huge tsunami waves lifted them from the shallow coastal waters up on to the shore, splitting many open, with documented horrific results. One survey in 2006, over a year after the tsunami of Boxing Day 2004, identified 15 containers of confirmed nuclear and chemical waste in eight coastal areas, showing the wide geographical spread of the issue. Another researcher documented illnesses directly attributable to the waste, including widespread cancers and gruesome birth defects.

A 2005 United Nations Environmental Programme (UNEP) report cited uranium, radioactive, and other hazardous deposits leading to a rash of respiratory ailments and skin diseases breaking out in villages along the Somali coast. According to the UN, at the time of the report it cost US$2.50 per ton for a European company to dump these types of material off the Horn of Africa, as opposed to US$250 per ton to dispose of them cleanly in Europe.

The UNEP report confirmed that waste washed up on Somali shores caused serious health problems: 'Contamination from the waste deposits has caused health and environmental problems to the surrounding local fishing communities including contamination of groundwater. Many people have complained of unusual health problems as a result of the tsunami winds blowing towards inland villages. The health problems include acute respiratory infections, dry heavy coughing and mouth bleeding, abdominal haemorrhages, unusual skin chemical reactions, and sudden death after inhaling toxic materials.'

No one knows how many more canisters still lie off the Somali shores, slowly seeping their poison into the sea and the food chain. The planet's most unfortunate nation, ungoverned, devastated by civil war, drought and famine, its oceans pillaged, now also had to suffer toxic and radioactive waste causing sickness, deformity and death.

The Somali fishermen watched helpless from the shore, until someone had the idea to go out and get something back from those exploiting and destroying their ocean. They started heading out to sea from ports such as Eyl, Kismayo and Harardhere – all now considered as pirate dens – to challenge the foreign vessels. The names under which they operated, such as the National Volunteer Coastguard of Somalia or the Somali Marines, are testament to the fishermen-turned-pirates' initial motivations.

Nobody seems to dispute that this is how piracy started in Somalia. The fishermen would motor out to a boat that was indisputably fishing in their waters, board it and demand a fine – a payment for fishing there.

And for a time this is how it was.

04

ONE OF THE OLDEST PROFESSIONS

For as long as men have gone to sea in boats, there have been other men in boats looking to attack and rob them.

In the era of the great civilisations of Egypt, Carthage, Greece and Rome, the Eastern Mediterranean was never free of the scourge of piracy. The cities of these empires needed supplies from the furthest reaches of their territories. Nests of pirates operated from bases among remote islands or along the North African coast, preying on the slow-moving galleys that carried the food and treasures to build and feed the new phenomenon of these huge cities. With carriage by ship being the only practical way to transport valuable goods, especially precious metals, the high seas were fertile hunting grounds for pirates.

Those early pirates also knew the value of hostages, and would hold any persons of wealth or with political status to ransom. Even

Julius Caesar was once captured by pirates – although on his release he raised a fleet to find and crucify his former captors.

The pirates who roamed the seas in the days of the great European empires of Britain, France, Spain and Portugal have morphed in folklore from villains to Johnny Depp-styled heroes. While the Spanish plundered the riches of the ancient civilisations of Central and South America, swashbuckling buccaneers raided the easy pickings of heavily laden treasure ships making their way home to Europe.

Later, many of these brigands of the high seas were legitimised as privateers – with their vessels independent of any navy, but carrying letters of marque to loot enemy ships in the almost constant state of war between the European naval powers.

The sea routes from the East Indies carrying the exotic treasures of India and the islands of Asia – including spices, silk and ivory, as well as silver and gold – also attracted pirates, and the jungle coast of East Africa and its estuaries and islands offered them countless hiding places for their bases.

By the 20th century, with modern ships and communications, piracy seemed to have died out save in a few isolated locations.

One long-standing hotspot of piracy is West Africa's Gulf of Guinea. Today, oil tankers are the favourite target of pirates whose booty is the valuable cargo of fuel that is quickly trans-shipped on to smaller tankers, taken ashore, and sold on the black market almost openly.

These pirates tend to be land-based criminals, mainly from Nigeria; organised gangs who will not hesitate to use extreme violence. Piracy here is easy and big business, in a country rife with corruption, and offering countless hiding places in the small private ports and docks that proliferate in the massive Niger delta. The huge Nigerian oil industry is in chaos, and pirates take advantage of that. Around two-thirds of attacks in this region occur while tankers are stationary – either at terminals, on moorings waiting to discharge their load, or while trans-shipping cargo – unlike Somalia, where all attacks are on moving vessels.

Violence is a trademark of the West African pirates, but they have no interest in taking either the tanker or crew hostage – only in stealing the valuable cargo. It's a highly organised and profitable criminal business – from the pirates who actually board the tankers and the smaller ships on to which the oil is unloaded, to the private harbour facilities that are the link in the chain of supply to the black-market street buyers of the fuel. It is proving so lucrative that analysts fear its geographic scope is spreading.

Another high-risk pirate area is the Malacca Strait between Malaysia and Indonesia. The late 20th century saw a resurgence in the piracy that had been almost a tradition there: piracy in the Malacca Strait is nothing new – it's been going on for hundreds of years. Like the Gulf of Aden, the 885-km-long (550 miles) stretch of water is a bottleneck for ships. It's the principal route for oil tankers from the Middle East to East Asia, carrying one-third of the world's crude oil shipments and one-fifth of the ocean's sea-borne trade. With as many as 70,000 ships passing through these waters every year, slow-moving vessels are an easy target. Despite the advice given to cargo boat captains to increase speed to deter pirate attack, this is rarely possible in the shallow and crowded navigation of the Strait.

Like the pirates of old, these modern-day bandits generally board a ship to steal money, food and anything else they can find. Occasionally, the more sophisticated will have smaller coasters waiting on to which they offload a ship's cargo. Although taking crew members is not unknown, these are almost akin to smash-and-grab crimes. Averaging up to 100 incidents a year, often the pirates will simply take everything of value that is on board and leave. The ship's cash float is usually their principal target, although anything that can be taken will go – the crew's televisions, clothes, any electrical items, phones and computers.

The jungle, rivers and creeks that line the Strait provide plenty of hiding places for the fast boats that dart out on their opportunistic raids. As it's merely a theft of equipment that belongs principally to the ship owner, crews are not going to put up a fight. It's not generally a hostage situation, and no multimillion dollar ransoms are sought – unlike Somalia, both Malaysia and Indonesia on either side of the Strait have strong functioning governments offering no place to take and hold a hijacked ship until a ransom is paid.

Piracy in Somalia has evolved into a different creature. Rather than a quick in-out raid for loot, Somali pirates generally aim to capture a ship with minimum casualties, then hold the vessel, its crew and cargo to ransom for millions of dollars. They are in it for the long game – average times between capture and release run into many months, and sometimes years.

Seychelles Ambassador Ronny Jumeau was a member of the Contact Group on Piracy off the Coast of Somalia (CGPS) while Permanent Representative to the UN at a time when Somali piracy was at its height. He was intimately involved in the issue.

'The difference between Somalis and other pirates is that the Somalis control ports and anchorages that they can bring the ships into. The pirates of West Africa do not control ports. They have to deal with the issue at sea. If you hold a boat at sea with hostages then you have a Captain Phillips situation – anything can go wrong. Once you take the ship into a port, you can take the hostages off the boat and hide them in the hinterland. Now the shipowners have got to pay money because even if you want to have a raid to rescue them, you can't do it unless you know exactly where they are ... and if they scatter the hostages, then you have really lost control of the situation. In West Africa what they do is hit a ship, take whatever they want, and leave.'

In the early days of Somali piracy, those who seized trawlers without licences could count on a quick ransom payment, since the boat owners and companies backing those vessels did not want to draw attention to their violation of international maritime law.

Once the potential of the unprotected ships in the Gulf of Aden was spotted, with the chance of huge rewards from large ships (that were in no way affecting the livelihood of Somali fishermen), local piracy grew into a more widespread criminal enterprise. At the peak of their activity, the pirates were holding more than 700 crew members and over 30 ships.

Instead of a desperate last-ditch effort to protect their original livelihoods, piracy had mutated into an opportunistic way of making easy money. The shipping industry was taken by surprise. With no naval protection and no security, vessels large and small fell prey to Somali pirates. The statistics show an astonishing rise and peaking in piracy within just a few years. The EU Naval Force (EUNAVFOR), one of the principal anti-piracy naval coalitions in the region, has only kept figures since its inception in 2008, but the data tells its own history of the phenomenon of Somali piracy.

Simply put, the incomes received by the pirates rocketed as they became more proficient in negotiations. In June 2005, the Kenyan merchant ship *Semlow*, carrying UN food supplies for tsunami victims, was seized by pirates en route from Mombasa, Kenya, to

Figures from EUNAVFOR (http://eunavfor.eu/key-facts-and-figures/):

	2008	2009	2010	2011	2012	2013	2014
Suspicious events	8	59	99	166	73	20	4
Total attacks	24	163	174	176	35	7	2
Of which pirated	14	46	47	25	4	0	0

NATO's figures show a similar trend:

		2008	2009	2010	2011	2012	2013	2014
Somali Basin	hijacks	8	26	26	4	2	0	0
	attacks	11	58	68	52	5	5	0
	disruptions	N/A	15	88	52	16	6	0
Gulf of Aden (incl. IRTC)	hijacks	33	18	12	1	0	0	0
	attacks	42	67	33	29	7	1	0
	disruptions	N/A	47	56	21	7	2	0
Arabian Sea	hijacks	N/A	1	7	19	5	0	0
	attacks	N/A	5	31	48	10	0	1
	disruptions	N/A	N/A	3	23	14	0	1

Bosaso, Somalia. The ship was held for 100 days until a Somali businessman persuaded the pirates to release it without payment.

In April of the same year, however, a Hong Kong-owned liquefied petroleum tanker, MV *Feisty Gas*, was hijacked and held for some two weeks before payment of US$315,000.

By October the stakes were rising. Somali pirates seized the bulk carrier MV *Panagia*, which was transporting a cargo of coal from South Africa to Turkey. The Ukrainian-based company that owned the vessel reportedly paid US$700,000 to a representative of the Somali pirates in Mombasa, Kenya.

In 2005 the average ransom paid per ship was around US$150,000; from then on, it rapidly escalated. By 2010 the average ransom paid had risen to US$5.4 million.

This was no longer the work of small bands of illiterate fishermen. Most pirates today are no longer themselves displaced fishermen but members of nomadic land-based clans who generally have little or no knowledge of the sea. Rather than poor fishermen seeking redress, today's pirates are more akin to drug dealers – they are flash, have status, cars, machismo, money, and they get the girls...

Originally referring to the dispersion of the Jews beyond Israel, the word 'diaspora' has come to mean the dispersion or spread of any people from their original homeland. In the Somali context, it has come to mean expatriate Somalis living around the world. Somalis are great business people and have been successful in many fields. Just because they live outside the country, the strong family and clan allegiances don't disappear. The money they send back home to their extended families is often the difference between survival and starvation.

However, a criminal few of the Somali diaspora have seen piracy as a potentially good investment with excellent rates of return. A businessman stands to lose his initial investment if the gang of pirates he sends out to sea is apprehended – he would lose a couple of outboard engines attached to rudimentary fibreglass boats that have seen better days, together with a few guns and some fuel. If his motley crew were to come up trumps, then for an investment of a couple of tens of thousands of dollars, he could expect a potential ransom of many millions.

As with any criminal enterprise, the financiers behind it are virtually impossible to trace or identify with any certainty, even by organisations such as Interpol. It's virtually impossible to bring prosecutions against anyone other than the foot soldiers – the ill-fed ruffians actually sent out on the boats to do the dirty work. There have been many theories, including links to terrorist organisations, but the financiers are first and foremost businessmen. Some of the profits will bankroll legitimate businesses such as hotels, transport companies and property; other investors will choose to go down the criminal route of trafficking people and arms.

There is no question that there is a business structure behind Somali piracy today. I have spoken with convicted pirates who talk of 'the Company', of having to sign for every item of stores and equipment before heading out to sea, and of the detailed arrangements in place for dividing up any ransom – with the financier receiving the lion's share. Sometimes a single wealthy businessman or criminal lurks behind a pirate group, sometimes a consortium of investors who 'buy shares'.

These financial backers are in many cases located in neighbouring Middle Eastern states, although just as easily in the West. They will never get their own hands dirty – that is the job of the pirates and the men on the ground, of whom there is an unending supply. In a nation where around half of the population exists on less than US$1 per day, the lure of pirates' wages is irresistible.

Somalis do not need to launder the money they make from piracy because their unique financial system operates on trust and honour, bypassing banks and other financial institutions. If a ransom is received, the profits will be disbursed to investors through the *hawala* money-transfer system. As the system often does not involve documentation, with most transactions done verbally, there is no paper trail. Although *hawala* companies in both the West and the Arab world have become more regulated in recent years, it is very difficult to track the money once it arrives in Somalia. This renders it almost impossible to trace monies received from ransom payments; since most are paid in cash, they simply disappear into the Somali community rather than ending up in banks or other financial institutions.

One thing is clear: the pirates who take to sea in small boats to hijack large ships receive very little of the proceeds. The 2011 UN Security Council Report of the Monitoring Group on Somalia and Eritrea collated and analysed all available information, and produced a picture of a remarkably structured business model:

'Pirate finances are usually managed by a "Committee", who organize an operation and are responsible for managing all the costs. The Committee members usually consist of a chair, the two principal investors, the commander of the sea-pirates and the commander of the terrestrial guard force. The Committee is supported in the financial aspects of its work by an accountant who is usually rewarded with a share equal to that of a guard.

Ransom payments must cover two types of expense: the "cost" of the operation and the "profit". After a ransom drop, pirate leaders deduct the operational expenses or "cost" from the total amount of ransom, before distributing the remaining money or "profit" to participants in the operation. The profit is generally lower than the cost and is divided between the investors (30%), the guard force (30%) and the sea-pirates (40%).

Operational cost: The "cost" of an average pirate operation typically includes the following:

- Committee members: usually 5 persons who collectively receive 5 per cent of the total ransom amount for their work in the Committee, in addition to the return on their investment;
- Provisions for pirates and crew, both on board the hijacked ship and onshore, including food, drink, clothes, vehicles, equipment, weapons, outboard engines, fuel, etc.
- *Shahaad*: a Somali social obligation to share wealth, whether in cash, or by showing generous hospitality, estimated at as much as 20 per cent of the total ransom amount. The elders of the local community where a hijacked ship has been held will ensure that they get their fair share.
- Cook(s)
- Accountant(s)
- Logistics co-ordinator
- Interpreter or negotiator
- Payoffs to other local militia groups
- Pirate leader and investor.

Off duty expenses like cigarettes, khat, phone cards and prostitutes are usually not included in the "cost". These are deducted from an individual's share before they get any balance.

Profits: Investors in an operation share roughly 30 per cent of the profit, according to their individual contributions. The remainder of the profit is distributed in the form of "shares" to the participants. An individual can play multiple roles in an operation/organization and therefore collect multiple shares or fees.'

An unlikely sounding partner for the piracy business is the *khat* trade. This stimulant is legally used in many countries, and extremely popular around the Horn of Africa; in Yemen, an estimated 40 per cent of the country's water supply goes towards irrigating *khat* crops. As drugs go, *khat* is one of the least harmful, and was only banned in the UK in June 2014. *Khat* is a mild stimulant, consumed by chewing the leaves of the plant. It has to be masticated while the leaves are still fresh, as within 72 hours it loses its stimulant effect. Until it was outlawed, daily flights would arrive at London Heathrow from Kenya with cargos of freshly picked *khat* that would be on sale in shops the same day. The city of Bristol, for example, has a strong Somali community, and had five shops selling the leaves, as well as 22 special marfish cafés where *khat* was chewed.

Khat is not a 'quick-hit' drug. Chewing *khat* is very much a pastime, similar to the chewing of betel nut in Pacific Island countries. It's a social experience and a *khat*-chewing session can last for many hours. The leaf tastes bitter so most *khat* users accompany sessions with cans of sweet drinks or heavily sugared tea.

Most pirates chew *khat* as a way of passing the time, staying alert and socialising with their fellow pirates. They may spend weeks or months trying to hijack a ship, guarding the crew on board a hijacked ship, or providing protection onshore. Since few young pirates can afford the daily consumption of *khat* for such extended periods, it is usually provided to them on credit by the investors and businessmen who control both the pirate network and the *khat* business. Accounts are meticulously recorded, and the return for the suppliers is huge, especially because they may charge the pirates as much as three times the market price. For *khat* bought on credit, this means that a pirate pays up to US$150 for one 'kilo' of *khat*, which normally sells for US$50 on the streets of Harardhere.

The connection between piracy and the *khat* trade clearly offers some pirate leaders a way both to invest their proceeds and to generate additional profits. A significant proportion of the ransom money is believed to be invested by pirate leaders in the *khat* trade via Somali businessmen based in Nairobi. Aircraft that fly *khat* from Kenya into Somalia often return to Nairobi with cash – an important channel for proceeds of piracy to leave the country.

With a sophisticated structure and additional avenues of revenue, piracy has turned into Somalia's only boom industry. In the years 2010 to 2012, an estimated 2,000–3,000 ragtag Somali pirates extracted ransoms of nearly US$430 million from the world shipping community. And the extent of the piracy plague is astonishing. In the six years between 2005 and 2011, the outlaws captured well over 200 vessels and close to 4,000 sailors. At the peak of their activity, at one time they were holding 32 ships and some 736 crew as hostages.

How was it indeed possible for the pirates to achieve such success? It was through a combination of factors that are mostly still present today.

The non-existence of a centralised authority and weak, easily corrupted regional administrations was the primary factor in a country offering countless bases from which the pirates could operate with impunity. In Somalia there was no risk of arrest – the greatest risk was of other brigands stealing a group's hostages or ransom monies. With little other employment available, there was an endless supply of young men keen to try their fortunes.

Add to that the seemingly limitless supply of ships off the coast of Somalia. International shipping relies heavily on the Suez Canal as a shortcut from the Mediterranean to South and East Asia; likewise, tankers shift oil from the Persian Gulf through the region; furthermore, all sorts of high-value vessels such as cruise liners ply the waters of the western Indian Ocean.

One other significant factor explains the success. Somali pirate attacks regularly yield million-dollar payoffs. By comparison, pirates in other areas of the globe are often lucky if they receive ten thousand dollars.

Traditionally, pirates hijacked vessels to steal money, cargo, and occasionally the ship itself. In modern times, it's hard to steal a ship, re-register it, and find a willing buyer. Stealing money, crew's possessions or cargo is generally not particularly profitable either – it is the marine equivalent of burglars getting away with one's wallet and home electronics system.

Somali pirates, by contrast, have developed their own highly specialised and hugely profitable business model. Where they began in time-honoured fashion with groups of armed men seizing a ship, the Somalis learned quickly that via extortion from international shipping companies and their insurers the rewards could be massive.

In a typical hijack, once on board, they hold ship, crew and cargo hostage, head for the Somali coast where they can anchor at liberty, and then commence negotiations for ransoms of many millions of dollars. Time is on their side; they can sit it out where they are for as long as they want. Each day the clock ticks against the shipping company for whom the vessel remains out of action while their costs rise. The expenses of a ship and crew held hostage and not earning revenue mount up quickly – estimated at some US$17,500 per day for a bulk carrier.

Most navies are unwilling to intervene in hostage situations for fear of innocent deaths, so the pirates hold all the strings. Under pressure from crews' families, the majority of shipping companies or their insurers sooner or later pay the ransom to ensure the safety of the crew and return the ship to active service.

In 2010, pirate income derived from ransoms was estimated at US$238 million. That compares with a gross domestic product for the Somali nation as a whole of just under US$1,100 million in the same year. However, by 2011, pirate ransom income dropped to US$160 million, a downward trend that has been attributed to intensified counter-piracy efforts – efforts I was to witness at first hand during the course of my research.

05

HOW TO BE A PIRATE

A sleek steel-grey warship lies at anchor in the sheltered waters of Port Victoria, Seychelles.

The sea is flat calm, the morning sun already hot in a clear blue sky, just a few clouds obstinately sticking to the caps of the thickly forested mountains rising steeply behind the town.

A Maersk container ship is unloading alongside the main jetty, containers swinging as they are craned on to waiting trailers that scurry purposefully alongside the quay. The colourful and speedy *Cat Cocos* ferry passes behind, laden with holidaymakers heading for Seychelles' second largest island, Praslin. Small fishing boats criss-cross the water, and against the fishing quay two purse-seiners, rafted one alongside the other, discharge their cargoes – tens of thousands of large silver tuna. It could be just another day in Seychelles. Except for the fact that Seychelles is at war, and the warship is one of the numerous EUNAVFOR vessels engaged in the combat against Somali pirates.

The ship is crammed with every type of technology, its multiple navigation systems able to pinpoint any spot on the ocean to within one metre, its powerful modern engines capable of speeds up to 29 knots. Its principal weaponry includes naval guns, Mauser Auto-cannons, SAM missiles and Harpoon anti-ship missiles; on board wait a vigilant team of the most highly trained assault marines. The crew of 230 professional seamen live in comfortable quarters with every luxury including wifi, flat-screen TVs, hot showers, laundry, and comfortable beds with clean sheets. The food on board is produced by a kitchen of professional chefs. A fully equipped medical facility is capable of dealing with everything from toothache to gunshot wounds.

The two battle-ready Lynx helicopters in its stern hangar have a top speed of 320 kph, their own refined weaponry including air-to-surface missiles and a heavy machine gun, state-of-the-art navigation systems and long-range surveillance capabilities. The warship is equipped with everything that the 21st century can provide. It's here to combat an opponent with none of these advantages – but who still seems unbeatable.

In the foreground, on a patch of waste land overgrown with grass and puddled from the morning's monsoon rain, lie some of the opposition. A ghost fleet of captured Somali pirate vessels, now abandoned and rotting. The boats are much as they were when captured – there was nothing of the slightest value to remove from them. There are clearly two types. The larger models, known as whalers, are around 23 feet long: open fibreglass boats powered by an ancient inboard engine. Much of the space is taken up by rusting fuel drums. The ashes from a long-extinct cooking fire lie just alongside them.

The hulls have been patched many times, with makeshift repairs to fibreglass where the boats have been holed at various times during a long life of hard use. Some have been roughly painted blue above the waterline – maybe a naive attempt at camouflage. Few have any markings, although crudely painted on the bow of one is 'Hobyo Boys' – referring to the Somali city of Hobyo, a notorious pirate haven. The single inboard engines are rusting badly, but weren't in a much better state when the boats were captured. In the engine compartment is just one control lever – the further it was pushed forward, the faster the boat would go. Steering is via a hand-controlled rudder, the helmsman sitting at the stern the whole time the boat was at sea, often for weeks – no expensive autopilot systems here. Navigation was by virtue of a handheld compass; some of the luckier crews had a primitive GPS with the co-ordinates of their home village stored, so they had a bearing to follow when they found prey or ran out of food and water.

The smaller boats are little more than skiffs, around 15 feet long – again fibreglass, but this time powered by faster, although aged 50hp outboard engines. These are modest open boats that one would feel nervous about taking anything more than 100 metres (330 feet) beyond a harbour breakwater. None of these boats looks safe enough to take out of sight of land. Yet they were all captured up to 1,000 nautical miles (1,850 km) from the Somali beaches where they were launched. All that is missing from this ghost fleet are the weapons and the crew.

Weapons are stored elsewhere in a police-evidence compound – ancient AK-47s manufactured many years ago and filtered down to this last use after many conflicts, together with a handful of rocket-propelled grenades. All that remain of the on-board arsenal, these weapons at least were not flung overboard in the last moments before arrest.

And the crew – between 11 and 13 scrawny malnourished boys and young men per boat – are mostly now locked up for decades for their acts of piracy. These men may have spent several weeks at sea, under a relentless sun and at the mercy of storms, voyaging far distant from their villages in the hope of capturing a prize. They are illiterate, uneducated, and generally aged between ten and their early twenties – although few actually know their age as there are no records back home. These youthful adventurers left in the urgent hope of securing a better life for themselves and their families, and endured long periods at sea in the harshest of conditions with limited food and water and no shelter.

In the words of Commander Enrique Cubeiro of the Spanish EUNAVFOR contingent, these men are nothing short of 'remarkable...' – reluctant respect offered by a man whose job is to stamp out the scourge, but remains so professional a seaman that he can acknowledge the seafaring bravery – or desperation – of others.

Incredibly, in the war between the two ridiculously imbalanced fleets, the pirates were for a long time winning. Avoiding detection by the most sophisticated radar systems, tiny dots on a huge ocean, they proved near impossible to contain. When the first spate of piracy crossed from Somali shores to the territorial waters of Seychelles – a million square kilometres of ocean rich with shipping of all types – the two Seychelles Coastguard cutters were totally unable to cope. Seychelles government ministers described it as 'like trying to patrol the whole of Texas with just two cop cars'.

The pirate's techniques were simple and effective. The larger boat, known as the mother ship, would be home to the pirates, plodding through the Indian Ocean towing behind its two skiffs – the hunting dogs. Low-lying and with no metal structures, the pack would not register on any but the most sensitive radar systems – and would literally slink below the net.

Sometimes a number of packs would hunt together. A large ship can be seen from a good distance away at sea – even if the bulk of the ship is below the horizon, its superstructure will just show. Three mother ships and their hunting skiffs spread in line 20 km (12 miles) apart could effectively cover shipping lanes for a distance of 160 km (100 miles) or more. Other crews would hunt alone, unnoticed in the ocean's vastness, seemingly innocuous until they struck.

At first, pirate activity was limited to the Somali coast, and the entrance to the Gulf of Aden, but as larger numbers of international warships patrolled those seaways, the pirates' tentacles reached ever further out into the Indian Ocean. Like a plague they spread – south through Seychelles and along the African Coast, and east almost as far as India.

No matter how container ships try to vary their routes to stay clear of areas of known pirate activity, they still have to visit the usual ports on their endless circuits of the Indian Ocean and have no choice but to run the gauntlet of pirate-infested zones. Any shipping heading for the Gulf and up through the Red Sea to the Suez Canal was funnelled into narrow shipping lanes, where the pirates' fast small boats darted in and out like barracuda cutting into a school of fish.

The pirates know the commercial fishing grounds, where the huge tuna seine-netters work. These are among the most valuable catches for a pirate. Every day a vessel is not fishing costs tens of thousands of euros, and its owners are often willing to negotiate a speedy release of their ships. Such vessels are, however, difficult to take, bristling with well-armed expensive security guards.

We had filmed on board one of these, the MV *Alakrana*, a mean sleek fishing machine. Fast, and with the latest fish-catching technology, below decks was a huge, modern, well-lit, stainless-steel fish-processing area.

Alakrana had already twice been the victim of pirate attacks. On the first occasion, the boat and crew had been held for 47 days until a ransom of around US$3 million was paid. The second attack was beaten off by an on-board armed security team. While the *Alakrana* continued to fish the region, she was one of a reducing number.

In 2006, 226 Japanese vessels were fishing in the High Risk Area – by 2011, this number had more than halved.

Inshore fishing grounds are well known too. Fishermen have no choice – that is where the fish are, where they have found fish for generations, and where they must go to bring home a catch and make a living.

Walking around Seychelles central market early on a Saturday morning, already crowded and vivid with fresh local fruits and the colourful outfits of the locals shopping for an early bargain, I got talking to fisherman Beatty Houreau. He pointed out to me just how few fish were available in a nation where fish is the staple diet. Restricted to fishing south-east of the islands, where the coastguard could offer better protection, not only did the catch size fall, but the size of the individual fish caught was also falling – clear evidence that these less productive areas were rapidly becoming overfished. It was a sad irony that piracy that had its roots in disputes over fishing rights was having a similar effect on the fishermen of a neighbouring country.

'The hostage-taking by Somali pirates is creating fear in our fishermen. It's creating panic within the families of the fishermen. The fear is there. Will my husband, will my brother, be the next one to be taken? The crew of the boat just leaving port, will that be the next one to be taken? It is creating a major psychological impact on our families and on the fishing community.'

And he spoke of some of his fellow fishermen who at the time were still being held hostage by the pirates.

'I understand they are alive but not well. Held hostage in a foreign land, with an AK-47 behind your back, a man cannot be well.'

Leisure yachts, such as that sailed by British couple Paul and Rachel Chandler, are a more random find for the pirates – a matter of pure luck. There's no second-hand market among wealthy Somalis for captured yachts, but there's always the chance that a fine ransom will be paid for a wealthy owner. There are also tourist charter boats, operating at dates and in locations that could easily be discovered by anyone making a quick internet search – and although the pirate crews don't have that facility out at sea, those onshore directing their movements certainly do. These boats advertise their itineraries for sailing, fly-fishing, eco tours and diving holidays well in advance. Only the wealthy can afford trips lasting a week or more to the outer island groups of Seychelles, and to capture a boat with a mixture of rich Western tourists from several countries would be a real jackpot.

Cruise liners are the prize target. When the MS *Costa Allegra* was disabled after an engine room fire at the end of February 2012, some 200 miles (320 km) from Mahé, the world held its breath. Having sent out an SOS, the ship was drifting helpless in a region with known current pirate activity. Bearing over 600 passengers from 24 nations, she would have made the ultimate pirate trophy. Help scrambled from hundreds of kilometres around, the first to give a tow being the Seychelles-based purse-seiner MV *Trevignon*. Salvage tugs and the Italian Navy were close behind.

I watched them bring the huge cruise liner safely to Port Victoria, a small armada of escort ships bustling around while the *Trevignon* tenaciously but slowly towed her salvage into harbour. The worst the passengers had endured was a couple of days without power – unpleasant, but nothing compared to what could have happened if pirate boats had been first on the scene.

Pirate tactics have evolved as the pirates themselves have learned the key to more successful attacks, and in response to the increased naval presence in their hunting grounds.

In the early days, they would post a lookout on top of one of the small cliffs and hillocks that are a feature of many parts of the Somali coastline – the superstructure of a ship can be spotted dozens of kilometres offshore when the weather is clear in the sunny Indian

Ocean. The gang would quickly launch a skiff with an outboard, grabbing whoever was around to jump on for the ride, then head out to intercept the unfortunate vessel.

As the pirates became more organised, the classic hunting pack developed, consisting of an open whaler with an inboard engine, towing two fast attack skiffs behind. These mother ships, laden with a dozen or more barrels, some containing fuel and some water, were equipped to spend weeks at sea. Food supplies were usually little more than sacks of dried spaghetti, occasionally supplemented by any fish they might catch. Often, once they got clear of land and into the shipping corridors, they would simply turn off the engine to save fuel and wait, drifting wherever the currents and winds took them, until the first sign of a target. They would pass long days, with most of the crew sleeping under a tarpaulin in the bow to protect them from the burning sun, while a few kept watch, listlessly scanning the horizon in all directions, searching for the first hazy outline of a vessel that could bring them millions in ransom cash.

As naval patrols became more frequent and efficient, a new scenario emerged. Pirates would head out to sea to capture one of the hundreds of regional fishing boats or cargo dhows plying the Gulf – as well as fishermen from all the countries around the area, the narrow strait between Djibouti and Yemen has always been a busy local trading route. These captured boats could then be used as mother ships in place of the old open whalers. The pirates would haul their skiffs on board and conceal them, so that the boat looked like any other craft going about its business in the region. Furthermore, the captive crew could be used as a human shield against patrolling naval ships, which were reluctant to open fire if innocent people were on board.

In addition to the innocuous appearance that such a vessel provided, allowing it to get much closer to their prey, the pirates could travel further afield, in greater comfort, stay at sea for longer periods and be less affected by the weather than in their old open boats. On occasion, the pirates would use a hijacked merchant ship or even pleasure yacht for this purpose. Such is the havoc wrought by the pirates that any blip on the radar is now generally treated by skippers as potentially a pirate ship.

While this new mode of piracy was spreading its tentacles ever further, other teams reverted to the early days – a small skiff at sea in the busy Gulf waters suddenly darting out from the pack of otherwise blameless fishing boats in an opportunist attack.

Whatever their target, once the prey is sighted the pirates' tactics remain much the same. Once a sail or the first hint of a ship's superstructure is spotted on the horizon, they are energised into action. Like hyenas, they stalk their prey, gradually inching closer as dusk falls. Day and night in this region near to the Equator are fairly equally balanced, and from sunset to dawn the pirates have around 12 hours to close in on their victim.

On board the mother ship, excitement and anticipation mount – capturing a hostage vessel is the reason they put themselves forward as crew; this is why they have spent weeks at sea and undergone so many hardships. By morning they could be rich men. The pirates are all talking nonstop like overexcited kids, none listening, each telling the others what they will do, and how they will be first over the side, first to the bridge, first to take the captain and win the ship for themselves. Their share of the prize money is already being spent in their minds – that luxury SUV they will buy, the house they will build, the parties they will enjoy, the women...

No one sleeps during the night – the mother ship buzzes with childlike anticipation as the helmsman at his wooden rudder steers them slowly ever closer to their quarry.

The guns and grenade launchers have all been kept bound in plastic sheeting since they left Somalia, protecting them from salt and water. They are now almost ceremoniously unwrapped, checked and rechecked, magazines of bullets loaded, grenades attached to launchers, spare magazines and grenades tucked in pockets of ragged jeans and filthy shirts, or occasional pouches.

As dawn approaches, the attack skiffs are pulled close, each boat is boarded by a steersman who revs the engine, casts off the tow rope and pulls alongside to pick up the attack crew – usually four or five to each skiff.

Grappling hooks, ropes and boarding ladders – ordinary metal ladders with a crudely attached curved end for hooking over a ship's rail – are already on board the skiffs, as they would take up too much space on the mother ship. Several yellow plastic containers of petrol with red screw tops are also already on board – it could be a long chase.

The steersman holds the skiff close alongside as weapons are carefully handed across – they are far too valuable to risk losing now into the sea. The remaining attack crew then clamber over and when all are aboard, the driver guns the engine and heads towards the unwitting kill, just now appearing as a smudge in the grey light of first false dawn.

The skiffs, smaller lighter boats, can generally achieve speeds of up to 25 knots – faster than most of their prey. Despite this, the majority of attacks end in failure. Seas may be too rough for the skiffs to attain full speed, their engines may break down, the target may be just too far ahead and beyond the range of the skiff's fuel supplies. In addition, skippers of cargo ships are now trained in evasion manoeuvres, such as executing sharp turns to kick up a large and confused wake, making it difficult for the skiffs to get close enough alongside to try to board. There may also be armed security or other anti-piracy devices acting as successful deterrents to boarding.

If they manage to take a larger ship, the pirates will invariably steer as quickly as possible towards the Somali coast to start ransom negotiations. Smaller vessels such as fishing boats may become a more convenient replacement for the mother ship, their crew locked up under guard, the Somalis ransacking the boat and then continuing in their quest for more valuable prey.

06

FIRST ENCOUNTER

From the outset, an essential ingredient in writing a book about Somali pirates has got to be talking with Somali pirates. I knew where I could find plenty of them – many serving sentences counted in decades rather than in years. Would they be willing to talk to me?

I'd stocked up with several packs of cigarettes – currency favoured by inmates the world over. I'd prepared my questions. I'd even brought a camera in the hope that some might agree to a photograph. Now it was all down to fate. No interviews, no book – as simple as that. How would they feel about talking with a Brit when our navy might have been the one to capture them, and was still actively hunting their colleagues out on the open ocean?

People I'd spoken to had even suggested that there was an element of danger in being alone with desperate men with nothing to lose. 'They take hostages!' But my apprehension as we reached the prison wasn't for my personal safety; it was that I might leave empty-handed, with no interviews on my pocket Dictaphone.

On the drive up the steeply winding forested road to the Seychelles mountaintop jail, my translator Abdullahi Yerrow Salat had warned me that it was a strong possibility none of the Somali prisoners would wish to speak with me. Abdullahi is a Somali who holds Kenyan nationality and is contracted by the United Nations Office on Drugs and Crime. Except during piracy trials, when back-up interpreters may be called in, he is the only Somali-speaking interpreter in the country.

When I arrived at the prison, the governor Superintendent Maxime Tirant was even more pessimistic about my prospects of success.

'Interpol came to try and interview the Somalis; a mystery throat infection swept through the Somali wing, though nowhere else in the prison. The guys from Interpol came every day for a week, but not a single Somali was well enough to get out of bed to speak with them. But when the weekend came, every one of them was up and about again – a miraculous cure!'

The main prison accommodation block lay inside a compound surrounded by a wire fence topped with coils of razor wire, guards armed with machine guns overlooking it from towers roofed with corrugated iron. I was meeting the prisoners, however, in a small room in the two-storey administration building outside the main compound, a room that seemed to have many uses – as classroom and guards' rest room, and for visits. The walls were papered with optimistic and jolly handmade posters similar to those found in prisons around the world: half a dozen photos stuck on a sheet of coloured A2 paper of the guards-versus-prisoners soccer match with handwritten captions under each; of the prison pantomime; childlike coloured pencil drawings done by prisoners; and also, unusually, architects' plans of the proposed new women's prison. Along the walls, beneath the posters, were ranged stacks of variously coloured plastic chairs.

On the steps up to this first-floor room, an old dog lay snoring in the sun. On my arrival, I passed a single barrier for vehicles separating us from the outside world, manned by an unarmed Gurkha who did not even take my name; strangely, Somali prisoners seemed to be roaming freely.

My translator explained that these Somalis in their denim-blue tops and trousers were out on a work party. Building works were still going on at the prison and that was their task. None of them had ever tried to escape – on a small island there was nowhere for them to go, and in any event they were all afraid of the Seychellois.

Maalin Daud Olat was the first of the Somalis that I interviewed, and he insisted on having his friend Mohamed Hassan Ali come in with him. I learned later that Maalin was respected among the Somalis, had a lot of influence among them, and was in effect checking me out. If I passed the test, others would talk to me – if not, then he and his friend would probably be the last I would get to speak with.

To smooth things over and get off to a good start, I passed Maalin a pack of 20 Marlboros. He looked at them with disgust and then pointed to a pack of just ten Mahé Kings, the local cigarette. My first lesson – whether because they were American, or maybe just because of the taste, not a single Somali wanted the 20 packs of Marlboro, and all preferred half the number of Mahé Kings. Maybe someday the local cigarette factory will do a spoof of the Marlboro advert using a pirate on a boat ... or like the soap powder ads we are bombarded with: 'Nine out of ten Somali pirates prefer Mahé Kings...'

Maalin was 39 years old – by a long way the oldest of the Somalis that I interviewed in Montagne Posée prison. He was small, skinny and balding, with a beard. He told me he'd had only four years of schooling. He was from Mogadishu. He'd never taken part in the fighting there but he'd seen a lot.

When I explained to Maalin that I was writing a book and wanted to put all sides of the story, including the Somalis' side, he seemed happy to talk.

'I was captured by the Spanish on 28 January 2011. I am serving a ten-year sentence. I do not accept that I am a pirate.

In the fighting in Mogadishu, I lost my two elder brothers and my younger sister. There is no life to be had in Mogadishu. I was working in a factory making plastic water bottles.

When I left Somalia, the intention was to head for South Africa. I had paid to go on the boat. You can't go through Kenya because of the wars in the south of Somalia, which is why we went by sea.

I left my wife and family in Somalia. The plan was to go to South Africa as an immigrant, and when I got settled to send for my wife and two children. But because of this sentence, we are now divorced.'

I had seen several of the skiffs and small open boats that had been captured by the Seychelles Coastguard stored on waste ground close to the harbour. I wanted to get an idea of life on board – for me, the thought of spending days, weeks even, in burning sun and hundreds of kilometres out to sea was impossible. To Maalin, it was very ordinary.

'There were 11 of us on board and a skiff behind in case of emergency. The drums on board – some contained fuel and some water. There was enough room at the front for us to sleep six at a time. During the day, we had a plastic cover to protect us from sun and rain.

We ate breakfast, lunch and dinner on board, and cooked on charcoal in an old metal drum.'

So what actually happened – why was he here in prison?

'The big boat had engine problems and we had been drifting for a long time. We saw a ship so sent some of the crew to get water. The ship fired on them so we left. A helicopter came and we were arrested.

We had no weapons on our boat. We were taken to the Spanish boat and beaten – the Spanish are very bad people. We were treated very badly on board that ship. If I have a chance, I will sue the Spanish government because we were beaten up. The Spanish actually burned our boat. They had no cause to treat us as they did. After five days we were brought to Seychelles.

I am appealing against my conviction. We were only travelling, not pirates.'

It wasn't the tale of a life of piracy that I had hoped to hear, but if he was still in the appeals process protesting his innocence, then he was hardly going to admit being a pirate to a total stranger.

'But if I don't win my appeal and am sent back to Somalia, I want to do my sentence in Mogadishu – not Puntland or Somaliland.'

As I was soon to learn, while certain countries such as Seychelles had undertaken to prosecute and imprison pirates, even with international funding for improved prison facilities there was no way they could continue to accommodate an ever-increasing number of Somalis. It's a problem that is only going to grow – there are now over twelve hundred suspected or convicted pirates detained in 21 countries around the world, with the majority in those that have agreed to become trial centres. In a small country like Seychelles, this has resulted in a high percentage of Somali inmates, with its own consequent problems. In a larger country like Kenya, it has stretched prison capabilities beyond capacity. These are not short-term prisoners with early release dates – some will spend the next two decades or more behind bars.

Once a conviction is secured in one of the trial centres, the ultimate aim is to transfer the pirates back to Somalia to serve their sentences, not always easy in such a fragmented country, where at times even the police and army do not get paid, let alone prison staff...

With funding from the United Nations Office on Drugs and Crime (UNODC), new prisons have been built in Somalia and convicted prisoners sent there to serve the balance of their sentences. In Puntland, the country's first new prison in 30 years was opened at the end of 2010. UN finance has also built a new prison in Somaliland and upgraded facilities in the prison in Mogadishu.

Maalin talked about this at some length and insisted I write it down so someone out there might hear it, and it was a common theme among many of the others I spoke to. They were insistent that if they were transferred back to Somalia to serve the balance of their sentences, they went to a prison in their own region.

'I don't trust the other regions – we are all different clans. We are always at war. I want to go back to Mogadishu prison. There have been tribal clashes for 24 years. If I'm sent to prison in other lands, they are our enemies and we would fear for our lives. If the UN would put people in prisons where they come from, that would be much better.'

This was an illustration of the depth of the clan system – convenience of visiting for family came a very low second, if indeed mentioned at all.

Then Maalin seemed to reflect for a minute, and changed his tune, as if it were the first time this thought had come to him.

'But I would prefer to stay in prison here. It's better, even though it's a foreign country. It's a bit freer here than in Somalia. I get four months a year remission here – only three in Somalia.' Remission is discount on sentence for every year served, building up credit towards early release. 'And when my sentence ends in Somalia, they may not let me go – they may ask for a bribe, for money, before they release me.'

I wanted to find out more about how he was coping, and about life back home in Somalia.

'It's my first time in prison and I'm facing many challenges. I'm missing my family, my animals, life back home. I have goats, sheep, camels – not a lot, just a few. They are at my parents' outside Mogadishu.

Before 1991, Somalia was a good place to live. We had a good government, peace, law and order, everything was good. I don't think it will get like that in the future. Ever since 1991, it's just been fighting and war.'

Maalin was a quietly spoken and apparently mild-mannered man. I had no idea whether what he was telling me was the truth or just a story made up for court. I told him that I sympathised with his story. I also explained that what I wanted was to speak with some people who would admit to being pirates, so I could find out what that is like, and why they did it?

Maalin seemed to get twitchy, restless, and it was clear he now wanted to leave. He stood up and walked for the door, followed by his friend Mohamed, who had remained silent throughout, before turning round with his final words.

'I have never had 200 dollars in my life. I have never had a single dollar from piracy. I am not a pirate. But I am here for ten years. Maybe your book will help me?'

The door closed behind him and that was the end of my first interview with a pirate – or at least with a man convicted of piracy, but who claimed he was innocent.

I thought I had said something wrong to cause that sudden departure but no, my translator assured me, it was time for prayer. Like him, the Somalis were Muslim, and had to pray five times a day. I may be naive, but I'd never thought of pirates having religion...

Once they had gone, I went down to have a chat with the governor to let him know how things were going. Outside his office, Maalin and Mohamed were sitting on the grass enjoying one of the cigarettes I had given them. They were waiting for a guard to escort them back through the gates into the main prison compound. Although the whole interview had been conducted through the translator, Maalin suddenly seemed able to speak English.

'Mohamed would like to speak with you after prayers, and there are others. I will come back if you have more questions for me. Please tell my story. There are many bad men here – many pirates – but we are not all bad. I think we should talk some more.'

I explained that I would be back on Monday; this seemed promising. Maybe I would get some real pirate tales after all. The next request surprised me.

'When you come back on Monday, can you bring a book for me – any book – as I am learning English?'

07

A PRESIDENT ON THE FRONT LINE

There can be few more enviable jobs than being President of one of the planet's most beautiful strings of islands. With a population of just 90,000, Seychelles' 115 islands, with a total land area of only 455 km² (175 square miles), are scattered like jewels across a sea area of 1.4 million km² (540,540 square miles) of the western Indian Ocean. As might befit those living in one of the most desirable tourist destinations in the world, the Seychellois are a happy and prosperous Creole nation.

The last thing that James Michel could have expected when he became President in 2004 was to be faced with a scourge of the oceans that everyone thought had died out with Blackbeard – piracy on a huge scale. He never for one moment dreamed that he would ever find himself in the nerve centre of a naval battle at sea, making life-and-death decisions.

The President was looking relaxed when I met with him, wearing an open-necked shirt and casual trousers. It was mid 2014 when we spoke, and the tide seemed to have turned against the pirates. But no one could doubt what a challenge Somali piracy had been to him.

'When it came, it was a surprise, a shock, because we were not expecting it to happen. It really was a tidal wave of piracy because suddenly they had moved south from the Gulf of Aden and started operating deep in the middle of the Indian Ocean. Seychelles having the most proximity to the Somali coast, they were very active in our area. They were targeting every ship that was operating in the region. Our fishermen were operating there; we also had cruise ships in that area. We are a maritime nation and the sea lanes are the highways that connect us to the rest of the world.'

And the pirates were highwaymen threatening those highways.

We were in State House in the centre of Victoria, the only town in Seychelles. It's a grand mansion, a testimony in understated elegance to the British colonial powers of bygone days, as is the replica of London's Big Ben clock tower that marks the entrance to State House's imposing driveway, although now stranded on a traffic island at the town's busiest crossroads. Both mansion and clock tower were built a century ago for the British governor, in the days of imperialism when no expense was too great for the representative of the British Crown, even in the smallest and most far-flung corners of the empire. Past Governors bore such quintessentially British names as Sir Eustace Twisleton-Wykeham-Fiennes, and Sir Percy Selwyn Selwyn-Clarke, after whom the town's central market is named. President Michel had met me in the Salon des Gouverneurs, the official reception room where he receives visiting heads of state, royalty and ambassadors.

I've met with President Michel several times before, but I've never known him to be as passionate about any issue as the threat of Somali piracy to his nation.

'Our fishermen were being taken as hostages – it was a big challenge to try and bring them back to Seychelles. But I said to myself – no Seychellois will remain there indefinitely in Somali hands as hostages. And of course one of the problems we had was the security of the sea lanes, because we depend a lot on the outside world in terms of our livelihood. We import almost everything and the price of commodities went up, insurance went up, because of the insecurity of the sea lanes. Piracy hit at a time when we were really fighting for our economic survival and working on an economic reform programme, and what it cost us at that time – 2010 to 2011 – was about 4 per cent of our GDP. It was massive.'

Seychelles had found itself thrust unexpectedly into the front line of the most bizarre war of the 21st century.

'We found ourselves in the forefront of what was happening, and we had to take the initiative in order to get the international community to come and take their responsibility in the fight against piracy. Because the problem of piracy was not only a problem for Seychelles, it was an international problem; it threatened the security of the sea lanes. A lot of traffic has to go through the Indian Ocean, and what was happening was threatening the interests of other countries even very far away.

I knew that we could not tackle that level of piracy on our own; this is when I made a call on the international community to come and take part in preserving the sea lanes and to protect Seychelles that was suffering the brunt of the attacks. For far too long the world had forgotten about Somalia, and left Somalia and the Somalis to their own devices, and it had developed into a lawless state, and also a breeding ground for terrorist activities. There was no government. They were ruled by clans of armed tribesmen and by terrorists. There was a need for the international community to take its responsibility and restore the rule of law in Somalia. Unless this was done, we would not resolve the problem of piracy. And this remains relevant up to today.

Until we restore the rule of law in Somalia, piracy will not disappear. It may have died down a bit, but it will not disappear completely until they have a proper government, rule of law, proper police force, proper coastguards – until then, piracy will always be a possibility in a country that has for too long been plagued by lawlessness.'

Initially, the reaction of most of the international community was a little indifferent, not realising how serious a threat piracy was. President Michel did it the old-fashioned way. 'I wrote to all the international leaders of the world, mainly Europe, America and the United Nations Secretary-General. I tried to impress on them the need for the international community to take the matter in hand. Because it was not just a Seychelles problem – we were not the only ones being affected. The world needed to get together to fight piracy.'

The letters he wrote were the catalyst for international action. Soon afterwards, the British Prime Minister David Cameron called an extraordinary meeting in London with the participation of the United Nations and other world leaders. At last the world started to focus on Somalia and its problems.

Evidence of the international commitment to assist Seychelles in the fight against piracy is everywhere around the country: patrol aircraft donated by India and China; coastguard ships and patrol boats provided by the United Arab Emirates (UAE), China and Britain; a new courthouse capable of dealing securely with trials of over a dozen suspected pirates at a time, funded by China; and the new UN-funded mountaintop prison.

'The help we have received from around the world has been apolitical. We have had assistance in different ways from many countries and this has helped us develop our capacity to address the problem.'

I asked him if he had any sympathy with the pirates, who are seen by some as the Robin Hoods of the high seas? He was unequivocal in his response.

'Unfortunately, whenever any crime is committed, some people always try to find justification for it. There has been illegal fishing, there has been toxic dumping – the whole world knows that. But this is no reason to start organised crime, going out to sea and taking people hostage, and affecting the security of the oceans – there is no excuse for that. It is organised crime and it has developed into a very profitable business for the warlords of various Somali clans. Whatever way you look at it, I see it as a form of terrorism. Putting the lives of innocent people at risk on the high seas to me is a form of terrorism.'

Recently enacted legislation gives Seychelles the power to prosecute suspected pirates arrested not only in the country's territorial waters, but anywhere at all on the planet's seas, and allows for prosecution even if no act of piracy has taken place – merely on suspicion of being involved in piracy. The massive sentences being handed out by its courts can run into decades. To many, these new anti-piracy laws are seen as draconian. The President didn't agree.

'I know that we were one of the first countries in the world to come up with a tough legislative framework to fight piracy but it was necessary. We were courageous enough to do it – we had to deal with piracy wherever we found it on the high seas. And I think it has proved to be a wise decision and we have been able to play a pivotal part in dealing with piracy.'

Did he feel that there was perhaps a degree of complacency in many quarters that the problem had been resolved? After all, the statistics seemed to suggest that piracy was no longer an issue.

'The problem is not completely resolved. I think it is like a cork on a fizzy bottle. Remove the cork and it all spills out again. If the problems in Somalia are not resolved, piracy – although it has died down a bit – will come back, and perhaps stronger than before.

The problem is the rule of law in Somalia – well, even more than that – the reorganisation of the whole country. There is hope now – there is a government, but there is still a lot of instability. As long as the instability remains, as long as there is no proper organised economic development, you will still have the problems that exist in a lawless state and piracy will return.

I know it is not easy – it is easier said than done. It will take not one year or two years, it will take many years, but it is something that has to be done if we want the problem to be permanently resolved. And what makes it more difficult is the presence of terrorists – the Al Shabab – who will try to destabilise the government – any government that they are not part of.

But if the international community policing the waters of the Indian Ocean withdraws, and the will to restructure Somalia diminishes, then we will be back to square one.'

James Michel has been one of the world's most proactive leaders in the fight against Somali piracy. Are there any personal moments that really stand out for him? As he told the stories, I was no longer talking to the politician but to the man, speaking passionately, lost in memories of incidents in which he had been deeply personally involved.

'Two occasions stand out for me. They involve our fishing boats and our fishermen. The first one was very vivid. A fishing boat was taken by the pirates. We got information and we sent our coastguard ships after them. The hostages had been taken on board the pirate ship – it was an Iranian dhow which they had captured. They had been transferred from the fishing boat to that, and they were towing the fishing boat behind. While they were on that boat our coastguard vessels reached them. So we tried to talk to them through loudhailers. They failed to respond and continued.

We fired warning shots – they still didn't stop, and fired back with their Kalashnikovs. They also had an RPG on board and fired that too. So it was a decision I had to make – I was personally at the Command Centre. It was a very difficult decision to make. Our hostages – our fishermen were on board – they were heading straight on for Somalia – our coastguard boat was there, and they were threatening at the same time as we got nearer that they were going to shoot the fishermen if we tried to board their ship. I had to protect my people.

There was an Iranian dhow here in the harbour in Victoria. We got the captain and we found out exactly where the engine was situated. It was the same type of boat, according to the information that we had from our coastguard vessel. So I gave instruction to the captain of the ship to fire just above the engine to ensure that the boat would sink but we would not hit the engine causing the boat to catch fire, as if it caught fire it could explode. So firing just above, the boat would start to sink.

My thinking was – the instinct for survival. If the boat is sinking, the pirates will not start thinking to harm the fishermen – they will start thinking about saving their lives. They will jump in the sea. And our fishermen will also jump in the sea, and we can go in and rescue them.

So – it worked. We fired, the boat started to sink, and the pirates all jumped in the sea, forgetting the fishermen – it was a fight for survival. Because these pirates were not professional fishermen, not professional seamen. As soon as everyone was in the water our coastguard moved in, rescued our fishermen first, and then after that we rescued the pirates. In the firing, one of the pirates was wounded, but all our hostages were freed unscathed.

There were two operations like that and both times we managed to bring our fishermen back unharmed.'

It was a mesmerising tale. In such a tiny country as Seychelles, everyone knows everyone. People whom he knew personally, whom he had met and whose families he knew, would have been among those captured by the pirates. His had been the final responsibility, the finger on the trigger, and both times his people had been rescued unharmed.

The other moment that stood out for him was meeting Rolly Tambara (see Chapter 29) and Marc Songoire, two elderly Seychellois fishermen who had been held hostage for over a year, during which they had been treated extremely harshly. Although he would not confirm it, I knew that James Michel had been personally involved in every stage of the 12-month negotiations to free these two grandfathers.

'We managed to bring them back, and when they disembarked at the airport, you could see the pain in their eyes of what they had been through. Just going and hugging them was something beautiful inside. I said "Welcome back, my brothers."'

08

FIGHTING THE WAR ON PIRACY

The Lockheed P-3 Orion is not the sort of plane that you will normally see at a civilian airport. This American four-engine turboprop aircraft has been in military service since the 1960s, since when P-3s have seen operation in spheres as varied as the Cuban missile crisis, the Vietnam War, Iraq and Afghanistan – but nothing has been stranger than their current role: hunting pirates.

Depending on sea states and atmospheric conditions, from the heights at which they operate P-3s can see skiffs from around 32 km (20 miles) away, dhow-sized vessels from 80 km (50 miles), and larger ships, merchant vessels and oil tankers from considerably further. They also do intelligence surveillance and reconnaissance along coastal areas, looking for potential signs of pirate activity on land as well as at sea.

Flying daily from their base in Djibouti, P-3s of the Spanish and German navies spend up to ten hours a day patrolling vast tracts of the western Indian Ocean. In addition to these P-3s, Luxembourg is also contributing a shorter-range twin-turboprop Merlin, contracted from a civilian company. These EU Naval Force (EUNAVFOR) planes are part of the larger co-ordinated operation to eliminate piracy in these seas, one clear and visible response to President James Michel's appeal to the international community for a co-ordinated commitment to tackle Somali piracy.

Squadron Leader Geoff Fleming of the British Royal Air Force, currently attached to EUNAVFOR, refers to them as MPRAs – Maritime Patrol and Reconnaissance Aircraft.

'The number of patrol aircraft and the nations providing them is always changing. The other operations – NATO's Ocean Shield and Combined Maritime Force (CMF) also provide aircraft when possible. CMF rely a lot on US forces. The Australians and New Zealanders have provided MPRAs to them in the past. And we have the independent deployers as well. The Japanese presently have two P-3 Orions, one of which is always out on daily patrols.'

Obviously the principal aim of the mission is to locate suspect pirate vessels or activity, similar to the role of a traffic cop on the lookout for stolen cars.

'When you spot something at sea, the first job is investigating to identify the vessel to establish if it is a suspicious contact and worth closer investigation. If pirates are confirmed or suspected on board, the nearest warship is tasked to investigate.'

The electronic optical camera below the nose of the plane can record high-resolution images for post-mission analysis. Of particular interest are any vessels on their High Interest Shipping List – boats suspected as having been taken over by pirates that are now being used as mother ships. Geoff explains that the MPRA will record every vessel in its designated patrol area.

'It's good to get an overall picture of the pattern of life – what ships are out there. It's also good for the merchant ships to see us too, so that they know we are there and give them that reassurance.

Sometimes it's just an overt presence that works as a deterrent. Sometimes the sight alone of a reconnaissance aircraft is enough to spook pirates.'

The EUNAVFOR website recounts one such occasion when just the sight of a patrolling plane and the knowledge that they had been spotted was enough to make a pirate crew abandon the vessel they had taken:

'On Saturday 26 April 2014 the master of a dhow spoke of his relief after six armed pirates, who had taken his vessel and crew hostage, fled the scene after sightings of an EU Naval Force Spanish Maritime Patrol and Reconnaissance Aircraft.

The master confirmed his ordeal to members of the Boarding Team from the EU Naval Force flagship, FGS *Brandenburg*, after the German warship had closed the sea area to investigate the dhow.

The master stated that the pirates had forced him and his crew to sail to the Gulf of Aden, where they had planned to use the dhow as a "mother ship" to attack merchant ships at sea.'

On this occasion, the ship's captain reported that the pirates had taken with them electronic and personal items stolen from the crew. It could have been far worse...

The planes are often the first responder to an incident, sometimes even able to bring it to a satisfactory conclusion on their own before the arrival of warships. Another incident from the EUNAVFOR website recounts an oil tanker in the Gulf of Aden sending out a distress call that they were under attack from pirates. A Spanish P-3 aircraft was first at the scene and the crew could clearly see the pirates attempting to board the tanker, which was travelling at full speed and executing evasive manoeuvres. Although not armed, the P-3 made three passes over the tanker at low level, each time dropping a smoke bomb. After the third pass the pirates had been thrown into such disarray that they broke off the attack.

Geoff explains that the benefits of aerial patrols are obvious.

'You can cover larger areas of the sea with an MPRA than with a warship so we term it a force multiplier. You space your ships around the area of operations, and then if anything happens, the MPRA is there to guide the ships to the scene. It's a tightly co-ordinated operation, in co-operation with all the other forces out there.'

The EUNAVFOR website records another time when the MPRA located a clearly suspicious incident and remained at the scene until the navy could arrive to take over. On this occasion, the multinational co-operation is clearly apparent, as an Australian plane assisted the Russian Navy to reach a pirated Russian tanker.

'On this day, one of two AP-3C Orion maritime patrol aircraft operated by the Royal Australian Air Force in the Middle East responded to a distress call on the international maritime emergency channel from a civilian vessel. The Orion crew was tasked to identify if the ship's crew were in difficulties from a suspected pirate attack. Arriving on the scene in the Gulf of Aden, the aircrew observed an oil tanker, the MV *Moscow University*, lying dead in the water with three small skiffs – of the kind used by Somali pirates – pulled up alongside. Communications were established with the tanker's crew, who confirmed that they were in a safe location but in need of assistance against pirates who had stormed aboard and were roaming the ship. The request for help was relayed and the next day the 23 members of the tanker's crew were rescued unharmed by a Russian warship which was nearby.'

Geoff told me of another recent incident that again highlighted the seamless co-operation between the various forces and nations patrolling the High Risk Area.

'An oil tanker issued a distress call to the UK Maritime Trade Operations (UKMTO) on the evening of Friday 17 January 2014, reporting that it was under attack from a skiff. The attack was repelled by the tanker's armed security team, and the skiff then headed to a dhow which was lurking nearby, apparently being used as a mother ship.

The dhow was located by a Japanese maritime patrol aircraft operating out of Djibouti; a helicopter from the Japanese warship *Samidare* went to investigate. The EUNAVFOR flagship *Siroco* was then able to close distance to the dhow and launch its own helicopter and boarding team.

As they got close to the dhow, the helicopter crew and boarding team observed that people on board the dhow were throwing equipment overboard, deepening the suspicion that the dhow was indeed the reported pirate mother ship. Once the *Siroco*'s team boarded the dhow, five Somali suspect pirates surrendered, and the dhow's captain confirmed that his boat had been seized several days previously and had indeed been used in the failed attack on the tanker.'

In addition to the international naval forces, individual nations also have their own coastal protection. India is a major player in the war. The pirates have reached across to Indian shores; all of India's seaborne trade with the Middle East and the West passes through the High Risk Area, and its fishing vessels have also been targeted by piracy. The Indian Navy, air force and coastguard are extremely vigilant both in their own coastal waters and in supporting international efforts. Indeed, every country in the region has its own forces on permanent high alert.

The MPRAs are just one part of the jigsaw of assets in the air and on the water that form the ring of steel around the Somali coastline. There are also helicopters on board many of the warships that can be used for reconnaissance and tactical operations at closer range to their base ship. Unmanned Aerial Vehicles (UAVs) – more commonly known as drones – have also been deployed, particularly by the US Forces; their greater range and longer flying time means they can spend more extended periods in searching and observing the sea areas furthest from land. There is, of course, additional intelligence supplied by the lookouts on the thousands of ships transiting the region. All of these create a cobweb that is increasingly hard for the pirates to break through.

Occasionally, though, it is not the state-of-the-art technology and naval ring of steel that is the cause of the pirates' downfall, but their own egos.

In January 2013, Mohamed Abdi Hassan (best known by the nickname 'Big Mouth') announced to reporters that after eight years of successful piracy he was giving up the business to concentrate on his legitimate dealings. During that period, his name had been linked with some of the most infamous hijackings, including the Ukrainian ship MV *Faina*, which was carrying Russian-made tanks and weapons, released after payment of a US$3.2 million ransom; and the Saudi-owned supertanker MV *Sirius Star*, freed after two months and a US$3 million ransom being parachuted on to its deck.

A UN monitoring group report at one stage alleged that Big Mouth was 'one of the most notorious and influential leaders of the Hobyo-Harardhere Piracy Network'. The piratic event he will remember the best is of the relatively insignificant Belgian dredger *Pompei*.

After Big Mouth's public retirement announcement, and dissatisfied with trials and arrests where only the foot soldiers were ever prosecuted, the Belgian authorities designed a sting operation to bring this self-confessed pirate leader to justice for the seizure of the *Pompei*.

When it became clear that an international arrest warrant would achieve nothing inside Somalia, undercover agents working through an associate known as Tiiceey persuaded Big Mouth that they wanted to make a documentary about Somali pirates based on his life, and asked him to be an adviser on the film. He took the bait, unable to pass up the chance of such publicity and glamour. In October 2013, Big Mouth arrived with his companion at Brussels Airport, but instead of the expected red-carpet treatment, both were arrested.

'He's one of the most important and infamous kingpin pirate leaders, responsible for the hijacking of dozens of commercial vessels from 2008 to 2013,' the Belgian prosecutor announced, adding that, 'All too often, those persons stay out of the frame and let others carry out their dirty business.'

Big Mouth could now go to prison for up to 15 years for piracy and for 30 years for hostage-taking. His colleague Tiiceey is a former governor of the Somali region of Himan and Heeb, and is suspected of aiding Big Mouth's pirate organisation.

I got first-hand experience of aerial anti-piracy operations when I spent a day patrolling with the Seychelles Air Force (SAF).

On final approach, the single runway of Seychelles International Airport most resembles the deck of an aircraft carrier, being built totally on reclaimed land, and surrounded by sea on three sides. Based in a hangar adjoining the runway is the small Seychelles Air Force, with whom I was to spend a day on pirate patrol. I'd arrived early; a rainstorm had just passed through, but already the concrete stand in front of the open hangar doors was steaming dry. Inside the hangar, one of the crew meticulously polished the glass dome attached to the front of the plane's nose containing the camera lenses.

Over a coffee, we discussed today's flight, patrolling west of the islands towards the limit of Seychelles territorial waters. Apart from the pilot, I was surprised at how young the rest of the aircrew appeared. Inevitably, in a country as small as Seychelles, it turned out that I had friends in common with one of them, and the conversation quickly passed from pirates to surfing.

Inside, the plane was almost bare. At the back were two twin seats incongruously adorned with the sort of cream-coloured seat covers one would find in a car sporting furry dice in the windscreen. The rear door was a Perspex affair that could be rolled up during flight, with a length of red tape strung across it as a reminder of the long drop below. All down the left side of the cabin was a long rectangular fuel tank, the plane having been specially adapted for long-range patrol missions.

Forward on the right, just behind the cockpit, lay an impressive array of computer screens with a single seat for the operator, who worked a complex computer-game-type of joystick as he rotated and zoomed various cameras. One screen showed the tracks taken by a target vessel, often an indicator of suspicious activity – the track taken by a genuine fishing boat would be very different to that of a pirate skiff.

Our take-off was delayed until an Etihad-operated Airbus from Abu Dhabi had landed and taxied to the terminal building to disgorge its passengers. As the islands finally fell away behind us, and we were staring at vast tracts of empty ocean, the analogy of trying to patrol Texas with just two cop cars returned to me. Although the sky was clear and visibility good, there was a small swell and a stiff breeze was whipping up whitecaps everywhere. How could we possibly ever locate a small pirate skiff in that seemingly endless sea?

The patrol was fairly uneventful; we logged every vessel that we saw, but most were clearly going about their normal business. What was amazing was the power and magnification of the on-board cameras. While to a crewman on a ship – or indeed a pirate – we would have been so high and distant as to be barely noticeable, from the plane we could zoom in on individuals on deck and clearly make out what they were doing. A great deal of incontrovertible evidence has been provided by these cameras to support prosecutions. Pirates, when approached by a warship, often jettison any incriminating weapons and ammunition, not realising that their every action is being captured on film.

Only as we were heading back towards the islands did the crew suddenly become agitated. I'd been provided with headphones and a microphone so I could hear what was going on over the engine noise, and now listened in as an apparently deserted fishing boat was spotted, stationary, in a location where no fishing usually took place. Radio calls to the boat received no response. The radio operator called in a coastguard cutter to take a closer look, while we circled above.

As the cutter approached, the pilot took a close pass and someone appeared on deck, initially clearly blinded by the sun and rubbing his eyes before waving to the plane. Then the radio sparked into life and the voice identified himself as a Seychellois sea cucumber fisherman. The divers were all underwater below the boat collecting sea cucumbers, he was the cook and though he was meant to stay alert, he'd actually been down below taking a nap.

It was all plausible, particularly as at that moment a couple of divers appeared, surfacing alongside the boat; by then, the coastguard cutter was coming alongside and launching its inflatable with an armed boarding party. Thus, a suspicious incident turned into an exercise, although as the pilot pointed out, 'You never know when it will be the real thing...'

09

A RELUCTANT HOSTAGE

'You can die in Somalia just for your flip-flops. One guy can see you in the street in your flip-flops and he doesn't have any. He asks you for them and if you say no, you can have a bullet in your head. That's how bad it is...'

The first Seychellois ever to be taken hostage by Somali pirates, Gilbert Victor had been forced to take part in the attack on the MV *Maersk Alabama*, which subsequently featured in the *Captain Phillips* film starring Tom Hanks. He had spent over six months as a hostage, and then almost drowned when the boat taking him ashore to be released sank in heavy surf.

'You die there, they say you drowned, they leave you on the beach. They are not going to bury you – they leave you on the beach.'

It had been clear from the outset that Gilbert didn't want to talk with me. Calls went unanswered, when I eventually managed to speak with him his answers were evasive, and promises to meet 'sometime in the next few days' or 'maybe we can do it tomorrow' were left totally vague. As a tropical storm lashed the palm trees outside, we finally sat facing each other across a table. Gilbert looked ill at ease. Some people enjoy the attention and near-celebrity status that comes with being a freed hostage. He just wanted to forget, and every interview simply reopened the wounds.

I'd eventually tracked him down at a small marina on Seychelles Mahé Island, where he was working on another boat. He'd gone back to sea soon after his release, and was preparing a charter yacht for its guests.

'Yeah, but that's my life – I've been doing it for over 30 years now. What can I do? If I was a carpenter, I'd go and do some furniture, but I'm not.'

Gilbert had been delivering *Serenity,* a 38-foot (11.5-metre) catamaran, from Seychelles to Madagascar with a small crew. It's how he earned his living.

'The Indian Ocean was always a good ocean to sail. We were always happy to just go sailing, put all the lights on, play music. That's what happened to us – when we were caught, we were playing music. That's why we never heard these people coming. We only knew we were being caught when we saw the man on the boat. Nobody ever thought that one day the Indian Ocean would be like this, with pirates coming after you.'

In the cabin preparing lunch – a bonito he had just caught – Gilbert heard a bang from the stern. At first he thought they had hit a floating obstacle.

Climbing out on to deck to investigate, he was confronted by four men, barefoot and ragged and holding guns; five more glowered up from a battered fibreglass skiff tethered to the *Serenity*.

'Who are you?' he asked. He was scared, of course, but also perplexed.

'We are Indian Ocean coastguard.'

The one who spoke stared at Gilbert for a moment. He seemed young, but clearly in command, less jumpy than the others. Gilbert noticed that his teeth were crooked, the front ones overlapping.

'Look, my friend,' Gilbert said, 'these are Seychelles waters.'

'No, no,' the man answered. 'You have islands. We have water. We Somali pirate.'

Gilbert's captor Abduwali Muse was soon to become infamous but at this stage, to Gilbert, the skinny, ragged young Somali with the crooked teeth was just 'Little Captain', as he only stood at just over five feet tall.

'He later told me that he was only 17 and was not the leader of the gang, but he was, because when he caught me he was boasting, and all his friends were telling me – there's the boss.'

Gilbert was clearly finding telling his story difficult. His narrative was punctuated by long pauses, broken only when I asked a question or made a comment that prompted him to continue. Often when people have told a story many times it becomes polished and flows easily from them. Not so in Gilbert's case – I was having to draw every detail from him, and half-expected that at any moment he would bring our meeting to an end.

Gilbert was ordered to set sail for the Somali coast. He'd had no chance to make radio contact and as far as Seychelles Port Authority knew, *Serenity* had just disappeared from the chart.

'So nobody knew – because for all this time that we were going to Somalia without any contact to the Seychelles, there was so many things people would be thinking – maybe an accident, got sunk, maybe have bad weather. I learned later that people were already saying Mass for us...'

From the very first, the scariest part of being held hostage was that his captors seemed to have no idea what they were doing. Uneducated, scrawny kids, armed with AK-47s that they never put down – little more than boy soldiers, smelling powerfully of stale sweat, skin erupting with sores after several weeks on an open boat far out at sea. Their behaviour was frighteningly erratic – apparently friendly one moment, pressing a gun to his temple or in his mouth the next, and firing wildly by his head or feet. They claimed to fear no one.

'These people, they told me that they don't worry about the world – it's the world that worries about them.'

They didn't really seem to have a plan – just to head back to their home shores with their catch. That was a terrifying voyage – the trigger-happy pirates' mood swings meant that at any time they might just kill their prisoners. There were no means of communication save for gestures and the international language of a pointed gun.

All the while Gilbert was sailing, one or other of his captors was standing over him with a loaded AK-47 to ensure he pulled no tricks. Gilbert had broken down in tears the first time a gun was put to his head, and through the whole voyage his nerves were frayed, he slept little, and remained in constant fear that any random moment could become his last.

Gilbert had always been immensely proud of his work, and kept any boat he was delivering in the most immaculate condition, but before his eyes *Serenity* was being trashed by the pirates. They ripped open every cupboard and hatch, helping themselves to whatever they saw. Gilbert's own clothes were taken from his cabin and worn and discarded by the Somalis; food and drink stores were plundered; debris and unwashed dishes and pans littered the boat. When the toilet blocked, the pirates continued to urinate and defecate in it till it overflowed. The wanton and needless sacking of the boat just brought Gilbert down even further.

After two weeks, *Serenity* anchored off the Somali coast some 400 nautical miles (740 km) north of Mogadishu, after calling in at a number of ports along the way. An older Somali came on board, and he spoke some English. He told Gilbert that they were to be released – but only once a US$3 million ransom had been paid. To the Somalis, Gilbert must have seemed a rich man – sailing a luxury catamaran, he had to be worth a sizeable sum.

Three million dollars. The Somalis might as well have asked for free trips to the Moon. Gilbert lived in a tiny house on the hillside behind Victoria. He knew no one who could raise three thousand dollars, let alone three million.

The older Somali turned out to be a negotiator on the pirates' behalf. The demands were phoned through to a mediator in Seychelles. At least people back home now knew they were alive.

Little Captain had disappeared once they reached the Somali coast, but within a few days he was back on board, and with his gun again to Gilbert's head told him that he would be taking them back to sea. *Serenity* was to be the mother ship, towing the attack skiffs behind. This would be pure luxury for the Somalis, who were accustomed to hunting from small open boats, and a yacht was far less likely to be suspected as a pirate vessel. Gilbert was being press-ganged into piracy.

For a week he steered *Serenity* wherever he was told, Little Captain's orders being backed up by a home-made bomb in a glass jar filled with nails strapped under his seat. 'You call navy, I blow you to Allah.'

The first prey was a Taiwanese fishing boat *Win Far 161*, and after that was taken by the pirates, conditions for Gilbert got worse – he and his crew were moved to the overcrowded quarters of the fishing boat, already home to 30 Taiwanese fishermen.

'So that was when everything went wrong. Everything went very bad because we were all different nationalities, so there we were under guns all the time being watched by these people.'

Meanwhile the Somalis had spotted a far bigger target.

'The guy who caught us – Little Captain – he was the one who attacked the *Maersk Alabama*. He was with us when he did that.'

Having stalked the *Alabama* throughout the night, Little Captain and three others boarded the attack skiff, laden with a boarding ladder, grappling hooks, AK-47s and RPGs, while the *Win Far 161* headed on for the coast of Somalia with its harvest of hostages.

The fate of that attack crew is well known. Little Captain – his real name Abduwali Muse – was the sole survivor of the attack.

Gilbert subsequently identified his photograph to the FBI, resulting in his indictment for the two additional acts of piracy, and he is currently serving a 33-year sentence in the tough Federal Correctional Institution in Terre Haute, Indiana – known to inmates as 'The Terror Hut'.

But Gilbert's ordeal was only now starting.

Anchored back off the Somali coast, at first progress seemed to be made in the negotiations – Gilbert was even allowed to speak directly with the mediator in Seychelles, and his hopes were high.

'They would come and give you the cell phone and say speak to the guy for my money. The last time when this guy talked to me it was a Thursday and he said, "Look Gilbert, we are coming to the weekend. We cannot do anything now but definitely early next week we are coming for you." If you were in my place, what would you do? You'd be happy – I'm going home! And then next week nothing; what do you do? You go down again. That's when you start crying again and then from that day, it was 12th June, nobody talked to us again.'

Negotiations for their release seemed to have broken down. From that day in June, for the next three months they heard absolutely nothing. The world seemed to have forgotten about them, and their own world became the confines of the trawler. Gilbert despaired. There seemed no hope.

Conditions on board the Taiwanese tuna boat were intolerable. The hull of the ship created oven-like heat in the scorching sun; overcrowded with too many bodies in a confined space, the stench was rancid and hygiene impossible. Youths toting AK-47s, increasingly angry that no ransoms were being paid, constantly threatened them. With nothing to do but sit and ruminate, morbid depression set in.

Occasionally, if his captors were distracted, Gilbert managed to sneak up to the bridge and briefly use the ship's phone.

'If I got a chance I was stealing the ship's phone and calling my wife saying, "Look, what's going on? Have you heard anything?" – And all the time, no. I was risking being shot by stealing the phone.

'When you are hostage and these people want money from you, they will never treat you right. I mean you just sit there and all the time they come to you asking "Where's the money? No money, you don't go home." So that's when you start saying "I don't have that money, Seychelles doesn't have that money." That's when you start thinking you will never go home, because who's going to pay?'

To the Somalis, the hostages were just commodities.

'They will tell you if one man dies then another one comes. Just think how bad it can be if one guy said to you if you die, another one will come.'

Gilbert had given up all hope of ever seeing his family again when, over six months into the ordeal and with no explanation, he and his crew were told to get into a small boat to go home.

'And we ended up being capsized 200 metres from the shore. Just imagine being held prisoner on a boat for six months where the order was you sit and sleep, you sit and sleep. No exercise – and then there you are in the Indian Ocean in rough seas, big swell coming on to the beach. But you know you have to be strong, you don't just say you are going to die. Better you die in front of your family...'

By this point, Gilbert had asked that we turn off the cameras. Three years on and the scars were still too deep.

'I don't want you to show my face on TV with me crying, because if my children see it... If I was someone living by myself, I would tell you the story but I have my children, I have my wife – I don't want her to see that.'

By now I was feeling that I had pushed far enough. Reliving his experience was clearly distressing for Gilbert. I told him how much I appreciated him giving me his time, and as I was packing up asked if there was anything else he wanted to say about the pirates.

'Pirates – no, they are not. These people are gangsters, kidnappers or whatever you can call them. But definitely they are not pirates. They're hijacking boats, they are hijackers. It's just like somebody says to you they hijack a plane. Will you call them Somali hijackers – that's what these people they are, kidnappers. They never take anything from the boat; they don't want your food or anything like that – they just want to say "Ok, we got you here – you give us $3 million or $4 million before you go home." That's ransom – if someone is asking ransom for your release, you have been kidnapped.'

Gilbert is a big man, but the occasional tear had been running down his cheek, and it was time for us to leave. As we shook hands, he told me that this would be the last interview he would ever give. He's been offered a lot of money to sell his story, but isn't interested. He just wants to put it all behind him and get on with life.

10

COMPLAINTS ABOUT THE FOOD

I reflected back on Gilbert Victor's tale of life as a hostage during the break in my first day of interviews at the Montagne Posée Prison in Seychelles. So far, the two men whom I had met seemed a far cry from the pirates Gilbert had described to me. It was hard to imagine the man who had asked me to bring him a book so he could study English being an AK-47-toting terrorist of the shipping lanes.

While my interviewees Maalin Daud Olat and his companion went for prayers, I set off looking for something to eat. The only place was the Gurkha guards' mess – an outside kitchen shaded by a tarpaulin, where bat curry was the only choice on the menu. I had tried to strike up conversation with a couple of these former Nepalese soldiers, now on contract to guard pirates on this Seychellois mountaintop, but although they were friendly our common language was limited to just a few words. When I climbed the stairs back to the classroom that was my base for the day, stepping over the still sleeping dog that did not seem to have moved since my arrival that morning, Maalin's companion, and perhaps his second in command or 'minder' within the prison, was waiting for me.

Mohamed Hassan Ali was large, slightly plump, with a beard; soft and gentle-looking – or perhaps deceptively so. Incongruously, he wore an 'I ♡ New York' badge on the collar of his red-and-white polo shirt.

He was serving a sentence of 21 years. Aged 39, he told me he was from Mogadishu and had once had a family but 'not now'.

'I had no education. I learned to be a mechanic from age eight; I joined a garage at ten and was there till I was 18, when I started fishing. I was a fisherman. I had worked as a fisherman and as a mechanic repairing boats since 2002. We fished a company's boat, at sea for 20 days at a time, even a month. The catch would be sold to the company, expenses deducted and the remainder shared between the crew. More often, we would just go out overnight, throw our nets about three in the afternoon, haul them in in the morning and return to shore with our catch as we had no freezers on the small boats.

Before the pirates scared them away, the foreign ships were always taking our nets. We would fish for shark mainly, but also for any fish we could get, with 50-metre-long (165 feet) nets. We would link as many as 25 of these nets together then hold a spotlight. But the foreign ships would come through during the night and tear up our nets and we would lose them.

Because we were only 55 km (35 miles) from Mogadishu, we could sell the fish we caught, but further north there was no market – if they caught fish, there was no one to buy them. The sharks, we sold both the fins and the meat.

This should have just been another ordinary fishing trip. Adale was our port of departure. There were 25 of us with three skiffs on an Iranian fishing boat. It was my first trip on the Iranian boat but I'd done trips like this on other boats.'

Adale is one of those sad reminders of colonial Italian prosperity and stability in Somalia. It was a halt, a station on the long-defunct

South Somalia railway system that ran 70 miles (115 km) between Mogadishu and what is now Jowhar. As well as passengers, the line carried products from plantations along the way to the Port of Mogadishu – bananas, coffee and cotton. No train has run for more than 70 years.

'We left Adale on a North Iranian boat with Iranian fishermen. The boat was named *Tahiri*, although in court it was called something else like *Jelbut 40*. There were freezers on board to preserve the fish we caught. On the second day, we were attacked by a Danish ship *Absalon* 40 miles (74 km) from Somalia and taken on board. We spent 22 days on that ship before being landed in Seychelles. They treated us well on board, but the portions of food were small.'

I later told Lieutenant Commander Jacqui Sherriff at EUNAVFOR of this complaint about the on-board cuisine on the navy's vessels. Interestingly, she said this was a deliberate policy, not to starve the Somalis, but because having been used to smaller amounts of food, the navy didn't want to make them unwell!

Mohamed continued his story. 'Of the 25 of us, four were landed in Seychelles, four in Kenya and the other 17 released. They said they could only take four of us in Seychelles as the prisons there were full – the same day another British warship had landed 14 prisoners. The Iranians did not say they had been hijacked, and we had no guns or RPGs on board. We were told we had attacked *Tahiri* and our skiffs were proof. I believe we were found guilty because of the tension here in Seychelles. Two of their fishermen were being held in Somalia so it was a political decision.'

These two fishermen were the elderly Rolly Tambara whom I was later to meet, and his friend Mark Songoire. It is certainly true there was a massive groundswell of sympathy for them in Seychelles and a resultant anti-Somali feeling. While they were still held hostage, I had filmed crammed church services all around the islands dedicated to their release.

'When he sentenced us, the judge said "I will do you a favour and give you 21 years' imprisonment." I think he thought he was being funny. Three of us got that – the juvenile who was 16 years old got 14 years.

I feel so bad. We had done no wrong. We were nowhere near Seychelles – just fishing 40 miles (74 km) from Somalia. I'm 39. Twenty-one years less remission means I will be 53 years old before I am free. I may even die before that. I have lost my life, my wife, my family, lost everything.

I'm waiting for an appeal but I have no hope as both my lawyer and the judge were Seychellois.'

I wanted to learn more about life in Mogadishu.

'From 1991, there has been no good life in Somalia. Central government fell in '91. In the tribal clashes of '92 many lost their lives, many more all their belongings. There was the great hunger in '93. UNOSOM [United Nations Operation in Somalia] came and made centres to give out porridge, maize, soya. When people get this help they feel better. UNOSOM left in October '95 and from then till now there have been lots of presidents, lots of warlords, all claiming territory.

In the fighting in Mogadishu I lost my wife, brother, and two uncles.

I am scared they will transfer me to a prison in Puntland – they might keep me in and release real pirates who pay them. And the roads, the distance, no one could ever visit me from Mogadishu.'

Mohamed told me that one of the others who had been arrested with him was waiting outside and would confirm his story. The mandatory pack of 10 Mahé Kings cigarettes exchanged hands, and I spoke briefly with Abdul Ahmed Mohammed. He was now 18 years old but due to his youth at the time of trial received the discounted 14-year sentence. Adale was his home town. He had never been to school. From age 15, he drove a cargo truck. His mother was still alive; his father had died while he was here in prison.

He confirmed word for word Mohamed's version of their arrest, and shared the apparent bemusement that many of those I was to speak to felt. 'How do you see taking someone from their own coast, bringing them to a foreign country, and giving them a very big sentence when they were just fishing to provide for their family? How can that be justice?'

As with many of those I interviewed, Mohamed and Abdul were very persuasive and passionate about their innocence. On my first day in the prison, I had met three alleged pirates, all of whom had argued their blamelessness. I decided to call in at the court on my way back to my rented cottage to do some research of my own and try to pull up a copy of the judgement in the *Tahiri* case – I had already learned that piracy cases were known by the names of the ships pirated rather than the names of the defendants. The judge's clerk was glad to help – in fact I could find the judgement online.

When I read it that evening, the prosecution's version of facts was somewhat different to what Mohamed had told me. The Danish warship *Absalon* had been observing a known pirate camp 53 nautical miles (100 km) south of Hobyo for over a month. The fishing dhow *Tahiri* had previously been moored up alongside a ship that was being held by the pirates, and had subsequently been released on payment of a US$10 million ransom. For this reason among others, *Tahiri* was suspected of also being taken by the pirates.

When *Tahiri* slipped from its moorings after dark, *Absalon* tracked it, and at dawn launched its helicopter, which reported what the judge termed 'Several piracy indicators on board, including armed persons of Somali origin.' The Commander of the warship also told the court that skiffs and hooked ladders were aboard.

Absalon ordered *Tahiri* to stop and fired warning shots but the boat failed to comply. The Danes then fired on to the boat, hitting the funnel, water tanks and fuel tank but *Tahiri* still kept going. Only after flash bang grenades and tear gas were fired into the wheelhouse did *Tahiri* stop, enabling the Danes to board her. On board they found nine Pakistanis, five Iranians, and 25 Somalis. No weapons were found except some booster charges for RPGs, but Commander Fjord Larsen told the court that before his men had managed to board, he and his crew had watched the Somalis throw a large number of weapons and ammunition overboard, including RPGs and AK-47s.

Although he did not give evidence at his trial, Mohamed Hassan Ali did talk when interviewed by the police. He confirmed that he was a mechanic on board, stating that the Iranians and Pakistanis on board were not hostages but 'our business partners'.

None of the hostages appear to have given evidence at the trial. Convicting men of piracy without requiring anyone who had actually been pirated to give evidence to say it had happened did seem to me, well, unusual... I spoke later with a prosecuting lawyer who explained to me the difficulty of getting subsistence-wage Asian fishermen to a foreign court to testify – the problems indeed of tracking them down at all many months later when a trial eventually takes place.

11

AN UNWISE TARGET

Sometimes the pirates get just a bit more than they bargained for.

Operation Atalanta, otherwise known as European Union Naval Force Somalia (EUNAVFOR-ATALANTA), is the first joint naval operation by European Union forces, and represents part of the international effort to combat piracy off the coast of Somalia. Among the multi-national fleet was the Spanish warship SPS *Patiño*, technically known as a Supply Class Fast Combat Support Ship. She carries a crew of 148, as well as some 20 aircrew for her helicopters – of which she carries up to five – and while on Operation Atalanta, she also carried a complement of marines: a total of around 180 highly trained frontline Spanish servicemen.

The honour of being flagship of the fleet rotates among the ships and nations making up the EUNAVFOR contingent at any time. At that particular time, *Patiño* held the position of flagship of the fleet. In the hours before dawn on 12 January 2012, the ship received some unexpected visitors – Somali pirates. Shortly afterwards, I joined the ship for a routine patrol.

As we were leaving harbour, Commander Enrique Cubeiro told me the story of the surprise dawn attack. Very relaxed, in his dark blue, short-sleeved, open-necked tropical naval kit, his tale was interspersed with brief orders to his junior officers on the bridge.

'About 45 minutes before sunrise, we were attacked by a group of pirates in a small skiff. It was still dark, and a day of seas so rough we had picked nothing up on our radar, so for us it was a very big surprise. With sea conditions like these, no one on board would have expected a pirate attack.'

The crew were at breakfast when a lookout reported a skiff very close to the stern of the ship, trying to attach a ladder. They immediately alerted the bridge who called Commander Cubeiro, who was at the time in his cabin, and told him that a group of pirates were trying to board *Patiño*. As he arrived on the bridge, the pirates started firing – not at the bridge, which is at the bow of the ship, but at the rear superstructure where the bridge would be on most cargo ships. There were four marines on the aft deck and they immediately returned fire; there was an exchange of shots for about 30 seconds. The pirates obviously had second thoughts, and the skiff turned and headed away from the ship. Commander Cubeiro was astonished; *Patiño* was supposed to be hunting pirates, not pirates hunting the warship!

'We were now at battle stations. The first job was to find the pirates – not easy as their small skiff had no clear radar signal among the big waves. We started to execute a search – it was getting light by now – and as soon as possible, we launched a helicopter. The helicopter found the skiff within six minutes, about 6 miles (11 km) from the ship. The Djiboutian officer on board hailed the pirates and told them to stop, but they ignored him. So the helicopter had to fire a few warning shots – that stopped them.

Three of the Somalis had bullet wounds, from the earlier exchange of fire with our marines, so our priority was to transfer them from the skiff – not easy in those seas. They were operated on in our hospital on board and all survived.'

Commander Cubeiro had been telling the story while overseeing our departure from harbour. Now he handed over command of the ship, and we left the bridge and crossed the deck to the stern, passing open hangar doors in which mechanics were working on two large helicopters. Heading up several flights of steel stairs in what seemed to be a tower crammed with pipes and vents, he pointed to sunlight streaming through bullet holes in the aft superstructure. The attack had been so recent that as *Patiño* was still on patrol, there had been no opportunity to head into a shipyard for repair work to be carried out.

In another hangar, among coils of cables and stacks of barrels, was the pirates' attack skiff, which had been hauled aboard. It was crudely built of white fibreglass and had certainly seen better days, as had the old 40hp Yamaha engine on its stern. In the conditions that day, it had only been capable of 15–16 knots, far less than the speed of *Patiño* in pursuit.

'They said it was a mistake – they hadn't meant to attack a warship. They had thought it was a merchant vessel with the bridge at the stern. So they thought that would be okay – as they hadn't meant to attack a Spanish warship, they should be set free. It was all one big mistake.'

The pirates knew that at that time the EUNAVFOR policy was to take all weapons and dump them back on the Somali coast. Commander Cubeiro and his fellow officers were almost amused by the idea; this had been a clear attack on a Spanish warship, so they were headed for trial in the Spanish courts.

When I was picked up from *Patiño* by a Seychelles coastguard boat at the end of our day's patrol, I looked back at the ship and realised that the pirates' mistake had been an easy one to make.

Patiño doesn't have the classic lines of a sleek warship. There is superstructure both fore and aft, and two huge gantries midships. She had been moving slowly 50 nautical miles (92 km) off the Somali coast – in fact, waiting to escort a food aid ship into Mogadishu. In the grey, flat pre-dawn light, her silhouette was very similar to that of a slow-moving and vulnerable cargo vessel that would have been easy prey for the pirates.

Despite everything, as one seaman speaking of others, Commander Cubeiro had expressed what seemed to me to be a sneaking respect for the pirates. When I had asked him what his views were on them, he had thought carefully.

'The pirates showed,' and he paused to think how best to put it '... tremendous willingness. It was a day of very rough seas – waves three to four metres. It was very windy and quite far from the Somali coast. They must have been at sea for more than three to four days. So for me, it was ... impressive that they stayed in these conditions all this time at sea.'

The contrast between the pirate skiff and this ship of war could not be more marked. On *Patiño*'s bridge at least a dozen specialists hovered around a range of electronic screens and devices, radar, controls and navigation systems, while others came and went with a busy sense of purpose, wearing their smart uniforms of dark blue, short-sleeved, open-necked shirts, bright yellow insignia on the shoulders, and matching caps. The rails of the ship bristled with powerful high-velocity machine guns, belts of bullets running from metal ammo boxes. We'd been shown the ship's clinically clean operating theatre where five scrubbed and gowned medics were setting the broken leg of a crewman who had tripped and fallen badly while ashore.

I remembered the lack of instruments of any kind on the open skiff; the ragged clothing of the pirates and their open sores from sustained exposure at sea; their paltry weapons, and understood where Commander Cubeiro was coming from.

When they realised they were not being returned to Somalia but would be taken to Spain to face trial, the pirates' story changed from that of a mistaken attack, that they had somehow seemed to think would absolve them of culpability. They now stated there had been a seventh pirate on board who had been killed and whom they had thrown overboard – enabling them to claim that the missing man was the one who had fired the shots and had forced them to try to board the ship.

By the time the case came to trial, their story had changed again. They now said they were only fishermen who had approached the navy vessel in their skiff because they had lost their way, were hungry and needed help, and the Spaniards opened fire on them without warning. None of the versions impressed the judge. All six pirates were convicted and received sentences ranging from 13 to 17 years.

Patiño wasn't the first naval vessel to be attacked by pirates. In fact, in April 2010 there were two attacks on US warships within ten days.

On 31 March 2010, the guided-missile frigate USS *Nicholas* was tracking the pirates at long range off the Kenyan coast. Around midnight, a skiff containing three Somalis approached and opened fire. The *Nicholas* wasn't exactly a soft target. A warship that had seen action in the first Gulf War, it had no problem in dealing with a handful of ragtag pirates. The *Nicholas* returned fire, disabled the skiff, and detained three suspects before picking up two more from a nearby mother ship.

It's hard to think that the Somalis could have thought that the *Nicholas* was anything other than a naval vessel, unlike *Patiño,* where the mistaken identity was understandable. Assuming they knew their target, it's even harder to think that the three Somalis on the attack skiff really thought that they could take on and defeat the whole crew of an American ship of war.

Perhaps there is another explanation, and this incident is an illustration of how very unsophisticated and unaware of the world many pirates may be. Poor herdsmen and nomads who had lived a subsistence existence in the Somali desert and plains would have no idea what a warship looked like. They had no education, would never have watched movies, and maybe genuinely had no understanding of the target they were attacking. In that period, the pirates' success rates were extremely high. Perhaps they just saw an enormous ship and thought it would be worth a lot of ransom money.

Just ten days later, there was another pirate attack on an American naval vessel. While the *Nicholas* had been attacked in the southern reaches of the piracy zone, off the Kenyan coast, this attack took place to the northern end of their range. USS *Ashland* was at the time some 380 nautical miles (700 km) off Djibouti, in the entrance to the Red Sea, when shortly before dawn, a skiff with six pirates closed on her and started firing. The navy ship returned fire with two rounds from a 25 mm gun, which started a fire on the skiff. The pirates leapt into the sea and were picked up by a rigid-hull inflatable boat from *Ashland*. This attack may well have been a mistake, the pirates thinking *Ashland* was a commercial merchant ship. *Ashland* is actually an amphibious dock landing ship and, like the *Patiño*, has none of the sleek warship lines of most naval vessels.

Indeed, that is exactly what one of the Somalis said when the case came to trial in Norfolk, Virginia, in the USA. Hoping for a lesser sentence, he agreed to give evidence against the rest of the crew. He claimed to be the group's leader and testified that when one of his crew members fired an AK-47 at the *Ashland*, they thought they were attacking a merchant ship.

The case for the others was somewhat different – they claimed to have been returning to Somalia after ferrying refugees to Yemen, when they came across the ship in the Gulf of Aden. They said an AK-47 was fired in the *Ashland*'s direction to get its attention, so it could help them after they had been wandering around lost at sea. That version did not exactly tie in with the Federal Prosecutor's description of one of the Somalis standing and aiming a rocket-propelled grenade at the warship. Nor did either version impress the judge, who imposed sentences exceeding 40 years' imprisonment. Once again, when the pirates had attacked one of their own naval vessels, the country in question decided that the powers of their own courts were sufficient to prosecute the case there, rather than in an Indian Ocean trial centre such as Seychelles.

This was one of the rare times when there was a breach in ranks by the Somalis, with one giving evidence against the others, and also telling a different story to his colleagues. In almost every other piracy case that I was to investigate, the defendants seemed to have chosen a defence that all adopted and stuck with, even if it was often not the story they had initially told when arrested.

12

NAVAL FORCE HEADQUARTERS

Cherry blossoms were blooming in the London commuter suburb of Northwood. On one side of the road sat the detached houses and manicured gardens of well-to-do city workers; this was where the BBC's popular comedy series 'The Good Life' was filmed in the 1970s – a parody of middle-class shock horror at people not conforming to their perceived standards.

On the other side of the road, the cherry blossoms didn't quite conceal the state-of-the-art surveillance cameras and a heavy-duty wire mesh fence, topped with razor wire.

Once a country estate, before it was swallowed up by the relentless creep of sprawling suburbia, Eastbury Park was taken over in 1939 by the RAF's Coastal Command as an officers' mess, and the Battle of Britain was directed from the bunkers they built there.

Thirty years later, when the RAF no longer had a use for the complex, it became the location for the British Armed Forces Permanent Joint Headquarters (PJHQ) for planning and controlling overseas military operations. Another part of the complex became the base for NATO's Maritime Command (MARCOM).

I was there to visit a newcomer in this nest of military head-quarters – EUNAVFOR's Operational Headquarters, from where the EU's counter-piracy Operation Atalanta is commanded by a Royal Navy Rear Admiral.

From her rank alone I'd expected Lieutenant Commander Jacqueline Sherriff MBE to be a rather dominant and proper middle-class lady. The bright and engaging Royal Navy officer who came to escort me into the base after I'd cleared security – passport essential! – was a long way from that image, being relaxed, chatty and cheerful. It turned out that Jacqui's home was in the West Country, and as we walked to the building occupied by EUNAVFOR, we shared our dread of the Friday afternoon motorway traffic we would have to struggle through on our respective drives home later.

The large, open-plan office that Jacqui first took me into resembled many similar office spaces in private businesses, except that every section had a small national flag on a stick, and the people at the desks were wearing a wide assortment of their national military uniforms, ranging from camouflage gear to parade dress. Stationed alongside the 19 EU Member States at the Operational HQ of the EU Naval Force – the first ever EU combined naval operation – were military officers from three non-EU countries: Montenegro, Serbia and Ukraine.

Jacqui explained the involvement of those non-EU nations and the contributions they were making to the overall success of Operation Atalanta.

'At the beginning of this year, we had the Ukrainian Navy frigate, Hetman Sagaidachny, with a Ka-27 Helix helicopter and military contingent embarked, working with the EU Naval Force. Nations that do not provide a warship can supply military personnel. Serbia recently provided a small, highly trained military team to escort World Food Programme (WFP) ships through the piracy High Risk

Area. Using these small protection teams means that WFP vessels don't need a warship escort as they transit along the Somali coast, so the EU Force Commander can deploy the EU Naval Force warships more effectively to patrol the High Risk Area.'

In a conference room away from the collection of naval uniforms, Jacqui projected a map of the region on to the screen, and launched into a briefing she must have given many times before to visiting journalists.

'Somali piracy really spiked in 2008 and got the world's attention. The pirate attacks were having a significant impact, not only on maritime shipping and the €1 trillion-worth of international trade that is estimated to pass through the Gulf of Aden in to Europe and beyond each year. It was also raising concerns that the WFP ships, carrying humanitarian aid to the Somali people, could be pirated. As a result, the United Nations, with Security Council Resolutions in place, requested assistance from the EU and following an EU Council decision, Operation Atalanta was launched just ten weeks later in December 2008.

EU Naval Force warships, assisted by maritime patrol and reconnaissance aircraft, are at sea 24/7, deterring piracy in the High Risk Area and, whilst there, they also contribute to the monitoring of fishing off the Somali coast.'

I had previously liked the analogy of the EU Naval Force counter-piracy effort as being similar to trying to police the whole of Texas with a couple of cop cars – after all, it's a 4,800-km (3,000-mile) coastline and the Somali pirates have attacked ships as far away as the coasts of India and Madagascar. Jacqui had heard it before, and wasn't impressed.

'Our counter-piracy operations are intelligence-led and we conduct counter-piracy patrols in sea areas where the threat of attack is at its highest. So it's a bit like if you had the two police cars in Texas, there's no point patrolling cornfields if the burglars are operating elsewhere, in the towns and cities.'

And she reminded me that the EU Naval Force is not alone out there.

'The sea areas in which we operate are extensive, covering the vast waters of the Indian Ocean and Gulf of Aden, so we co-ordinate our efforts with warships from NATO, which has its maritime HQ based in the building next door, and the Combined Maritime Forces (CMF) operating out of Bahrain.'

Jacqui flashes up a map showing the locations of warships from all three counter-piracy task forces – they did indeed seem well-spaced along the Somali coast and concentrated in areas with the highest risk.

'What has been very successful is the tactical-level co-operation that has developed between the counter-piracy task forces over the past five years. At any one time we can have between 10 and 12 warships from the EU Naval Force, NATO and CMF operating off the coast.

There are also warships from countries such as China, India, Russia, Japan and South Korea operating in the areas. We now have navies from many different nations working together that traditionally would not have done so.'

Even the planet's most implacable enemies have worked together. The South Korean naval destroyer ROKS *Munmu the Great* received a distress call from the North Korean merchant vessel *Dabaksol* that it was under attack from pirates. *Munmu* launched a Lynx helicopter to assist while the warship itself headed off to help. The helicopter remained to protect the North Korean ship until the pirates aborted the attack. A news report stated that 'The North Korean sailors thanked the members of the *Munmu* before continuing on their way to India.'

Later, a member of the South Korean Joint Chiefs of Staff said: 'This is the first time that the South Korean Navy has rescued a North Korean ship from attack.' Intriguingly – possibly even prophetically? – the South Korean warship was named after the first king to achieve unification of the Korean Peninsula.

Jacqui felt that real progress was being made, but was also of the opinion that the world in general did not fully grasp what was happening.

'The real height of Somali piracy was in January 2011, when there were a total of 32 ships and 736 hostages being held for ransom by pirates off the Somali coast. With the 32 ships, including tankers, cargo carriers and smaller vessels, being held by pirates for ransom ..., you can imagine how the Somali coastline would have looked at that time. And the 736 hostages held by pirates in January 2011 – I don't think that the world really registered that figure. I remember when the 80 Chilean miners were stuck down a mine shaft and the world stopped, quite rightly, as they were brought up to the surface one by one – yet 736 hostages being held, I don't remember them getting that much attention. As I speak today, 39 hostages still remain in pirate hands, even after the 11 who were just released after being held for nearly four years.'

Pirate attacks have reduced significantly, due not only to the international naval operation, but also thanks to captains implementing a code known as Best Management Practices for Protection against Somalia-Based Piracy (BMP). This offers advice on how to avoid or, in the worst case scenario, deal with pirate attacks. Vessels also now employ armed security teams in case of incident; while their use has received some criticism, it is true to say that no ship carrying private armed security has been pirated.

I wondered whether, if piracy incidents remained low, there was a real danger that the international community might start to lower their guard and become more complacent.

Jacqui put up two comparative charts side by side, showing the tracks of vessels passing through the High Risk Area in September 2011 and during the same month in 2013. The red tracks were the ships with armed security on board, yellow without. Two things were clear – many more ships had armed security in 2013 than in 2011, but the charts also showed that some ships were once again transiting closer to the Somali coast; in 2011, most tracks steered well away from it. A number of ships were 'cutting the corner' again, saving on fuel and time.

There was also a white track shown on the 2013 chart that cut straight across the shipping lanes, from the Somali shore to the most concentrated part of the red and yellow tracks. This was the route of the most recent pirate attack. The South-West monsoon having just ended, two skiffs containing armed pirates attacked a cargo carrier 230 nautical miles (425 km) out in the Indian Ocean, due east of Hobyo. The pirates were repelled by the on-board security team. Three days later, a similar attack occurred on a Spanish fishing vessel a further 235 nautical miles (435 km) east, presumably by the same pirates.

'Both ships were able to repel the attacks, we were able to locate the pirates and apprehend them. But the pirates only have to get lucky once, and if they get on board a ship they would, as in the past, demand millions of dollars in ransom payments. This, in turn, could reinvigorate pirate leaders to once again plan attacks at sea.'

While initially restricted in their brief, the need to extend the operating areas of the EU Naval Force quickly became apparent.

'Before 2012, we could only take action against the pirates once they came out to sea. The pirates knew this and so they would use the beaches to prepare their boats for an attack, loading fuel barrels and ladders, etc, and then in the dead of night they would quickly get out to sea. In May 2012, our area of operations was extended by EU member states to include the Somali coastline.'

Within days of its mandate being extended, EUNAVFOR struck lucky. For some time they had been observing what they described as a pirate logistic dump on the central Somali coastline near Harardhere, a known pirate haven. At first light of dawn, a ship-based helicopter was launched that headed for the dump. Their timing was good – there was a lot of activity and it appeared that a pirate mission was just about to launch.

At first the pirates were unconcerned. Some waved their arms at the helicopter, a couple raised their AK-47s. They were accustomed to helicopters flying over to observe them, but the helicopters never did anything other than take pictures. This time was different. The gunner at the side door of the helicopter opened fire, streams of bullets tearing into at least five fibreglass skiffs, leaving lines of bullet holes and destroying their outboard engines. The pirates scattered in every direction, some running to hide in the dunes, others spinning the wheels of their 4x4 vehicles, sand spraying everywhere in their haste to escape.

No pirate was injured – the helicopter gun crew had been tasked with leaving no casualties. The message sent to the pirates and their financiers was nonetheless loud and clear: they could no longer use the beaches with impunity.

What makes EU Naval Force different is the ability to deliver what Jacqui terms 'legal finish' – in other words, sending those suspected of carrying out acts of piracy for prosecution in a court of law.

'When counter-piracy operations began, there was some criticism. The public couldn't understand why after we had apprehended the pirates and destroyed their equipment, they were sometimes returned to the Somali coast. The legal issues are complex, especially when you are operating far out to sea in a warship, but since November 2009 the EU has signed legal agreements with the Seychelles, Mauritius, and more recently, Tanzania. These agreements allow for those suspected of piracy to be transferred to one of those countries for prosecution.'

As naval patrols have become more co-ordinated, the pirates have had to advance their own strategies and find ways to operate further out to sea, using pirated dhows and other vessels as mother ships to increase their range. In 2009, they were operating mainly in the Gulf of Aden, where they enjoyed rich pickings, with over 2,000 merchant ships a month passing through that area, most of them with little security on board.

'As the warships became more successful in apprehending them further out to sea, the pirates had to change their tactics again. What we've seen more recently is the pirates operating much closer to the Somali coast, on a more opportunist basis, nipping out to sea, testing the water.

In November last year, ten pirates came out to sea and it was just like a scene from the *Captain Phillips* film, with many people on the beach watching as the suspected pirates launched their boats. The EUNAVFOR German frigate FGS *Niedersachsen* was in the area conducting counter-piracy patrols and as the warship closed in on the scene, the suspected pirates were seen racing back to the beach, ditching their ladders overboard as they went.

Around the same time, the EUNAVFOR Spanish Oceanic Patrol Vessel ESPS *Rayo* apprehended six men 320 miles (515 km) off the Somali coast, which shows that when pirates can get a boat, an engine and fuel, they will still come out.'

In conclusion, piracy has reduced since 2012, but it would be wrong to think that the threat is over. Considering that pirates have received up to US$135 million in six years from ransom payments, and according to the World Bank a young man can 'earn' thousands of dollars as a pirate if he's successful, this represents a lot of money for a young Somali. Certainly for the foreseeable future, the maritime industry and counter-piracy forces will need to remain vigilant or there could be a return to the level of pirate attacks that were witnessed in 2009–2011.

13

TALKING WITH THE PIRATES

Back in Seychelles, Maalin Daud Olat had obviously put the word about that it was OK to talk with me. When I arrived at Montagne Posée Prison the following day after our interview, the governor pointed out several Somalis inside the wire compound gates waiting for their chance to talk with the British writer with the cigarettes.

Mohammed Bashir Mohammed told me he was 15 years old. He was a big guy, well built and 1.8 metres (6 feet) tall. He had grown a good chin beard, and permeated the room with a very strong adult smell of stale underarm perspiration. I would certainly have put him as being over 18, probably in his early twenties.

He was from Mogadishu and had never been to school.

'For many years we've had no proper government, a tough life. I've seen much fighting between Al Shabab and government soldiers.

I started work aged 11, looking after animals – that's the only work I've ever done. Then I got a job as a fisherman – this was my first trip. The boat was called *Volvo*, with nine of us on board. We were fishing for sharks. We spent eight days on the sea – the weather was very rough. It was always rain and cloud – we never saw the sun so had no idea which way to head to get back to shore. We just got lost, and then a ship arrived that we thought might help us; but it was a Spanish warship and they detained us. We had no guns on board or weapons of any kind.'

I remembered an interview I had done with a prosecuting lawyer when producing my documentary; he had told me that the 'innocent fisherman' defence was the stock case put forward by the Somalis. I was seeing a pattern develop. Get cigarettes off the English guy, tell him you are blameless, spin him the usual story. Pretending that I knew more about his case than I actually did, I decided to push him a little. 'But I thought that when you were arrested there were no nets on the boat?' He looked surprised that I apparently knew so much detail.

'We had lost many of our nets in the storm but still had just a few on board – we had set the nets and would have gone back to haul them in, but in the storm we got lost and couldn't find them to haul them... We lost most of our nets and our catch in the storms and rain. All nine of us are here waiting for trial.'

I had no idea of the prosecution case against him and his colleagues and no trial date had yet been fixed, so the evidence had not been tested in court. If he and his colleagues were indeed pirates, they had shored up the 'innocent fisherman' defence rather well. The first pirate groups that had run that defence had not had a scrap of fishing gear on board. These guys at least had some fishing gear, and a credible reason for not having more.

And as to his age – well, if convicted and the court accepted he was only 15, his sentence could be as much as half of that imposed on adult members of the gang. No wonder that so many Somalis claimed to be under 18. I was only to find out later just what an issue this was becoming for the prosecutors, and how they were tackling it.

Next in line to talk to me – and collect his cigarettes – was Abdikadir Mohamed Hassan. Wearing an orange T-shirt and green trousers, he told me that he was 12 years old. He was the first supposed juvenile that I believed was under 18, but the shadow of beard on his chin and top lip told me he was probably older than he claimed. He had been arrested in February 2014 and was awaiting trial – no date had yet been fixed.

His story was similar to that of the first Somali I had spoken to, Maalin Daud Olat, that he was an innocent economic migrant who had paid for passage out of Somalia, to head for a better life in Saudi Arabia. I was sceptical again; the same defence themes were cropping up time after time.

He came from the Gedo region, which lies on the border of Kenya and Ethiopia. The translator told me that it's the driest place in Somalia. He had lived a nomadic lifestyle with his parents, who had around 30 goats for milking. 'We move with the rain.'

He had gone to live with an aunt in Mogadishu, a five-day journey on the bus, looking for work.

'I got a job there in a small hotel, serving water and juice. I spent 21 days in Mogadishu before my aunt's son said he could make a deal to leave Somalia and go to another country as illegal immigrants. He took me to a middle man called Osman who sent me to the boat. I paid Osman US$200.'

At this stage, I began having serious doubts about his story – how did a 12-year-old son of nomadic goat herders manage to raise US$200 in a country where that was a year's income for some? Abdikadir had his answer ready, even if it didn't really ring true.

'That came from contributions from my mum and aunt and from all the family. We got on the boat in Mogadishu harbour. The crew looked like Indians. I was told that we were going to Saudi. I'd been told there would be a lot of Somalis on the boat but I'd been misled – there were only five of us. It was night when I went aboard, but it looked like a cargo boat, as they were unloading when I got on, and there was wheat on the floor of the room I was taken to.

After 20 days at sea, we were approached by a Saudi warship and taken on board ... on suspicion of piracy. We had no weapons.'

This case was pending so I could not find out the prosecution's version of facts or any court judgements. Maybe his extended family did raise the fare for him; it is very much the Somali way to help one's extended family in any way possible. He may have had relatives who already lived abroad and who sent money to help and support the family back home. If the captain was people-smuggling, carrying illegal immigrants to Saudi Arabia, he himself would have faced imprisonment and possible confiscation of his ship, so he could well have been making up the piracy story to protect his position. True or not, it was certainly more original than the 'innocent fisherman' defence.

I asked Abdikadir how he was finding things.

'I have big problems in prison here for four reasons. 1. I miss my parents. 2. I failed in my mission to get to Saudi. 3. I'm in a foreign prison. 4. Local inmates threaten me because I am so young. When I come outside, they threaten me as a young boy; they push me out of the food lines, they bully me and pick on me.'

As I walked out of the prison to my car in the hot afternoon sun, I felt frustrated. I was talking to pirates – of this I had no doubt – but I wasn't getting my story. I wanted to find out what drove men to take to the sea in small boats to try to capture huge ships; I wanted to find out what life was like on those boats; and I wanted to find out what it was actually like to seize a ship and its crew. I was getting no answers, just implausible protestations of innocence and unlikely stories. I was getting nowhere...

14

OUTWITTING THE PIRATES

Stephen Barbe had just arrived back in harbour after 18 days at sea and he and his crew were unloading their kit on to the fishing quay before heading home. All had bottles of chilled Seybrew beer, condensation dripping down the outside in the 30-degree-plus afternoon heat. Their boat *Faith* is a 33-foot-long (10-metre), fibreglass fishing vessel. They dive off it for sea cucumbers, which are bought by a Chinese trader who dries them before they are shipped to Hong Kong.

Beer bottle in one hand, Stephen took me around the boat showing off the bullet holes, now repaired with fibreglass although their location was clear to see. He graphically described to me where one of the pirates was shot – 'There was blood and bits of flesh all up here and here' – pointing to the shelves in the small galley where dried foods were stocked. Pulling away bags of rubbish from under the sink, he also showed me where one bullet had come through the side and struck a gas bottle; luckily for him and the crew, it had been an empty one.

In the tiny bow cabin of the boat was a jumble of six bunks criss-crossing under and over, squeezed in to provide a home for the crew during their weeks at sea. Stephen pointed out a cluster of bullet holes at the head of one bunk and their exit holes on the other side of the cabin, all now roughly repaired. The crew had been cowering on the cabin floor as the bullets passed just a couple of feet above their heads.

Stephen suggested we go across to the bar on the quay, the 'Bar Peser' in the local Creole, 'Fishermen's Bar' in English. It would be cooler and more shaded there, and we wouldn't get in the way of his crew unloading *Faith*. It was well before midday, but already the bar was doing good business, and there was the loud banter of men who had spent too long at sea and had been dreaming of a cold beer or three. I'd paid for my interviews with the pirates in cigarettes; it looked as though I'd be paying for the story of a former captive of the pirates in beers.

'I was fishing not far from home – about 45 nautical miles (85 km) offshore. I could still see the land.

It was early evening, about 7pm. It was still light and the sun was just setting. I was searching for a fishing ground that I know – it's not on the chart. I was in the wheelhouse when I saw two of my crew on the front deck with their hands up. Then I heard something banging on the side of the boat. I told my cook to go and look what was happening; he came back and said there were pirates on board. I really didn't believe him – I thought that the crew were playing a joke on me – so I went to have a look for myself. When I came out, I saw that there were about 11 of them with guns.

I tried to go on the SSB [marine single-sideband radio transceiver] to make a distress call but I didn't have time. They came in the cabin with their guns and told me to put everything down. They told me to turn off all the equipment and all the lights. The sun had gone down by now, the moon hadn't yet risen, and it was totally dark out on the water. Then they had a small torch with them, which they used to signal and two more boats came alongside. One was a skiff with an outboard and one was a bit bigger with lots of barrels on it – the mother ship.

They said we were to go to Somalia. I told them that I didn't know the way. They kept saying that I must know, so I gave them a route but it wasn't the right route – it would have taken us to the south of Somalia, to Kenya.'

Stephen drained his beer and looked expectantly at me; I brought another couple across from the bar and reminded him where we'd got to – him giving them the wrong bearings.

'Yes, they know a bit about navigation, these guys – they could navigate by the stars – and they knew I was taking them off course. They weren't stupid. They shouted at me – threatened me, pointing their guns at me – until I came around to the correct course. I was the only one who they kept out – they locked the rest of the crew in the cabin.

The last thing I wanted to do was go to Somalia, so I tried to figure out something.

About a day later, we met a cargo ship. The Somalis got really excited, talking and shouting among themselves. Some of them got their weapons and got into the skiffs to chase after the cargo ship. They didn't get close, though they did fire three RPGs at it but they didn't hit. I just saw them going up, then fizzling out into the sea. I could see the cargo ship increasing speed and turning away from them – the sea was a bit choppy and the skiffs couldn't go at full speed. I heard the ship's captain on the VHF radio sending a warning of pirate attack in this area. So I knew that there would be some sort of patrol in this area, maybe a ship or a plane, something like that.'

I tried to imagine the scene. *Faith* was a tiny boat, and with Stephen's crew together with all the Somalis on board, it must have been seriously unpleasant and overcrowded. These were the typical pirate tactics I had been told about by Lieutenant Commander Jacqui Sherriff during my visit to EUNAVFOR HQ – the Somalis using vessels they had seized as mother ships to increase their range and make them appear less like pirate boats.

Stephen continued. 'I talked to my crew – I said that we had to try and do something to stop the boat so that when the patrol arrived, they could see us and realise we were in trouble.

We carried on that night. The next morning when it got light, I knew the patrols would be out and searching. So I told the Somalis that we had to change the oil in the engine. I told them that the engine was losing oil and if we didn't stop to do this, the engine might seize up. I'd been trying to make friends with the Somalis just to calm them down because they were really jumpy, really angry a lot of the time.

I topped up the engine with oil. There were two of them came down with me and they were watching me all the time. But while I was pouring the oil, I used my foot to close the seacock. The seacock is the intake of sea water that circulates in the engine to cool it. I knew that they would try and blame me, but as they had seen me do nothing with my hands except pouring oil they couldn't make out that I had done something wrong. With it closed, the engine started to overheat and then it stopped. They were getting angry. 'Captain, what's the problem?' I pretended I didn't know. They went down to the engine again with me. I started taking the engine apart piece by piece. I told them it might be the pump so took the pump off and started stripping it down. I knew there was nothing wrong with it but they didn't, so I made it look like I was really trying to sort it out.

When the engine stopped, we were just drifting. Eventually we saw a plane. It circled around several times before leaving so I know it would have given the coastguard our position and our registration number, so they would know who we were.

Eventually I had to solve the problem – I told the Somalis it had been the pump – but by then, we'd been drifting all day and I knew that I had given the coastguard time to get to us. I also told the Somalis that we couldn't run at full speed because if we did, the engine might blow up and then we would never make it to Somalia.

The coastguard ship *Topaz* arrived at about 6 in the afternoon, just before sunset. They hailed us to stop, but the Somalis threatened me with guns and said to keep going. They let me speak with the coastguard on the radio, and I told them that I couldn't stop because they were all pointing their guns at me. They said to tell the coastguard to leave us, that we would not stop. The coastguard came back saying that if we didn't stop they would sink the boat. We still didn't stop, so the coastguard started shooting at the waterline of the boat, trying to sink it.

Then the coastguard boat came in closer and began firing into the boat. One pirate was close to me – he got shot in the arm. And there was one at the back who got shot in the legs – he died afterwards. The pirates then came to the stern and started throwing their guns over into the sea. They all had AK-47s – they looked really old weapons and a bit rusty.'

I waved at a passing waitress for a couple more beers. I was mesmerised by the story. I didn't think Stephen could be much older than 30, yet his cool thinking had saved both him and his crew spending months as hostages in Somalia. How did he feel about it all now?

'I'm back at sea again. I'm a bit scared but I'm more careful. I like this job – I wouldn't give it up. I don't use lights at night. That's a problem because we used to be able to work at night but we can't any more, so we are catching a lot less and having to stay at sea way longer. And now navigation is dangerous – all the boats are in total darkness at night so there is a very real risk of collision and sinking in the fishing grounds. Most boats don't have radar and you just have no idea if there is another boat right ahead of you.'

One of his crewmen appeared in the bar just then; Stephen was needed as the van had arrived to collect their catch. As he left, I thought once more of the cruel irony that the piracy phenomenon that had started over fishing rights was now taking simple fishermen from other nations as its victims.

15

BEST PRACTICE

Whether a ship has a full arsenal of anti-piracy devices or absolutely none, tactics have been devised to minimise the risk from pirates, and these have been codified in a small booklet known in the shipping industry as BMP4 – a much shortened abbreviation for 'Best Management Practices for Protection against Somali-Based Piracy', the '4' relating to it being in its fourth edition.

BMP4 is the bible for any skipper transiting the High Risk Area for piracy, which on a map spreads from Madagascar in the South to India in the East, and all along the African coast into the Gulf of Aden. It's also handy for shipowners whose vessels are operating in that area to help them prepare their vessel and crew for a pirate attack.

Within the information provided are observations on how the weather, particularly the monsoons, affect pirate activity. The western Indian Ocean has two basic weather patterns – the North-East and South-West monsoons reflecting the seasonal switches in wind direction. The lulls between these are most favoured by the pirates – 'Pirate weather' as one skipper told me. BMP4 notes that because attacks are launched from small skiffs, any sea conditions creating waves over 3 metres (10 feet) are going to make pirate operations difficult – although having said that, such conditions did not prevent the attack on the Spanish warship *Patiño*.

BMP4 notes how piracy has evolved from a couple of small skiffs with powerful outboards darting out from the shore; through the longer-range pattern of a larger open whaler carrying fuel and water on which the pirates ate and slept, towing the attack skiffs behind it; to the current pattern of commandeering pirated fishing dhows, common throughout the region, or small coastal freighters as the pirates' mother ship.

As naval activity has locked down the Somali coastline, pirates have been forced further out into the open ocean to find prey. With their skiffs often hauled aboard their captured ships and covered with tarpaulin, these vessels look far less threatening than the classic whaler towing two skiffs, and enables them to infiltrate the shipping lanes far more easily – a 21st-century version of the wolf in sheep's clothing. An extra bonus is that the crew of the pirated ship held on board can at times offer a human shield – most navies have proved extremely reluctant to attack vessels with hostages on board for fear of 'collateral damage'.

On board the larger mother ships, the pirates have a far greater range and the ability to stay at sea for considerably longer periods. They are also less affected by weather conditions. The safety offered by the periods in between 'pirate weather' may be a thing of the past.

BMP4 recommends two fail-safe means of foiling a pirate attack – high speed and on-board security teams. As yet, no ship travelling at over 18 knots has been pirated, nor has one with armed guards. This should not breed complacency, however, as with the stakes so high the pirates have shown themselves extremely adaptable. Already, with the massive reduction in pirate successes, shipowners are reviewing use of both tactics. Both cost money, and shipping is a business with tight margins. A slower-moving vessel without armed security costs thousands of dollars per day less to operate.

There is a lot of common-sense advice in BMP4. It sounds obvious, but good watch-keeping is essential; on a ship travelling in a straight line on an apparently empty ocean for thousands of kilometres, keeping watch can be boring, and often amounts to an occasional glance outside and reliance on radar alarms. Pirate skiffs slip under the radar – they have no more radar signature than the crest of a wave – and if no one is physically looking out for them at all times, the outlaws can be aboard before anyone knows it. Doubling the number of crew on watch, shortening their rotation to keep them fresh and alert, and investing in good binoculars and night-vision optics are all good advice.

It's easy counsel to give, but the pirates' targets are commercial vessels. These are tankers and container ships: merchant ships staffed by the minimum of crew, with perhaps a dozen or so merchant sailors for whom keeping watch is just one of many on-board daily chores. By comparison, warships carry a couple of hundred professional naval seamen aboard.

On a long voyage when several weeks are spent at sea, life for the crew of a merchant ship slips into a fairly easy routine of eating, sleeping, watching DVDs, drinking coffee, having a smoke and a chat, and carrying out on-board tasks. Many ships are manned by seafarers of several nationalities, often extremely lowly paid and on occasions not very highly skilled. Suddenly to expect such crews to have the manpower and watch-keeping capabilities equivalent to those of a much larger and more highly trained military crew in order to carry out BMP's recommendations can at times be optimistic. It's not unknown for badly manned vessels to run aground, actually hitting islands! In other words, the chance of such poorly crewed ships spotting an approaching skiff is remote. This is not meant as criticism of merchant seamen in general – most are extremely professional – but the pirates have only to get lucky once...

BMP does not just deal with precautionary advice. In the case of an attack, BMP recommends that the first aim is not to let the pirates get close enough to attach their boarding ladders and climbing ropes. Engaging top speed is the first response, and then if the pirate skiffs get close, making small sharp turns will create more wash and make it more difficult for the pirate skiffs. It warns that larger turns will slow the ship and actually make it easier for the pirates to get alongside.

Water cannons or fire hoses blasted on to the attackers can provide a highly effective screen of water – although it can be dangerous operating these manually, as anyone doing so will be exposed to shots fired from below. Even using the ship's ballast pumps to flood water on to the deck and over the gunwales can render it difficult for the pirate skiff to stay alongside and makes climbing up the steep ship's side far more tricky.

If the pirates manage to scale this sheer steel wall, then an effective razor-wire barrier is essential as a last defence against them reaching the deck. As pirates will target the bridge with gunfire and RPGs to try to force the ship to stop, enhanced bridge protection is suggested, from sandbags around the doors to security grilles for the windows.

But if every security measure has failed and the pirates succeed in getting aboard, then the final resort is a citadel – a secure place to which the whole crew can go and ideally control the ship. A citadel is something BMP advises that every prudent shipowner should install.

The citadel should firstly be hard to find. In the vastness of an ocean-going ship with steel bulkheads everywhere, a hidden door somewhere deep in the ship can be incredibly hard to find. If, like me, you can get lost on a car ferry, think how difficult it could be to locate a well-concealed location on a huge industrial vessel.

Even if it is found, it should be secure against entry from the outside. The pirates will have few skills in opening vaults, and there is no way they can themselves remain safe, firing RPGs or machine guns in the confined space of a ship's hold.

The citadel should have plenty of supplies of food and water, ventilation and toilet facilities – the crew may be there for quite some time. Good communications systems are also essential. Some citadels even have a dual set of controls for the ship. For a small coastal freighter, this might be an excessive expense, but for large modern ships with valuable cargoes that might otherwise be ransomed for millions, it is essential.

For the pirates, seizing the ship is just a part of the deal. They need to steer it back to the safe shores of Somalia, and for that they need at least some of the crew. Few pirates have the skills to drive an ocean-going tanker or container ship. As previously described, they also need the crew as a human shield – most navies will not risk killing innocent crew members in an armed military action to retake a pirated ship.

If the ship is shut down and going nowhere, however, and if the crew are safe in a secure citadel, then military action is a real option.

For the pirates, if the ship is dead in the water; if they have no hijacked crew available to steer the ship; and if the helicopter circling above warns them of military vessels close behind, many will cut their losses and jump ship while they can. If they stay to fight, Special Forces have a clear playing field on which to operate, knowing every moving person they see is not crew but a pirate.

One example of the successful use of the citadel was the rescue of the German container ship MV *Taipan*, which had been hijacked by pirates 500 nautical miles (930 km) east of the Somali coast. The crew shut down the engines, sent out an SOS and locked themselves in the ship's secure room, deep in the bowels of the vessel.

The Dutch naval ship HNLMS *Tromp* was first at the scene, and reported the ship dead in the water with two pirate skiffs tied behind it. When it became clear that the pirates had no intention of leaving the *Taipan*, a spectacular rescue operation was launched by Dutch marines. The pirates were all confirmed to be in the bridge area of the ship, so the marines launched their attack at the bow. While their Lynx helicopter hovered above the ship, and its machine gun laid down suppressing fire, the marines abseiled down ropes from the helicopter on to the containers stacked on the ship. Making their way across the tops of the containers, and then along the narrow gangways of the ship, the marines continued to fire on the pirates, then stormed the bridge. All of the hostages were freed safely, none of the marines was injured by Somali gunfire (one was slightly injured in landing from the helicopter), and the ten Somali pirates quickly threw down their weapons and surrendered.

It was a textbook mission, worthy of Hollywood, and the whole action from the moment the helicopter lifted off from the deck of the *Tromp* to the final surrender of the pirates, weapons thrown away and hands over heads, was captured on a head camera attached to the helmet of one of the marines and later released by the Dutch Navy. To watch a real-life recapture of a ship taken by Somali pirates, it's all there on YouTube.

Lieutenant Commander Jacqui Sherriff of EUNAVFOR summed up the value of citadels on board pirated ships. 'Because the pirates didn't have access to the crew and their lives were not in danger, then the Dutch Navy could go on board and take the ship. It's when we've got an AK-47 to the head of a hostage that it's just too dangerous. People say to us all the time, why don't you just go in and go and get them; it's the safety of life that we have to consider.'

16

THE CONTAINER-SHIP CAPTAIN

There's something mesmerising about watching a large container ship being loaded and unloaded. So much is happening all at once. An apparently unco-ordinated ballet of cranes swinging containers, dock workers hooking and unhooking chains, scurrying trucks hauling away containers and dashing back just in time to receive the next. Nobody seems to be directing operations but it runs like clockwork. Standing on the quay alongside one of these huge ocean transports, with tiers of 2,000 containers piled high on their deck, the sheer massive scale of the ships is daunting.

The MV *Maersk Weymouth* was tied up to the jetty in the bright sunshine of an African port. It appeared to be an identical vessel to the *Maersk Alabama*, which had been so dramatically pirated and rescued. As I watched the hustle and bustle, a small Asian figure in a white polo shirt had been close by, talking with an extremely tall, black-skinned man in a hard hat and holding a clipboard, who was clearly some sort of shipping agent. Their conversation ended, and the smaller of the pair wandered casually across and asked what my interest was in the ship. I explained my project and was stunned when he responded: 'Would you like to come aboard? This is my ship – I'm the captain.'

As we climbed several flights of stairs from deck level to the bridge, I learned that the ship was built in 2009, and was one of almost 200 Maersk container ships plodding through the world's shipping highways. Passing through a seemingly endless maze of identical corridors, stairs and doorways as we climbed five storeys, we didn't see a single person; most of the dozen or so crew were out supervising the loading and unloading. Even out at sea, the small crew must seem lost in the vast empty spaces of the ship.

Only days earlier, I'd been on the busy crowded bridge of *Patiño*, the Spanish warship. The bridge of the *Maersk Weymouth* was just as big, stretching the full width of the ship, but empty other than the captain and his orange boiler-suited engineer, who brought us cans of cola.

Towering over all the other dockyard structures and the town beyond, gazing over the tops of the stacked containers, it made me marvel, and not for the first time, at the sheer bravado of the handful of scrawny illiterate Somalis who would pirate such a giant on the high seas.

The captain came from the Philippines and had only recently joined Maersk, a decision he was already regretting, not because of the company itself but because of the routes he had been allocated. The interview was difficult due to his limited English.

'I'm new to this ship but have already had six pirate encounters. If I'd known my assignment was in this place, I would not have signed on to this vessel. I would not have joined the ship. But that's life – I'm already here and under contract so we must finish our contract. By the end we will be used to pirates. I don't like this kind of work here. My previous company, I was working the Asian routes; Asia has no problem like this.'

This ship's trading circuit meant that it was rarely out of the pirates' area of activity – the High Risk Area (HRA). While most ships passing through the HRA are in transit via Suez, or shipping oil from the Gulf to the Far East, this one had drawn the short straw, with a route that kept it perpetually in the areas of highest pirate activity.

'Our route is from Madagascar, Seychelles, Oman, Reunion, and back on that circuit. From here we head to Oman – pirates again. The only really safe part of the voyage is in the very south, near Madagascar, but there are even reports of the pirates there now. Out here, you seldom see vessels – no ships – while in Asia you see ships all the time – lots of traffic, almost like cars, because it's always busy, good business. But here, no, virtually no ships, because of pirates. We are on our own on our route. What can we do? We are gambling our lives here, it's so dangerous. We are shipping fish in refrigerated containers from Seychelles to Oman, and we also bring their food here – all their food and meat – we bring food and take fish. But we are one of a very few ships working this route.'

Over at the chart table, he pulled out a chart that showed little more than the long straight Somali coast stretching to the Horn of Africa, and a vast expanse of empty sea. The chart was marked with pencilled crosses.

'We have seen pirates here, here and here... Often they are stationed across our track. We always take precautions. We have our radar alarm set for any boat that is within 10 miles (16 km), and if we see any boat within that range, we turn to run parallel so they can't close on us. If they change course when we have changed course, we know they must be pirates – if it was a normal fishing boat they wouldn't move. But if they change course as soon as we do, then we know that they are chasing us. So this area is very dangerous for pirates. We increase speed, they increase speed – also here is very dangerous.'

He tapped his finger on the chart, pointing to three pencilled crosses in a row running east to west at 90 degrees to the north–south route of the ship as it heads towards Oman.

'February 15, they took one vessel here right on our route. We always pass this side – 60 degrees,' showing a route that seems to go very wide to avoid Somali shores. 'They are often stationed here, there, there ... very dangerous.

Any ship at all that we see we give plenty of clearance; we change course so we are running parallel to it. If the other boat is obviously pirates, then we increase speed – this ship can do 18 knots. The pirates can't chase us for long – the most I've experienced has been a couple of hours before they have given up – they just don't have enough fuel and are not fast enough to close the gap and catch us.' He pauses. 'So far...'

'We just can't let them get close to us. The skiff boat we cannot let them alongside so we keep our distance. If they get close, then they will start shooting and we are in real trouble.'

What do you have on this ship to stop pirates? He laughs.

'Just wire – only wire – there's nothing.'

I'd already seen the razor wire wrapped around the rail along the whole length of the ship.

'And come look at this.' Outside the bridge is a pile of old plastic grain sacks now filled with sand, and at close quarters an extremely unconvincing dummy in a white boiler suit and yellow hard hat, propped against the rail. The dummy has a wooden broom handle in its arms, that is meant to look like a rifle, scaring pirates into believing there is armed on-board security.

'A dummy on deck – is that really going to save us? If they would give us arms it would be better – a machine gun, 50 calibre...' B B B B B B – he mimes shooting and laughs. 'But yes, it's very dangerous if the pirates get near – they have machine guns and grenade launchers. They will always shoot us. Just wire, no more, that's all.' He also has concerns for the safety of himself and his crew if they are taken hostage.

'The pirates have a hot temper – if the company will not listen to their demands, they will hit the captain, hit the crew, especially the master and officers. If negotiations are not going fast, they will hurt somebody or start killing the crew. It is a big problem. What is Somalia – they have no production, no minerals, nothing in the place. So what nation will be interested in stopping all this? Nobody, because the place is a bullshit place. The place is nothing. They only have pirates so that they can get an income.

We are not at peace – our minds are not at ease. We always pray to God. Every night we pray to God for safety here, because this is our life – pirates any time. We do not know what will happen to us. So I always quote this psalm, this passage from the Bible.'

And with Christian evangelical fervour he began quoting scripture, although not any psalm that I have ever heard of.

'The arm of the Lord is all powerful and his ear is all hearing, so I'm also asking him that he will cover me with his feelers. And because of his faithfulness, his shield and rampart, nothing is impossible to God. He says you can trample even the lion, even the serpent if God is with you and he will give you a long life. I am asking that he will cover the ship with his precious blood, shield the ship...'

An unusual prayer, but if one's working life is spent for weeks at a time driving a fairly slow-moving ship through pirate-infested waters – a modern ship worth multiple millions of pounds bearing an equally valuable cargo – and if one's ship is equipped with almost zero defences, then whatever prayer works must be all right!

It was three years since the *Maersk Alabama* had been taken by pirates in 2009, and only saved thanks to the courage of its crew and the American Navy SEAL operation to rescue Captain Phillips. Yet in 2012 this other Maersk ship, operating almost consistently in the High Risk Area, still appeared to have the most minimal of anti-piracy protection. Shortly before publication of this book I emailed Maersk to enquire if their security measures had by then improved. The reply from the Group Press Officer: 'For obvious security reasons, we do not want to provide details on the specific security measures onboard our vessels and therefore cannot go into details about how we protect our crews and vessels against piracy attacks. However, Maersk does use armed guards on its vessels on a case-by-case basis but only after a thorough risk assessment, following strict vetting procedures for guards employed as well as having clear rules of engagement.' So things appear to have moved on...

17

THE POLICEMAN WHO DIDN'T BECOME A PIRATE

'Are you Interpol?'

These were the first words of Abdirahaman Nur Roble, known as Balbal, aged 20, serving a 24-year sentence at the Montagne Posée Prison in Seychelles. He walked into the room with a roguish smile on his face. This guy was fast talking, very articulate and charming – not the archetypal image of a Somali pirate. Balbal means 'fast runner' as he runs fast, works fast, talks fast.

I explained who I was. 'I can tell you a good story. Do I get cigarettes?' Marlboro? 'No. I'll come back when you have some proper cigarettes.'

I explained that I was back on Monday to take photos, and would bring some then. 'OK, give me those and give me proper ones Monday.' He thought for a moment. 'And I will talk to you now, and maybe we will talk some more on Monday.'

It was day three of meeting pirates in the prison. I'd become just another regular face to the Gurkha guards as they waved me through the security post, although the old dog on the stairs still did not seem to have moved at all since my first visit.

After two days of nothing but protestations of innocence, maybe at last I had a pirate who would tell all? His was the longest sentence of those I'd talked to... I was intrigued.

And then the protestation of innocence, although Balbal's defence was the most innovative that I had yet heard. It was that he was armed and on board a ship because he was actually being paid to defend ships against pirates.

'I'd been working at sea in Puntland for seven months. We were an armed boat as we were guarding the foreign boats that came for our fish – from Bangladesh, Yemen, Oman, Iran, Pakistan... We would protect them. We were paid $100 per boat. There were six on our boat. When the foreign boats were about 20 miles (30 km) off, they would call our boss and we would go out, meet them, and bring them to the fishing area. The foreign boats don't fish. They dock somewhere and we guard them. They buy fish from the local fishermen till they are full, then they leave. And we make sure they are safe from pirates.

That day we were about 7–8 miles (12 km) off the Somali coast. We had gone out to meet a boat and escort it in, but our boat was old and had holes in it, the sea was rough, water was getting in, and we were starting to sink. A ship was passing that had left Bosaso for Dubai. We spoke to them on the radio. They said they couldn't turn back to Bosaso, but we could go with them, as there was another ship from their company coming into Bosaso and they would hand us over to them to take us into Bosaso.

We were 24 hours on that ship, then the other boat from Dubai arrived and they put us on board. About a mile off Bosaso, the captain said for us to get our weapons and get back in the skiff and head for shore. While we were doing this, a warship came and asked us to stop. A Somali speaker on the warship said for us to surrender, we want to know who you are. By then there were three warships. We stopped and surrendered – they said for all Somalis to go to the bow, so we did. Three small boats came, we were cuffed and blindfolded and taken to the warship. We had three AK-47s, two pistols and one machine gun.

I'd been doing this work for seven months with different people. There's a tuna factory in Las Khorey in the very tip of Somalia, not far from Bosaso. We were hired by them. In its time, it was the biggest tuna factory in Africa – it's still working.

No one from the ship came to court to say they had been hijacked. No one from the tuna factory came to give evidence. A juvenile with us got 12 years, all the others 24. I'm waiting for an appeal.'

It wasn't a bad story. Indeed, there was some degree of credibility to the concept. Despite all the problems, people from other fishing nations around the Gulf of Aden are trying to ply their trade off the coast of Somalia, particularly as, thanks to the pirates, fish stocks are recovering. If a foreign boat can buy fish cheap enough from the locals, and pay a hundred dollars for protection, it is good business. Life goes on – the seas off Somalia are not a desert of shipping; there are still fishing boats and ships bringing cargoes for Somali businessmen who will pay a little protection for safe passage.

I wanted to know more about this man and his background.

'I'm from Mogadishu. I've got two wives – one in Mogadishu, and one in Galkayo with a daughter there. Before I went to sea I was a policeman in Mogadishu for eight months. In the police in Mogadishu I had a gun, an M16, but no uniform as there were very few to go around. I have no education but I know my way around the city, and my main work was guarding a minister. I got paid for the first five months, but then no pay for the last three.

That's why Al Shabab get so popular – they pay their people; and if you work for the government, they tell you "Join us or we will kill you and your families". I never wanted to join Al Shabab, because they tell you "Go kill that person". Why should I kill an innocent person. Those guys killed my uncle – beheaded him. Al Shabab told me to kill someone and if I refused I would be killed myself, so I ran away. But I was wanted on the Al Shabab list so I left Mogadishu and ran away to Puntland.'

We were getting on well – easy conversation, lots of smiles, good body language. This was the man I felt would help me. I couldn't ask him to tell me the truth and admit he was a pirate – his appeal hadn't been heard and there was no way he would tell a stranger something different. Maybe he would help in another way.

My question: You must know everyone here in the prison, every Somali?

There was a pause while this was translated.

I want to talk to a pirate. Someone who will admit they were a pirate and tell me how it works.

He gave me long eye contact, thought hard, then smiled.

'There are no pirates here. There was one once who pleaded guilty, but he's now in prison in Somalia. I've never met a pirate.'

All the time, the laughter in his eyes, as we both acknowledged what a heap of crap he was telling me.

OK, but you must have heard some stories...

'No, I was on a team working against the pirates, so I don't know any pirates and never heard their stories...'

There was another long pause. Then Balbal pointed to the white vest the translator was wearing under his shirt.

'If you come back Monday and bring me one of those, I will ask around and see if anyone here has ever met a pirate...'

He stood to leave, then turned.

'I've heard that most pirates were brainwashed, and forced to hijack ships. In Somalia some are told to go – go to sea and bring a ship or a boat or you will be killed. So they are forced to go. They don't want to. Some go to sea because they are scared of

Al Shabab... Monday, yes, and you can take my photo and maybe I will have some more stories. And bring the vest, yes?'

And then a knuckle-to-knuckle salute as he left. I decided there and then that I would buy him the vest over the weekend. What with Balbal and Maalin Daud Olat both hinting that they might tell me more, I felt I was on the verge of a breakthrough and might get some real pirate tales.

Before they actually came to the door, I had no idea which Somali I would be talking to, so I had no chance of researching their cases before I met them. Today, although I didn't know it when I arrived at the prison that morning, all four pirates with whom I spoke, including Balbal, had been part of a six-man team, and had all been arrested together. Was one of them the leader, or was the pirate captain one of the two that I didn't get to meet? In his lengthy 60-page judgement before sentencing, the judge never identified any one of the six as being their leader, and sentenced all the adults identically.

The next member I was to meet of that pirate crew was Mohamud Ahmed, aged 15 from Galkayo – sentenced to 12 years as a juvenile, rather than the 24-year sentences imposed on the adult pirates. He'd had one year's schooling in Galkayo, and had never had a job. He had lived with his parents. They did not have regular work, occasionally some labouring but no permanent employment.

'I was ten when I started fishing. I left Galkayo to go to the coast to get work there. It was my first time fishing but it's easy to get work. I got a lift in a car – I paid to get there. When I got there, it's easy just to sleep in the bush, or stay in a small hut. We fished from Denola, it's on the coast, just a beach, no town. We would fish and the big boats from Yemen and other countries would buy from us.

Because I had been to school I used to do calculations, sums for the fishermen. I was like an accountant for them!

After fishing, I got a job guarding Iranian boats and it was while I was doing that – while I was on an Iranian boat – that I was captured. My Somali boss would pay me – tell me to go to this boat or that boat and guard it. We were guarding them against pirates and also against robbers and thieves who might try to sneak aboard. My boss was getting a good salary from guarding the boats.

I was armed – my boss gave me an AK-47 – I had never used one before. I had guarded anchored boats before – three different ones.'

From then on, his story to me was the same as Balbal's – innocent men who had been doing a job and been wrongly arrested and convicted.

He didn't mention the version he had told the Dutch when questioned on board not long after his arrest – that he had been promised US$3,000 for the hijack of a dhow that was to be used as a mother ship, and that when the Dutch warship approached, he had thrown his gun overboard.

The third member of this same crew that I spoke with was Abdullah Sharif Ibrahim, 26 years old and serving a 24-year sentence. Married with one son, his home was Garowe, the capital of Puntland, some 250 km (155 miles) from the coast. He'd worked as a mechanic for ten years, and had never had any form of education. He was a well-built, powerful-looking man, the sort I could imagine working out in a gym, unlike almost all the other Somalis who had been relatively scrawny. Incongruously, he had a tea towel over one shoulder; it turned out that he was tea boy for the guards for the day.

'I went to the coast, to Bosaso, to work as a mechanic repairing boats. I left my wife behind in Garowe. I was one year in Bosaso.

I'd been on the coast for a while. I wasn't making much money and by the time I'd sent some home to my wife, there was barely enough to live on. Then I was offered a new job – my new boss said I could both work as a fisherman and also guard boats on the coast. We would work on the boat, fishing from it, then guard it when it got back to the shore.' A variation from his colleagues, in that he told me he was to fish from the boat while at sea and only guard it when it was moored close to the shore.

'There was no evidence – we had been rescued by the *Burhan Noor*, which is why we were on board. The navy just came and accused us of suspicion of an act of piracy – we were detained before we were in sight of the Iranian boat we were supposed to meet, so they could not say who we were.' His argument was, of course, that if they had managed to make their rendezvous with the boat they were supposed to be guarding, the captain of that boat would have vouched for them.

Why did the captain of the *Burhan Noor* not say he had rescued you and that you were not pirates?

'The captain DID say that in my presence with the navy there, but the Dutch chose to ignore him – they just wanted to capture some Somalis – any Somalis would do, even innocent ones like us.'

Interviewed on board the Dutch Navy ship, his story, like Mohamud Ahmed's, was somewhat different. He was to get US$3,000, and in addition had received US$100 in advance for the hijack of a dhow. The weapons they had with them were thrown overboard when they were intercepted by the Dutch Navy ship.

Like his colleagues, he declined to give evidence at trial. It was interesting to me to witness at first hand this evolution of the pirates' techniques. Knowing that their usual *modus operandi* of an open whaler towing two skiffs was well-known to the coalition of navies patrolling the Somali coast, this was obviously stage one of a two-phase plan. Firstly, capture a dhow that could be used as a mother ship; then bring it to the shore, load the rest of the pirate crew aboard together with weapons and skiffs, and sail out into the shipping lanes posing as an innocent fishing boat until a target was found.

My final meeting of a very long day was with Mohamed – he would give me no other name, and as there were two other Mohamed's in addition to the juvenile among the six pirates convicted, I couldn't establish which one he was. For the first time, I had with me someone who fitted my image of a Somali pirate; jet-black skin and hair; thin, tall, and evil-looking.

Aged 23, with a wife and a son of four years old, he also assured me that he had been convicted with no evidence and given a 24-year sentence. There was a tension between us throughout the whole interview. As I posed every question, I stared into his eyes as I talked, waited as the question was translated, and then saw how it took him. He would think about his reply, tell it to the translator, and watch me intently as I listened to the English version. He knew and I knew that beneath the spoken words lay a deeper conversation...

This Mohamed gave the classic 'innocent fisherman' story – surprising, as it was totally different to the stories of his fellow crewmen and to the tale the court had heard.

'I'm from Bosaso, Puntland, from the city on the coast. I've never been to school. I'm a fisherman – have been since I was aged ten.

Six of us went fishing in one small boat. After four days, it got very rough and we had engine problems. We were picked up by a boat returning to Bosaso. It was a cargo ship from Dubai going to Bosaso. We were almost back at Bosaso when a warship came and said we were pirates and took us to Seychelles. I'm appealing against my sentence.'

A pattern had been developing during the day and the previous days – everyone was innocent and those who had already faced trial had been wrongly convicted. I maintained eye contact.

Would you tell me anything different after your appeal has been decided?

He grinned for the first time in our meeting. There was long eye contact – ten seconds or more, while he seemed to appraise me and consider his response.

'No.' And still the grin. I knew he was a pirate. He knew I knew he was a pirate. There was no way that he would tell me anything other than the 'innocent fisherman' story he and his fellows had settled on soon after their arrest and stuck to ever since. Well, stuck to in conversations with the outside world. I would love to have heard the conversations in their Somali-only prison block at night as they talked and joked about their pirating adventures.

Knowing I would be speaking with Balbal again after the weekend, I called again at the courthouse on my way home at the end of the day, and the same helpful clerk as before sourced the case papers for me. Unfortunately, the evidence didn't seem to be on the side of Balbal and the others with whom he was arrested, nor backed up by the captain and crew of the dhow.

Nor did any of the pirates' stories tie in with what they had said shortly after arrest. The Dutch had carried out interviews with the Somalis through an interpreter. These were allowed in evidence in court, despite having been carried out under Dutch military law on the high seas. This was perhaps unusual as Dutch military law is somewhat different to Seychelles criminal law, with different cautions and different rights for the detainee. It was a point taken by the defence during the trial, but not accepted by the judge, who commented: 'The information given on board the ship was clear and coherent; the statements were made much closer to the time of the incident with less chance of the accused persons getting their heads together.'

Balbal had told the Dutch interviewers that he was to be paid US$100 for the hijack of a dhow. He stated that they had weapons which were thrown overboard when they were intercepted by a Dutch Navy ship after they had hijacked a dhow with a Pakistani captain.

What the court heard from the prosecution was somewhat different to Balbal's version as told to me in the prison.

Although the *Burhan Noor* was an Iranian-owned ship, and its captain and crew Pakistani, the cargo belonged to a Somali businessman from Puntland. After the armed pirates boarded the ship and took control, he asked them to leave the boat but they would not; he was a man of influence and not a little wealth, so pulled strings, called in favours, and the Puntland government asked for help.

The ship was intercepted some 2–3 nautical miles (4–5 km) from the coast. When the German Navy vessel FGS *Sachsen* approached, the master of the *Burhan Noor* called them on the ship-to-ship VHF radio channel and asked them to stay away. He said there were six persons on board with guns and an RPG, who did not want the navy to board. There was someone standing right by him with a gun who had threatened that if the navy came aboard, both the *Burhan Noor* crew and the boarding party would be killed.

The skipper of the *Sachsen* called on the Dutch ship HNLMS *Rotterdam* for back up. According to the captain of the *Rotterdam*, the suspected pirates initially refused to surrender, threatened to fight them and even to kill the hostages. The court saw photo evidence of guns and RPGs, and pirates standing on the bow threatening the naval vessel with their weapons.

The *Burhan Noor* was still making way, getting closer to the Somali port of Bosaso – if it reached that harbour, all hope of rescuing the ship and hostages would be lost. *Rotterdam* therefore fired warning shots from the ship's main gun. After the second warning shot, the Somalis were seen to be throwing weapons overboard so a boarding party was sent to arrest them, all by now grouped at the bow of the *Burhan Noor*; the Pakistani crew were in the hold at the stern. When rescued, the crew stated that they were not fed all the time the pirates were on board. The captain had asked repeatedly for water; eventually, he was handed water in a cup that had diesel in it and told to drink it.

From the case papers, it didn't seem to me that they had been wrongly convicted, and the 24-year sentence reflected that this was one of the more unpleasant incidents of piracy.

When he arrived in Seychelles and was again interviewed, this time by the Seychelles police, Balbal's story and those of the others had changed from the one they had told on board the Dutch naval vessel. The Seychelles police never put to Balbal the content of his interview with the Dutch investigators (see Appendix 1 for a transcript of the interview of Abdirahaman Nur Roble by Seychelles police).

Above: John Boyle and a coastguard soldier out on anti-piracy patrol on board Seychelles Coastguard cutter *Topaz*. PHOTO © JOHN BOYLE

Below: UN Ambassador Ronny Jumeau. PHOTO © UN PHOTO/MARK GARTEN

Above: Aerial surveillance with the Seychelles Defence Force. PHOTO © JOHN BOYLE

Below: EU Naval Force officer aiming his machine gun at a pirate skiff. PHOTO © EUNAVFOR

Above: Maersk container ship in Port Victoria, Seychelles. PHOTO © JOHN BOYLE

Below: EU Naval Force helicopter picture of a skiff being launched from the coast – April 2013. PHOTO © EUNAVFOR

Above: Pirate boats: mother ship and attack skiffs. Note each attack skiff contains adapted boarding ladders. PHOTO © EUNAVFOR

Left: Mother ship and attack skiff photographed from surveillance aircraft. Note ladder and fuel drums. PHOTO © EUNAVFOR

Above: Pirate attack photographed from cargo ship. Note ladder and RPG at the ready. PHOTO © EUNAVFOR

Below: EU Naval Force flagship ITS *San Giusto* captures suspected pirates – November 2012. PHOTO © EUNAVFOR

Above: Captured pirates on deck of Seychelles Coastguard ship. Note the sores from many days at sea.
PHOTO © SEYCHELLES POLICE

Below: Arrested pirate in the back of a Seychelles Police truck. PHOTO © JOHN BOYLE

Above: Pirate mug shots. Note the facial sores in the bottom left photograph. PHOTOS © SEYCHELLES POLICE

Below: Arrested pirate being taken ashore in Seychelles. PHOTO © JOHN BOYLE

Above: Seized Somali weapons from a pirate mother ship. PHOTO © EUNAVFOR

Below: Captured pirate boat in Port Victoria, Seychelles. PHOTO © JOHN BOYLE
Inset from left: Captured pirate boat propeller, instruments and cooking drum. PHOTOS © JOHN BOYLE

I sat on my small terrace that night writing up my notes and watching the sun go down, as a cargo ship slowly crossed the bay on the distant horizon. It was exactly the same view that a pirate crew would have had as their first sighting of a target. I pictured the four Somalis whom I had interviewed that day attacking and boarding that ship. Speaking with them individually in the prison classroom, some dressed in prison work-party denims and others in ordinary casual clothes, there had been nothing too scary about them. My mind drifted and I could picture them, ragged and brandishing weapons, screaming commands and threatening the crew of the *Burhan Noor* in the first moments of capture.

I could picture Balbal in command, heading for the bridge to take control, moving quickly as his nickname suggested; thin, tall, evil-looking Mohamed would be a frightening sight, armed with an AK-47 and clearly happy to use it; muscular Abdullah, by his very silence a threatening presence; and boy soldier Mohamud, an unpredictable kid with a lethal weapon. I was glad not to have been on the bridge of the *Burhan Noor* that day.

18

THE LAW OF THE SEA

Where traytors, pirates, thieves, robbers, murtherers and confederates upon the sea, many times escaped unpunished, because the trial of their offences hath heretofore been ordered, judged and determined before the admiral, or his lieutenant or commissary, after the course of the civil laws;

The nature whereof is, that before any judgment of death can be given against the offenders, either they must plainly confess their offences (which they will never do without torture or pains) or else their offences be so plainly and directly proved by witness indifferent, such as saw their offences committed, which cannot be gotten but by chance at few times, because such offenders commit their offences upon the sea, and at many times murther and kill such persons being in the ship or boat where they commit their offences, which should witness against them in that behalf; and also such as should bear witness be commonly mariners and shipmen, which, because of their often voyages and passages in the seas, depart without long tarrying and protraction of time, to the great costs and charges as well of the King's highness, as such as would pursue such offenders...

The opening paragraphs of Britain's Offences at Sea Act 1536 identify many of the legal problems still faced in combating piracy almost five centuries later. Few pirates will ever confess their crimes, as I was quickly learning on my visits to Montagne Posée Prison, and these days *'torture or pains'* are not acceptable means of obtaining confessions! Also, from what the prisoners had told me, it appeared that witnesses are hard to bring to court, even in our modern world. Witnesses *'be commonly mariners and shipmen, which, because of their often voyages and passages in the seas, depart without long tarrying.'* Although rescued crews are enormously grateful at the time of their release, it's not easy to track down an Indonesian or Yemeni fisherman a couple of years later and persuade him to come to court.

The final problem that the 1536 Offences at Sea Act sought to address was where to hold a trial. It's a problem that 21st-century navies have also faced in dealing with pirates. The lawmakers at that time decided all trials should be held back home in England, no matter in what part of the British Empire the alleged piracy occurred. This was totally impractical in the days of sail, and the law was replaced some 150 years later to allow for acts of piracy to be 'examined, inquired of, tried, heard and determined, and adjudged in any place at sea, or upon the land, in any of his Majesty's islands, plantations, colonies, dominions, forts, or factories.'

The 20th-century United Nations Convention on the Law of the Sea (UNCLOS) was set up to define the rights and responsibilities of nations with respect to their use of the world's oceans. They didn't exactly rush to reach their findings. It took them from 1973 to 1982 to announce their conclusions. One of the principal issues was to decide what constituted a nation's coastal waters. Until then, these had been based on the Freedom of the Seas concept; in most cases, a country's coastal waters extended 3 miles (5 km) from their shores, this being based on the 'cannon-shot rule'. Beyond that were international waters, owned by none and free to all. By 1973, only a handful of countries claimed a 3-mile limit, the majority claimed 12, and some even claimed a 200-mile limit. This was to become an issue that turned out to be very significant in Somalia.

UNCLOS dealt with many other maritime issues. Only at paragraph 103 of the agreement did it get around to redefining piracy – just a couple of paragraphs before dealing with offshore pirate radio stations. It is hardly surprising that piracy was given such low ranking in importance: it was simply not a phenomenon that people thought would ever trouble the world again – like highwaymen. Britain abolished the death penalty for murder in 1965, but only got around to the abolition of the death penalty for piracy in 1998. It was just not considered a 20th- and 21st-century issue.

In the 1982 agreement, piracy was defined as consisting of any of the following acts:

> *(a) any illegal acts of violence or detention, or any act of depredation, committed for private ends by the crew or the passengers of a private ship or a private aircraft, and directed:*
> *(i) on the high seas, against another ship or aircraft, or against persons or property on board such ship or aircraft;*
> *(ii) against a ship, aircraft, persons or property in a place outside the jurisdiction of any State;*
> *(b) any act of voluntary participation in the operation of a ship or of an aircraft with knowledge of facts making it a pirate ship or aircraft;*
> *(c) any act of inciting or of intentionally facilitating an act described in subparagraph (a) or (b).*

Piracy at that time was not an issue at the forefront of anyone's mind. What UNCLOS failed to deal with was individual nations' powers to deal with piracy prosecutions. Today, EUNAVFOR, NATO and all the other navies on anti-piracy patrols in the Indian Ocean are like policemen of the seas. They keep the peace, carry out arrests and collect evidence. It is down to the legal systems of individual countries to prosecute the pirates, and that's where the problems have arisen: the headline-grabbing stories in international newspapers along the lines of 'Pirates freed without charges' or 'Somali pirates released back on to beach'.

Firstly, not every Somali at sea with weapons is a pirate. There are an estimated half a million weapons in Somalia – that's one for every 20 men, women and children. Hailing from a country a little like the American Wild West, it is not illegal for a Somali to have a gun. There is no central government to make or enforce a law against it. Therefore, Somalis having weapons on a boat does not mean they are pirates, and if there is no evidence of piracy, then navies are quite correct in releasing them and, if necessary, in helping them return to the coast.

The problem faced by navies is the procedure with obvious Somali pirates once captured. There are two issues – what to do with groups who are clearly pirates, who were heavily armed and towing fast attack skiffs, but who were not actually witnessed red-handed in an act of piracy; and what to do with those who could be prosecuted after being captured with clear evidence of committing piracy. The one thing that international navies cannot do is present such ruffians to Somali courts for prosecution – in the absence of any real government, there just is no legal system in place, no courts, prisons, police nor security, that could deal with the issue.

Many countries have taken the view that unless their own vessels have been attacked or their own people kidnapped, then they have no interest in prosecuting Somali pirates in their own courts. Thus, there have been few prosecutions brought in countries outside the region of East Africa. There are, however, notable exceptions.

In 2009, Somali pirate Abduwali Muse was sentenced in the US to 33 years and nine months in prison for hijacking the container ship *Maersk Alabama* in the Indian Ocean. Another example was the attack on the Spanish warship *Patiño*, which resulted in six Somalis being taken back to Spain to face trial.

Trials outside the East African region have, however, proved to be the exception rather than the norm, and trials in so many different countries have resulted in huge disparities of sentence.

Cabdullahi Cabduwily (also known as 'Abdu Willi') and Raageggesey Abdu Hassan Aji were each sentenced by a Spanish court to respective sentences of 439 years in prison for participating in the kidnapping in October 2009 of the Basque tuna boat *Alakrana* – on which I had recently been filming.

In 2010, five Somali men found guilty of piracy were sentenced in the Netherlands to just five years in jail. By contrast, in Yemen in the same year, six Somali pirates were sentenced to death, found guilty of killing two members of the crew of an oil tanker they hijacked. In the US, five Somali men were sentenced in that year to life imprisonment for piracy after attacking the USS *Nicholas*.

A further complication in European countries is human rights legislation. After they serve their term of imprisonment, the five Somalis who received five-year sentences in Holland should technically be returned to Somalia, although it is unlikely that this will happen because the Netherlands, like most European nations, is prohibited from deporting people to countries deemed too dangerous. When considering whether to prosecute suspect pirates, many countries have to ask themselves: 'Why bother?' Not only will they face the expense of a trial and of imprisoning such people, but they may also be obliged to support them on their release. The easiest option is just to dump them back on the beach...

Piracy is known as a crime of universal jurisdiction, which means that a country does not need a nexus – a connection to the incident – in order to claim jurisdiction over it. Normally, a nexus is required between the offence or offenders, and the prosecuting state – for example, the offence is committed within the jurisdiction of the state, or against a national of the state. Universal jurisdiction is very different – it applies to offences such as piracy, genocide, torture and slavery. Any country in the world can prosecute offences of piracy, wherever the offence has been committed, whoever the victim and whoever the accused.

If the country of the ship that is pirated chooses to prosecute and then imprison in its own courts, the issue is relatively straight-forward. But consider the hypothetical ship registered under a flag of convenience in Panama, owned by a consortium of Greek and Saudi shell companies, crewed by Indonesians and Filipinos under a Malaysian skipper, carrying a cargo owned by a limited corporation in Dubai, en route from Venezuela to Yemen, that is rescued in international waters by a Dutch warship. Who prosecutes and where?

The 1988 Convention for the Suppression of Unlawful Acts against the Safety of Maritime Navigation (SUA) partially solved the problem. It permits the master of a ship to convey suspects to another state – but only to the arresting state or to one with an interest. In theory, any of the countries in the hypothetical example above could prosecute.

In real terms, how many would be willing? A classic example occurred when 18 suspected pirates were detained by the Finnish minelayer FNS *Pohjanmaa* in April 2011, after they hijacked the Singapore-flagged vessel MV *Pacific Opal* in the North Arabian Sea, some 480 km (300 miles) east of Salalah, Oman. Almost three weeks after their arrest, all 18 were returned to Somalia without charges being brought against them – not for lack of evidence, but because no country could be found to prosecute such a large number. Finland, Singapore and Kenya were all invited to prosecute: 'The states either decided not to prosecute or could not provide intent to prosecute within the required timescale,' stated a EUNAVFOR spokesperson. 'With the *Pacific Opal* pirates, there was no state willing to prosecute them, and as EUNAVFOR cannot detain the suspects indefinitely, as this is in breach of the regulations of the European Convention on Human Rights, we decided to release them.'

Because of reluctance and the legal complications of dealing with pirates in their own courts, many countries initially reached an agreement with Kenya to provide funding in order that piracy trials would be heard there and convicted pirates imprisoned on its territory. Among those who signed agreements with the Kenyan government were the EU, US, UK, Canada and China. This worked well for a time.

To comply with international law, however, a Kenyan had to make the arrest, so the concept of 'ship riders' was introduced – each warship involved in anti-piracy operations was obliged to keep a Kenyan passenger on board, who would technically carry out any arrest. It was a ridiculous situation.

In April 2010, Kenya declared it was no longer willing to take on any more prosecutions and wanted to review agreements. Kenyan officials maintained that some nations had failed to offer adequate financial support to its strained justice system.

The UN and EU were quick to respond, providing a specially funded court at Mombasa's Shimo la Tewa Prison to hear maritime piracy cases.

The next problem emerged when a Kenyan High Court judge ruled in a case involving nine suspects that the country had no jurisdiction over piracy committed in international waters. Although that judgement was in time overturned, for the moment Kenya was no longer an option for prosecutions. In any event, Kenya had many internal issues of its own to contend with.

Where to send pirates for trial after capture was now a genuine issue for the patrolling navies. One small state – the tiniest in Africa, but the worst affected by Somali piracy – decided to grab the bull by the horns.

Seychelles had adopted the international definition of piracy, but amended Section 65 of its penal code to give it real teeth:

(1) Any person who commits any act of piracy within Seychelles *or elsewhere* [my italics] is guilty of an offence and liable to imprisonment for 30 years and a fine of R1 million.

(2) Notwithstanding ... any other written law, the courts of Seychelles shall have jurisdiction to try an offence of piracy whether the offence is committed within the territory of Seychelles or outside the territory of Seychelles.'

With the addition of just two words – 'or elsewhere' – Seychelles slashed through the complex questions of who could prosecute and whether they would be willing. They gave their courts the power to try an offence of piracy *wherever in the world it was committed.*

To meet the issue of those who were clearly pirates escaping justice because there was no clear evidence of them attacking a ship, Seychelles also extended the definition of piracy to include conspiracy to commit the offence; in the third clause, the new law stated:

'(3) Any person who attempts or conspires to commit, or incites, aids and abets, counsels or procures the commission of, an offence contrary to section 65(1) commits an offence and shall be liable to imprisonment for 30 years and a fine of R1 million.'

In short, pirates did not now have to be 'caught in the act'. Those who were clearly pirates, heavily armed and towing fast attack skiffs, but who had not actually been witnessed in an act of piracy, now faced prosecution and imprisonment.

This is similar to the offence of 'going equipped' in English and Welsh law. If a policeman finds someone wandering around after dark with an assortment of tools that have no good purpose other than to commit a burglary, then that person can be charged with the offence of going equipped to burgle, even though no burglary has taken place. At sea, this allows seizure of suspected pirate vessels and their occupants without having evidence of actual piracy. Some consider it harsh on all seagoing Somalis – unsurprisingly, some of those whom I interviewed in prison.

By agreeing to try piracy cases in its courts, and hold pirates both suspected and convicted in its prisons, Seychelles' actions had given EUNAVFOR what it most needed – 'legal closure'. No longer did an arresting vessel find itself powerless to do anything but give Somalis a nice meal, a slap across the knuckles, and drop them back to their beach, owing to a lack of international political will to prosecute...

Seychelles rapidly became the international trial centre for piracy, with the costs of new courts and prison facilities to deal with the accused borne by funding from the United Nations Office on Drugs and Crime (UNDOC).

Maxime Tirant, Superintendent of Montagne Posée Prison, told me that at one stage 20 per cent of its prison population were Somalis. He spoke of the problems caused by such a high percentage of prisoners as an ethnic minority who spoke none of the language of their jailers, and the cultural and overcrowding problems that resulted. The Somalis were also kept segregated from local prisoners, who deeply resented the damage the pirates were causing to their economy and fishing industry – and because the Somalis were holding some of their countrymen hostage.

This was something I'd discussed with Seychelles President James Michel and he had agreed that being the trial centre brought problems in terms of increasing the prison population, posing a burden on the national budget, and in needing to devote more resources to dealing with the trials and incarceration of the pirates.

'It creates that sort of problem but there are also benefits, as with the help of the international community, it has helped us provide better capacity in our legal system, and experience in dealing with certain types of trial that we were not used to before.

But what is more important is that it has enabled us to play a pivotal part in dealing with piracy in the Indian Ocean. Because unfortunately Seychelles found itself at one point alone, trying to do all that in the region. We had to sensitise the eastern African community about piracy. Most of them, they thought piracy was very far away – on the other side of the world – but when it started to hit them, then they realised how important it was. Mauritius has also signed agreements with certain countries to take pirates for trial. But we have really remained the centre and the bulk of the trials are carried out here.'

While the ultimate aim remains that Somali pirates are tried in Somalia, that is a long way ahead. For the present, legal and jurisdictional issues having been ironed out, suspected pirates are now successfully prosecuted and imprisoned in a small number of Indian Ocean countries.

19

FROM THE OLD BAILEY
TO THE BEACH

I had interviewed Michael Mulkerrins for my documentary, and he had at the time given me a good insight into the issues that arose in bringing piracy prosecutions. Michael was a British Crown prosecution lawyer, whose career path had taken an unforeseen turn. He'd previously been dealing with serious crime at London's most iconic criminal court, the Old Bailey, before finding himself seconded to the Indian Ocean to prosecute pirate cases. When we spoke, he had already conducted four separate trials involving 40 pirates, all convicted of piracy on the high seas, which probably gave him the record at that time of having prosecuted more pirates than anyone else on the planet. An unusual achievement in the 21st century.

We discussed Seychelles' piracy laws, which were in effect the tools of his profession.

'The obvious pirate attack involves boarding of a vessel, kidnap and holding it to ransom. To prove that act of piracy is relatively straightforward, providing we have the evidence from the crew who have been detained. We have in past cases called witnesses who were held hostage for days and weeks sometimes, who have been able to give evidence as to the conduct of the pirates – that they were armed, that they had RPGs, that they had threatened them and essentially told them to sail north-west to Somalia. That, from the lawyer's perspective, is a relatively easy equation.

The more difficult one is if a suspect skiff and mother ship are found in the Indian Ocean acting suspiciously a long way from the Somali coast – are they up to no good? They may not have committed any of the piracy acts that I have just mentioned, but the Seychellois have a residual law which says that if you are engaged or involved in a piracy act or you are prepared for piracy, then that too can be prosecuted. Even though we haven't shown that they attacked any ship, even though they haven't kidnapped any seafarers, even though they haven't made any ransom demand. This law helps us, where we've caught them at sea but they haven't been involved in any action. They might have been planning to, but we don't have the evidence.

An analogy would be if it were a land-based offence, that a policeman saw a very suspect transit van, knocked on the windows and there were six guys inside with balaclavas on the floor and maybe some very unusual tools or weapons inside. At home, we would have no problem at all arresting them and taking them to justice.'

I asked Michael about the principles governing the sentences the pirates received. He explained that it all depended on the seriousness of the incident: were weapons used, threats, violence, was anyone injured?

'We've had one case involving a French fishing vessel, a purse-seiner, that was pirated and a firefight took place between the French security forces and the pirates; hundreds of rounds of ammunition were exchanged on both sides, but nobody was injured. In that particular case, the pirates got 18 years. Each case is dealt with on its own facts, but one clear principle is that if there is an injury to a civilian, the pirates will be looking at more hefty sentences than would otherwise have been the case.'

He told me that none of the pirates had ever pleaded guilty, even in the face of overwhelming evidence. That was something that I was now discovering on my daily visits to the prison. At the time that I spoke with Michael, most defences put forward by the alleged pirates had been fairly unsophisticated; those I was hearing now were far more inventive.

'In all my cases bar one, the defence has been that we are innocent fishermen, we are out on the seas, and either our engine has broken down and we were looking for help, or we were asking for water. On each pirate vessel, there has been no evidence of fishing, of fishing gear, of fishing bait, of freezing equipment, of nets and the like.

On my last case, the defence was that they were economic migrants heading from Somalia to South Africa. This was a new one for me and from the lawyer's point of view needs a little more care to deal with it and disprove. OK, they didn't have fishing gear, but why would they – why would they have nets if they were economic migrants? But it just goes to show that the pirates are adapting their defences, because I think they know that running the defence of innocent fishermen is not paying them any dividends.'

I remembered this conversation some time later, when interviewing Maalin Daud Olat in the prison, and wondered then if this had been the same case. If so, then Michael had brought it to a successful outcome for the prosecution.

I had asked Michael if he had worked on any particularly memorable cases. He nodded.

'There is one case that stands out for me from the human perspective – the case of the *Talenduic*. All cases are known to we lawyers by the name of the ship pirated, rather than by the names of several defendants. The *Talenduic* and the *Cap Sainte-Marie* were both French tuna-fishing vessels. Large vessels, maybe 130–140 foot (40–43 m) in length, they are specially adapted for trawler fishing. They are very easy to pirate because the aft end is like a slipway into the water, out of which they roll their nets. They often fish in pairs as sister ships together.

The *Cap Sainte-Marie* had engine problems. She was dead in the water, in addition to which her nets were out and she couldn't get them in. Those nets weigh a lot – they are effectively a double anchor and when those nets are out they can't move; and she also had rudder problems.

Her sister ship *Talenduic* was nearby when the pirates attacked. The *Cap Sainte-Marie* was in real trouble. She couldn't move – she was literally a sitting duck. Fortunately, on board *Talenduic* were some French special forces as the on-board security team, so *Talenduic* acted as a protector and sailed around the *Cap Sainte-Marie* fighting off the pirates. There were actually divers in the water repairing the rudder as the firefight went on above them.

It's a nice piece of cinematography if Spielberg ever looked at it... This was the case in which the 18-year sentences were given.'

I asked Michael about the pirates themselves – what had he learned about them through his work?

'They've got nothing to lose, these guys; if they are successful, they earn money and respect back home; if they are not successful, they are expendable. We've heard stories about them being paid US$500 or the first one on the bridge gets a Mercedes ... but it is organised crime, there's no other way of looking at it.'

Clearly, in the short time since I had spoken with Michael, things had moved on. The defences run by the alleged pirates I was interviewing had become more innovative, the 'simple fisherman' defence being replaced with a variety of often ingenious tales. The requirements of the pirate crews themselves was also evolving as

Above: Freed hostage Rolly Tambara. PHOTO © JOHN BOYLE

Below: Rescued hostage Stephen Barbe. PHOTO © JOHN BOYLE

Above: Seychelles President James Michel (right), talking to John Boyle (left). PHOTO © JOHN BOYLE

Below: Freed hostage Gilbert Victor. PHOTO © JOHN BOYLE

Above: Defence lawyer Tony Juliette. PHOTO © JOHN BOYLE

Below: Prosecutor Michael Mulkerrins. PHOTO © JOHN BOYLE

Above: Somali pirates outside the courthouse in Seychelles. PHOTO © JOHN BOYLE

Below: Pirates about to stand trial in Seychelles Court. PHOTO © JOHN BOYLE

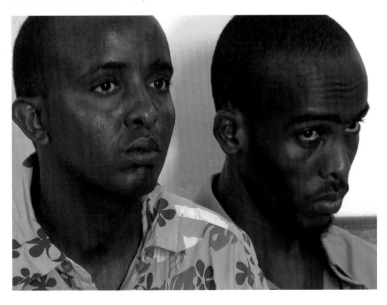

Above: Montagne Posée Prison's new wing, built to hold the growing population of Somali pirates. PHOTO © JOHN BOYLE

Below: Pirate awaiting sentence in Seychelles. PHOTO © JOHN BOYLE

Above: Young pirates in Seychelles hilltop prison, facing almost 30 years between them. PHOTO © JOHN BOYLE

Below: Maalin Daud Olat, currently appealing his conviction. PHOTO © JOHN BOYLE

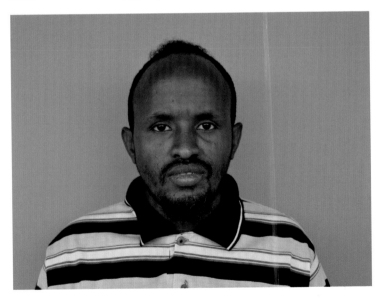

Right: Abdirahaman Nur Roble aka 'Balbal', 'the policeman who didn't become a pirate'.
PHOTO © JOHN BOYLE

Below: Abdullah Sharif Ibrahim, who claimed to be protecting boats from pirates. PHOTO © JOHN BOYLE

Below: Mohamed: innocent fisherman?
PHOTO © JOHN BOYLE

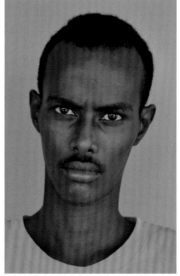

Above: FV *Naham 3* close to the Somali coast. Its crew were held hostage for over four years. PHOTO © EUNAVFOR

Below: Map showing locations of pirate attacks in 2010. MAP © JOHN BOYLE

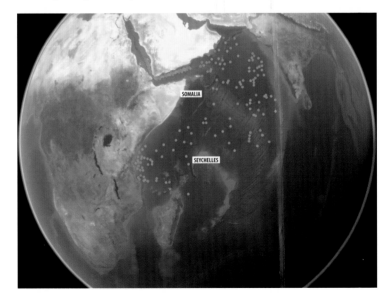

SOMALIA

SEYCHELLES

they now pirated dhows and other smaller vessels for use as mother ships. As both pirate operations and their defences grew more sophisticated to counter the prosecution's case, the lawyers were facing far more complex issues at trial. A new factor had crept into consideration. With the Court giving as much as a 50 per cent discount on sentences to those under 18, it was extraordinary how many Somalis were now claiming to be under that age.

Superintendent Maxime Tirant had told me more over a cup of tea in his office at Montagne Posée Prison. 'They give one name and age when arrested, another when they are interviewed, and once they arrive in the prison and have had a chance to speak with others already in the system, we usually get a third identity.'

I'd already identified this as a major issue. With no documents to prove even identity, let alone age, the Somalis I had met had given me ages that I had found extremely difficult to believe, often due to considerable facial hair growth and just general physical appearance.

Speaking with Michael Mulkerrins' successor after he had been rotated back to the UK at the end of his term, it was intriguing to see how things had developed.

The forensic science of age determination is more commonly associated with corpses and skeletons, whether at crime scenes or in dealing with the aftermath of mass disasters. Age at death can help investigators establish identities from among a potentially large number of possible matches.

Although age determination in living people is not so widely practised, it is in fact an ancient science. In the Roman Empire, young males were considered fit for military service from the eruption of the second molar.

In 19th-century Britain, a similar dental test was applied in certain situations – the age of criminal responsibility was set from seven years old, and the 1833 Factories Act made it illegal to employ a child below the age of nine. Even up to the present day, dental development is used as an indicator of a child's age in those parts of the world where births are not registered.

The discovery of X-rays opened up a whole new field of assessing age by examining bone structure and joint development. Other tools such as sexual development and even interviews with social workers have been used. There are four principal tools of assessment – social and psychological evaluation, physical examination, skeletal age and dental age.

Today, the science of age assessment in living people is principally utilised in dealing with unaccompanied minors who have entered a country as illegal immigrants.

Some minors arriving in the EU are subject to trafficking for the purpose of sexual exploitation, illegal labour or domestic labour. In many cases of trafficking, children are reported to be older than their chronological age. Yet there is still no consensus, even in European Union countries, on which methods must be applied when an age estimation of a supposed minor is needed.

The United Kingdom authorities usually only require an interview with the minor by a social worker. Austria insists upon an inspection by a doctor, a dental analysis and X-ray examinations. In France, a psychological interview is also used for age estimations of unaccompanied minors.

The science of age determination is one that Seychelles and other piracy prosecutors are now addressing.

Initially, the majority of suspected pirates who were detained in Seychelles were, on their own admission, over the age of 18. Judges have now started to draw a distinction between adults and juveniles, and have sentenced juveniles to shorter terms of imprisonment. It is frequently the case that, when detained, the suspected pirates will give what is likely to be their true ages to the detaining warships. They normally claim to be aged between their early twenties and mid-thirties. Once they have been accepted by Seychelles for prosecution, however, and are asked to state their ages in open court, it is common for the majority of suspected pirates to claim to be under the age of 18.

In two recent cases in Seychelles, medical experts from overseas conducted extensive examinations on suspected pirates who claimed to be juveniles. These involved a physical examination to measure features such as height, weight, and the development of any characteristics that may give an indication as to age. An X-ray of the wrist and hand was taken, to look at the degree of fusion of the distal radial epiphysis (the growth plate at the wrist end of the radius bone in the forearm). If these examinations were not determinative of age, dental X-rays were also taken, and comprehensive reports then prepared in respect of each individual.

It is accepted that there will be a margin of error when determining age via medical examinations, but this was also accounted for in the reports. In one instance, eight suspected pirates were medically examined. The conclusions reached were that seven out of the eight were over the age of 18 – in some cases, by three or four years.

I now understood why I was having difficulty believing some of the ages I was given by the Somalis I was interviewing.

The other issue that I wanted to discuss was the apparent lack of evidence in many cases from the people who had actually been held hostage – the captains and crews of pirated ships. Was there any truth in what the Somalis were telling me – that prosecutions were proceeding in the absence of that evidence? Many of the convicted pirates I had spoken with had felt aggrieved that, whatever the strength and quality of the evidence may have been, the court had heard only from the arresting navy and nothing from the alleged victims.

In conducting piracy prosecutions, not much seemed to have changed since 1536 – prosecutors faced the same problems as was noted in the Offences at Sea Act:

> *... and also such as should bear witness be commonly mariners and shipmen, which, because of their often voyages and passages in the seas, depart without long tarrying and protraction of time, to the great costs and charges as well of the King's highness, as such as would pursue such offenders...*

It's a regular problem securing the attendance of witnesses from overseas. It is often difficult to locate the witnesses. Even if they can be traced, if crew members who were held by the pirates are unwilling to give evidence, there is no way of compelling them to attend. Often it's too much trouble for them to turn up, they may lose their job, or they may be at sea for long periods.

As for other evidence, it was not uncommon in the early days to find RPGs, AK-47s, bullets and cartridges on board the skiffs, but it has become the norm for suspected pirates to discard such items overboard as soon as they suspect they are being monitored. Consequently, the type of evidence presented is changing.

Fortunately for the prosecutors, however, evidence in a piracy case can come from many different sources – not only from the crew of a vessel that has been attacked or hijacked, but also from the crew of the warship that detained the suspected pirates, from private armed security guards on board, and from aerial surveillance footage, among other sources. In addition, GPS evidence is becoming more prevalent, as the dhows or fishing vessels that are hijacked and used as a mother ship will often have a GPS device on board, and thus evidence can be obtained as to the location of the vessels at the time of an attack.

None of these incriminating factors reduce a pirate's sense of injustice, however, when he has been sentenced to prison for a couple of decades for an offence of piracy without a shred of evidence offered to the court from those who were allegedly pirated...

20

THE *ALBA STAR* CASE

I was to witness Seychelles' wide-ranging law in operation during my visit.

In the prison, Ali Jama Farah told me that he was 16 years old from Puntland. His trial had already taken place and he was waiting for the court's judgement. From the outset, his was not the most convincing story I had heard. He was certainly the most mature 16-year-old I've ever seen, already slightly balding.

He had had no education. He told me he was from a rural village in the bush called Iskambus, some 300 km (190 miles) from the coast – the interpreter said it was so small that I would never find it on a map. He lived with his dad and mum and family – they sell vegetables and clothes – sometimes depending on him to support the family. When I asked how he did that, he told me that he used to go fishing, sell some and bring some home. I was getting more incisive with my questioning now – how was it that he fished and brought fresh fish home, when they lived so far from the coast along dreadful roads? After thinking about it, he said that he and others get to the coast by car to fish. I wondered how he could afford to pay for a 300-km (190-mile) ride in a car but I left it there, my scepticism totally lost on him.

'There were six of us in a boat. We left in the morning, spent a night at sea, and the following night were taken by a boat from Holland. We had no weapons on board. We had fishing nets. We were fishing for shark. We can sell the meat at the market, and Arab men come to buy the fins to take back to their country.

I'd not been out on this boat before – the boat and people were new to me. We'd met in a village, discussed if we could work together, found a boat and went fishing. We left from a beach – a place called Omaan. It's an empty beach – just a couple of small timber shelters where the fishermen cook fish and sometimes sleep.

When we went to court, they made up a story and planted things on us. Seychelles think all Somalis are pirates. Yes, there are pirates but not all of us, and certainly not me. We could see the Somali coast with our naked eye, and there was no ship near us except the naval ship. In court, the prosecutor said we had attacked a ship. We had no weapons.

Where I come from, people do not carry guns. Where I live in Puntland, we have a president, government, ministers, police. The police will do operations against pirates – they will hunt for pirates.

In Somali, like anywhere, there are rich, middle and poor. I belong with those who fight for their daily bread – I am poor.

I was 14 and some months when I was detained – I'm 16 now – I've been here well over a year. I'm facing a poor life, being away from my family, being in prison. I get ten minutes every month to speak with my family on the phone. It's nothing.'

When I spoke with Ali Issack Ahmed, I did not even make a link that he and Ali Jama Farah had been part of the same arrest until I saw the court judgement, so different were their stories. He told me that he too was 16. In my notes, I see that I scrawled 'Nice tash!!!' as he certainly had the beginnings of a good growth on his upper lip. He was also from Puntland, a place called Hafwn, which he told me is little more than a beach that boats fish from. He was one of the best educated of the Somali prisoners that I spoke to, having spent one year and eight months at school. Most recently he described himself as having been working in an office for his uncle, delivering newspapers.

His version of the 'innocent fisherman' defence was an interesting twist and he had certainly covered all the bases.

'After I left that job, I went fishing for four months. Me and three others had a boat. One day we sent it fishing with a crew on board and it went missing, it didn't come back. We took a skiff and went looking for it. We ran out of fuel because we hadn't planned to be at sea long. We were caught by rain and storms and got blown 60–70 miles (100–110 km) offshore.

We had some fishing gear on board but only hooks as we hadn't gone to sea to fish – we had gone to find our lost boat. We hadn't taken much fuel and no navigation equipment as we had never intended going out to the high seas – we had wanted to go along the coast to the beaches to look for our lost boat. It could have been stolen or gone ashore because of problems. We ran out of fuel because we hadn't planned to be at sea long, and so got blown offshore.

We came across another boat 70 miles (110 km) off, with six men on board – they gave us some fuel. When we were about to leave, a helicopter came. It was shooting at us for about 90 minutes. Then a big plane came, then another helicopter, so we stopped, were detained and taken to a warship. When we were on the warship, we met the other six from the boat that gave us fuel – they had been detained too.

My trial is over and I'm waiting for judgement this month. I've now been here in this prison for one and a half years. The navy said that I attacked a ship – but no one came from the ship to say that I had attacked it. Can you help me?'

These two were the only alleged pirates I'd spoken to who hadn't yet received a judgement in their case. I was back in England before the judgement came through. The judge recited the facts.

Responding to a distress call from a Panama-flagged cargo ship, MV *Alba Star*, stating that it was being approached by two skiffs, the nearest EUNAVFOR vessel, the Dutch naval frigate HNMLS *De Ruyter*, despatched its helicopter and headed for the scene. The helicopter found no vessels in the area other than a large skiff towing a smaller one. The larger skiff had a hooked ladder on board, and other material covered by tarpaulins.

Because it was working at extreme range, the helicopter could not remain on station for long, but was soon joined by a Spanish Maritime Patrol and Reconnaissance Aircraft (MPRA); what is known as a 'hot handover' took place, so that there was continuous surveillance of the two skiffs, the helicopter heading back to *De Ruyter* to refuel.

As soon as the helicopter left, and apparently unaware of the MPRA observing from a distance, the two skiffs stopped and packages were dropped over the side. They then headed off in different directions at speed, the smaller with three men on board including Ali Isaac Ahmed heading directly west towards the Somali coast, the larger with a crew of six including Ali Jama Farah heading north.

Confronted by the Dutch warship, the larger skiff stopped without fuss and the crew were arrested. The smaller skiff was less willing to co-operate. It ignored warning shots fired by the *De Ruyters'* helicopter, ignored smoke-marker bombs dropped in front of it by the Spanish MPRA, and only finally came to a halt after warning shots from a second helicopter that arrived to assist. While no weapons or ladders were found on board, the navy search team found and seized aiming sights for RPGs and AK-47s – the suspects claimed they used these on land as binoculars. Three spent cartridges were found on the smaller skiff. There were also a number of mobile phones.

The evidence was not the strongest. No member of the *Alba Star* crew attended to give evidence in court so there was no direct eyewitness account of any attack on the ship, and the judge found the allegation of a piracy attack on that ship not proven.

However, the nine men faced an alternative charge brought under Seychelles' all-encompassing law that they 'jointly participated in the operation of a skiff with knowledge of the facts making it to be a pirate ship'.

Under cross-examination, the pilot of the MPRA conceded that although he had seen items being dropped overboard, there were no photographs of this, only infrared video, due to the high altitude at which he had been flying. He also conceded that he was unable to state exactly what was dropped into the water or even how many packages, although from the video it 'appeared to be two or three'.

Before announcing his verdict, the judge quoted from an earlier Seychelles case: 'The evidence is a combination of factors including the presence of equipment suitable for carrying out pirate attacks, the absence of a legitimate trade, the composition of the group, the position of the vessels, and the behaviour of the accused persons when approached by the authorities...'

The make-up of the classic pirate-hunting group – the large skiff laden with fuel and supplies, the boats' presence in an area far from fishing grounds, and the absence of fishing equipment – had all been stressed by the prosecutor. The judge listed seven factors he considered significant:

1 A hooked boarding ladder of a type not suitable for lawful activities and commonly found aboard pirate vessels ... observed from the air and in photographs
2 A smaller skiff with powerful outboard engines

3 A supply of food for approximately one week
4 A GPS unit
5 An RPG aiming sight
6 Discharged bullet casing
7 Mobile phones

The judge convicted seven of the nine defendants, including Ali Issack Ahmed and Ali Jama Farah, of jointly operating a pirate ship, finding the case not proven against the remaining two alleged pirates. However, he then appeared to listen carefully to the mitigation put forward by the defence lawyers of the convicted men. They argued that they were all first-time offenders, had not been armed with weapons at the time of their interception and did not retaliate at the time of their arrest, and that no person had suffered injury at their hands, or damage caused to any vessel by them. The judge also appeared to sympathise with their counsel's argument that a short sentence would enable them to return to Somalia and be reunited with their families. He passed sentences of six years' imprisonment on them all.

21

HOW TO DEFEND PIRATES

Tony Juliette's house was in one of the remotest parts of the island, and his directions along the lines of 'Turn left at the third big rock' had been in classic island style. The whole interior was open-plan, and a terrace ran the width of the front of the house, overlooking a jumble of huge granite boulders against which the Indian Ocean waves broke. On a large kitchen table were spread the papers of the current case that he was working on.

When I had asked around to find a defence lawyer to talk to about the piracy cases, his had been the first name I had been given. He had not been easy to track down; his one-room office in town never seemed to open, he did not use email and never seemed to pick up messages from his phone. Every time I'd gone to court to find him, I'd been told he'd just left or was not expected that day. I had almost given up hope of meeting him when, late one afternoon, he eventually called back, and invited me round for a beer.

He was welcoming and relaxed, smiling and friendly, and I immediately felt at ease as he opened a couple of bottles from the fridge and we settled in large comfy wicker chairs on the terrace, the gentle sea breeze warm and welcome after the heat of the day.

'I've been practising law in Seychelles for some time now. The first time that pirates were arrested and brought to Seychelles – the very first 11 – no one wanted to have anything to do with them. We are a very small island nation, and there was a very strong sense of hatred against them and what they were doing to the economy of our country. So you can imagine why very few people, especially in the legal profession, wanted get involved.

For a while they had no lawyer, so eventually the judge and the Attorney General called me in and asked if I would represent these people on legal aid. It was the first ever case of its kind in this country, and looked to be a challenging case, so I thought "Why not!"

Once I had agreed to take the case, the first problem that I encountered was the language barrier – they spoke not a word of English or French, and no one in Seychelles spoke a word of Somali. That's a pretty big obstacle! Eventually an interpreter was brought in from Kenya. But that was far from perfect, as the interpreter was appointed by the court and worked with the police and prosecution as well as with me. So I had no idea how far what I said to my clients remained confidential. But because this type of case was new to us all here, so much pressure was on me and there were so many constraints, I felt I had no alternative but to agree to this arrangement, otherwise it would have been impossible to proceed.

I would meet with the Somalis as a group. I found them to be very simple folk. I also found them to be very indifferent to the circumstances that they were facing. Despite having advised them of the severity of the charges they were facing, they did not seem overly concerned about the personal consequences to themselves. They seemed resigned to the fact that they had ended up in a situation where they would have to deal with serious consequences. They just didn't seem to care. It took a lot for me to explain to them some of the legal issues they had to deal with – they were at a loss as to what was going on.

I remember once I said to them: "You have all given statements that you were fishing. I'm your lawyer. Prove to me that you were fishing. Show me a line, show me a hook, show me a little bit of bait, a single fish head…" They just stared at me – that's the kind of people that they are.

They were very secretive and protective about their life in Somalia, and they would not tell me anything at all about what prompted them to go out to sea. In fact, they tried to display some ignorance about their own country. I asked them about their skiffs – there was a marking on one, a company marking. I asked them how I could get in contact with the company to try and help the case – they said they didn't know. They were very unhelpful: they would not talk about the reasons they got to where they were arrested at sea, save to say they were fishermen.'

So Tony was left to work on the Somalis' defence case with no help from his 11 clients.

Their charges split into three categories – commission of a terrorist act, membership of a terrorist group, and piracy. Tony felt comfortable that he could get the first two charges dismissed as there was no evidence whatsoever to support them, and legal argument would suffice. Piracy, though – he needed to examine the evidence carefully, and what he found surprised him.

The piracy case was founded on the allegation that the Somalis had fired on the Seychelles Coastguard cutter *Topaz* with sub-machine guns. There was no damage to that ship and no injury, nor any video or photographic evidence; simply the eyewitness accounts of the coastguard crew. Assessing the physical evidence, Tony began to have his doubts. Like any good defence lawyer, he was searching for weaknesses in the prosecution's case. A criminal case must be proved beyond reasonable doubt, and if Tony could raise enough doubt in the judge's mind then he had a chance of securing an acquittal for his clients. It's the classic question that lawyers always get asked – how can one defend people who are clearly guilty? That is not the issue – the point of a trial is, can the prosecution prove its case? The defence are there to find holes in the prosecution's evidence and try to raise enough doubts to get a not guilty verdict.

'Now, we all know that when you fire a weapon like the AK-47, shell cases are ejected and fall to the floor where you are standing. The amazing thing in this case is that when the Somali skiffs were apprehended, there were many weapons in them – AK-47s, handheld grenade launchers, lots of ammunition – they had not attempted to discard their weapons overboard. But there was not one single used shell casing that might indicate that there had been firing from the skiff at the coastguard vessel. It's inconceivable that they should have made no attempt to get rid of their weapons, but would have got down on hands and knees to search the floor of the vessel and throw used cartridges away.'

Interestingly, when Tony researched online and found the EUNAVFOR communiqué relating to this incident, it said that a French naval frigate *Floréal* (F730), assisted by a helicopter from that ship, had apprehended some Somali pirates and had received the assistance of the Seychelles Coastguard to take them to Victoria.

'Assistance ... my argument was that the Seychelles coastguard ship merely assisted the French and had never actually been attacked...'

Tony showed me the witness statements that he had prepared on the Somalis' instructions:

'We left Jazira Port (near the Somali capital Mogadishu) on 27 November 2009 with the intention of fishing. After being in the sea for three days, we encountered a storm, we got confused and our boat could not operate because it developed some problem. We also experienced heavy rain that led to the loss of our equipment and we were in that condition for 48 hours.

On 2 December at 0430 we were attacked... We were in the main boat at the time of the attack. Most of us were sleeping, however those of us who were awake initially saw a light similar to that of a torch. Thinking the light came from some fishermen, we sought help and instead were fired on and attacked.'

They claimed that the fishing equipment was on the boats that sank – two of the three vessels were sunk at time of capture.

While the presence of weapons on board might raise suspicion to those of us who live in more ordered societies, there is no rule of law in Somalia preventing possession and carrying of weapons and it is a way of life for many.

The trial took place in Victoria's old central courthouse, a classic Creole-style building in the centre of town, but not one built in anticipation of trials involving so many defendants. In the courtroom itself, in the absence of a dock large enough to hold them, the group of Somalis lined up on benches to one side, overseen by a couple of unarmed police officers. There was no holding cell capable of taking them, so during recesses they sat on the grass outside as the townsfolk and tourists went about their business.

The judge agreed with Tony Juliette's legal submissions and rejected the terrorism charges. Sitting without a jury, however, he found the piracy charges proven and sentenced all the Somalis to ten years in prison. Tony appealed the conviction unsuccessfully.

Doing his best for his clients meant that Tony was suggesting that the members of his nation's most revered service, the Coastguard, were not being truthful. It's a difficult allegation to make in such a tiny country, where everyone knows everyone. He hinted at the difficulties this had caused him.

'The international focus, coupled strongly with the local focus on the Somali pirate problem, has turned most Seychellois against the Somalis. We are a safe little country in the middle of the ocean, and we depend heavily on the sea for our survival. So you can imagine the hatred that our people had against these people, and you can imagine the difficulty as a lawyer trying to defend them. Folks don't understand that we lawyers have taken an oath to defend our clients on the basis of the evidence, and not to take into account any political, social, or other factors.'

Things have got easier since that first piracy trial.

'Over time, people have come to understand that everyone has the right to be defended against whatever crime they have been accused of. And there have also been Somalis arrested and released with no charges for lack of evidence – people have come to realise that we don't simply have a lynch-mob mentality here.'

So does he think that this first batch of Somalis were wrongly convicted? Tony doesn't answer, goes to the cooler to crack open another beer for us both, and changes the subject to tell me his personal and rather novel solution to the Somali piracy issue.

'As we know, pirates operate from Somalia in small boats with powerful 40–60hp outboard engines. If the international community were serious about the issue, then they could take measures and sanctions to prevent or at least limit the entry of these outboard engines to Somalia, as this is what enables them to get out to sea. Let in smaller horsepower engines to allow them to fish a certain distance from shore, but prevent the more powerful engines so they can't go so far out to sea. Outboards aren't manufactured there – they come from Japan. These are the most important tools that the pirates use in their activities. So why can't the international community use their pens and paper, their computers, their forces, to stop this? It's a very simple way of curbing the problem...'

Just then, Tony's mobile rang and he excused himself to deal with a long and complex call in Creole with his client for court tomorrow.

I stayed on his terrace, slowly sipping my beer, mesmerised by the full moon over a gently rolling sea. My mind strayed to the stark desert of the next landfall across that sea, and imagined camel trains laden with smuggled outboard engines crossing lonely distant borders...

22

OMERTA

'I am not a pirate and I've never seen one.'

As I was sitting talking to the interpreter, a large bearded man, eyes looking wildly in different directions, marched aggressively into the room. OK, now we've got trouble... There was an aura of violence, of aggression about him.

'Give me cigarettes and I will tell you my story.'

He was not one of those who had been waiting by the door for me to talk with; he was wearing the blue canvas outfit of an outside work party. I pulled a pack of Marlboro from my camera bag. He was not happy.

'I don't like these – they are American,' he spat out in disgust.

Sorry, mate, that's all I have ... tell you what. I'm back on Monday with my camera – if you agree to have your photo taken, I'll bring in some Mahé Kings. He still was not happy, but shoved five Marlboro inside his pants under the elasticated waist of his denim-blue prison trousers.

Ahmed Abdi Barre said he was 18 years old. I'd have put him in his mid-twenties. Bulkily built although not fat. The sort of guy to steer clear of in a bar, the sort who always seems to be looking for a fight. I certainly wouldn't have wanted him pointing a gun at me.

He was from Mogadishu, had a wife, no kids, and a 16-year sentence. Well, he'd been born in Mogadishu but now lived in Beledweyne, some 330 km (205 miles) to the north. Before he'd been arrested, he had been a cattle herdsman for six years, and worked on a farm before that. His was a tale of being an economic migrant, but heading north, not south.

'We were leaving Warsheikh. There were 16 of us. We had paid a Somali middleman for passage on an Iranian boat heading for Italy. Yes, Europe, to build a new life.

Al Shabab were killing almost everyone, beheading them, which is why I wanted to escape. My area is controlled by them. They ask you to join them – if you don't, they will cut your head off. So I was running from them, going to Europe for a better life.'

He had said that he had a wife – what about her?

'My wife,' he shrugged with disinterest, 'my wife, she would follow me.

We left harbour during the night and were detained in the morning by the Denmark Navy. I didn't know any of the other people. I'd never been on that boat in my life. I paid $250 for the passage.'

Two hundred and fifty US dollars? I didn't like him, and I really wanted to rip into this totally implausible story – to cross-examine him – the same impulse that the prosecuting lawyer must have felt as he stood to discredit this defence. Where does a fleeing Somali cowherd get US$250? Why of all places head to Italy? Did he realise that it was thousands of sea miles, around the Horn of Africa, through the Gulf of Aden, the length of the Red Sea, through Suez, and then through the Mediterranean, to one of the countries with the most vigilant sea patrols to counter illegal migration from North Africa?

But I also wanted to get him out of the room as fast as I could.

'Thanks, mate,' I was trying to convey as much sympathy as I could. 'Got to get on,' and turning to the translator, 'Who's next...?'

He seemed reluctant to leave.

'Tell them in your book that I want to be sent to a prison in Mogadishu. You tell them that.' Of course the world would be told, I reassured him.

From then on, although he was supposedly on a work party, most times I left the interview room he would be there. It turned out that he could speak passable English. He started hassling me for a 16 gigabyte memory stick so that he could watch films at night – he currently only had a two gigabyte stick. Would I be coming back tomorrow? Would I make sure to bring it?

While I'd cleared with the Governor the bringing in of a vest and a book for two other inmates, and a few local cigarettes were no issue, there was no way I was going to bring in contraband for a Somali pirate, and I made this very clear to him. He didn't seem to understand the word 'No'. Even when we were leaving late in the afternoon, he approached the car, to be told yet again and definitely 'No way!'

My instincts about him were proved correct when I read the court judgement in his trial. The Danish warship HMDS *Absalon* was patrolling off the Somali coast when they saw a fishing dhow with skiffs, ladders and weapons on board which 'were not related to normal fishing activities'. The boarding crew found 16 Somalis aboard, together with 12 members of the original crew – nine Pakistanis and three Iranians.

No weapons or ladders were actually found aboard save for one 7.62-calibre bullet of the type fired from AK-47s. Photographic evidence, however, showed splashes at the stern of the dhow on an otherwise calm day that were interpreted as evidence of pirating equipment having been dropped overboard.

Most telling was the evidence of the dhow's captain Ali Aktarhali; both he and one other crew member came to court to give evidence. A month before their rescue, they had left the Iranian port of Jabbar on a fishing trip. They were some 480 km (300 miles) offshore when they encountered the Somalis – nine of them in a small boat, all with guns and all firing at the dhow and its crew. Captain Aktarhali was forced at gunpoint to sail to the Somali coast. It took 70 hours to get there. As they were approaching the coast, a small boat met them and a boss named 'Mr Goodeye' demanded US$4 million in ransom. When the captain told him that the boat was worth nowhere near that much, he was not happy. As a result, the crew were kept seated on one side of the deck without food or water and without shade.

At their anchorage on the Somali coast were three other boats – two English and a Tanzanian: two cargo ships and a container ship.

They remained there for 11 days, only once being given food. Captain Aktarhali said they were treated very badly by the pirates, and the only water they were given tasted of diesel. During this time, there were many comings and goings with Mr Goodeye and several other people visiting the boat.

When they left Somalia, he was told that they were going to find a tanker. Sixteen Somalis were now on board, and all had Kalashnikovs, and there were also two RPGs. When they spotted the helicopter from the Dutch naval ship, the pirates started panicking and throwing weapons into the sea.

Contrary to the story told by the Somalis when interviewed by the police – that they had been heading to Libya or Italy as political refugees, depending on whom was being spoken to, after leaving shore the dhow had headed south-east for 80 nautical miles (150 km) – the completely opposite direction to heading for the Gulf of Aden and the route to the Mediterranean. The judge also commented that despite their claims to have paid US$400 each for their passage – which is what they had told the police, '... no documents or money were found on board, and none of the accused persons had any document or item with them that could have supported their claims that they were Somali refugees about to travel to a foreign country.'

The rest of the day at the prison fell into a familiar pattern. I could understand those who were still awaiting trial or judgement continuing to deny piracy, but what was to be gained from this silence from those who had been convicted and exhausted their appeals? It seemed like the Somali version of the Mafia's code of Omerta – the code of silence among organised criminals. It was still interesting to hear their back-stories of how they had ended up here, even though I was clearly going to manage no insight into life as a pirate.

It wasn't fair or proper of me to challenge the stories of those like Abdikadar Abdisalan who was still awaiting trial, so I simply let him tell me his tale. He was aged 17, from Galkyro, had received no schooling, and was single. In Galkyro he had a job, driving a small 15-seater minibus taking people around the town; he had been doing this for three years. Galkyro lies 515 km (320 miles) from the coast, in Puntland, so how had he ended up here, facing allegations of piracy at sea?

'I left Galkyro because the owner of the minibus took it away. I needed to eat and to provide for myself and my family as my parents are very poor and were depending on me.

Me and eight other men started work on the sea as fishermen catching shark. On the last trip, we left from Igo – a beach next to Adale. After three days we had engine problems. We were drifting for almost two weeks. By then, the sea was rough, the strong winds took us to the high seas, and we were taken by a Danish warship. We had only planned to be at sea for 12 days. When we had the engine problems and the sea got worse, we were rationed to one meal per day, very small portions, and when we were arrested, the water was almost gone.

We had no radio on board; no weapons; we had only four nets on board. We'd had many more but we had set them before we had engine problems so we couldn't pick them up. I only knew two of the crew on board – the others were new to me. This was my third trip out fishing.

We had no navigation equipment on our boat, not even a compass. We weren't planning on going more than 140 nautical miles (260 km) offshore. We would use the sun to navigate – it rises in the east, and Somalia is in the west where it sets.

I'm on remand waiting for my trial. I'm here by mistake – they claimed we had attacked a boat, a ship. We never attacked a ship – we didn't even see a ship.'

Another day, and still no prisoners accepting that they were pirates and telling me the stories that I wanted to hear. I wondered if I was just wasting my time. I remained hopeful that something would come of my second meetings with Balbal and Maalin, who had seemed to promise something more.

23

A HIGH PRICE TO PAY

Most of the Somalis I had spoken to had been involved in fairly low-key piracy, not headline-grabbing incidents; indeed, most ships taken by the pirates are average cargo vessels or large commercial fishing boats, but they are always looking for a jackpot, and occasionally they strike lucky.

The *Maersk Alabama* is probably the best-known ship taken by the Somalis – a fully laden container carrier, with ship and cargo worth tens of millions of dollars. If this were not enough to bring the case to world attention, the *Alabama* was also the first US-flagged ship to be captured by pirates in over 200 years, and the American response was immediate and dramatic – a story picked up by Hollywood, with Tom Hanks playing Captain Richard Phillips, master of the vessel.

Abduwali Muse and his cohorts began their piratic spree in March 2009, boarding two vessels in the Indian Ocean and taking hostages including Gilbert Victor and his catamaran; Muse was known to Victor as 'Little Captain' (see page 79). The brigands' escapade culminated in the capture of the *Maersk Alabama*, a 500-foot (150-metre) container ship headed to Kenya from Djibouti with a cargo of food aid for the region.

When the pirates were spotted, Captain Richard Phillips sent most of the crew to a secure room deep within the ship, while he and the remaining crew tried unsuccessfully to evade the pirates. After the ship was boarded, the crew members in the secure room were able to shut down the engines. The pirates went hunting for the hidden crew, with the result that the ship's chief engineer Mike Perry tackled and captured the pirate leader Abduwali Muse. An attempt was made to exchange him for Captain Phillips, but the pirates did not honour their side of the deal.

Two US Navy ships USS *Bainbridge* and USS *Halyburton* soon reached the *Alabama*, joined not much later by USS *Boxer*. Unable to control the ship, the pirates took to the ship's lifeboat, taking Captain Phillips with them as hostage – an American captain was a valuable second prize if they couldn't hold the *Alabama* itself. Aerial surveillance showed as many as four other foreign vessels, all captured by pirates and containing an estimated 54 hostages themselves, heading to the scene to pick up their colleagues and their hostage.

In an escalating situation, the pirates agreed to let one of the American ships take them in tow, and while Abduwali Muse was on board *Bainbridge*, believing that he was negotiating ransom details, Navy SEAL snipers were parachuted in, opening fire and killing the other three Somalis still on board the lifeboat. Captain Phillips was rescued uninjured.

It was one of the most publicised and dramatic ship rescues. Muse is now serving almost 34 years' imprisonment, and Captain Phillips is back at sea.

The pirates' aim is, of course, to capture a high-value ship and cargo, and a cruise liner would be the ultimate goal – crammed with wealthy people from many different nations, it would be their dream ransom scenario, with the value of the ship as the cherry on the cake. While cruise-ship companies are generally reluctant to disclose how much their liners are worth, it quickly became public knowledge that the *Costa Concordia*, which foundered after striking a rock in the Mediterranean in January 2012, had been built between 2004 and 2006 at a cost of US$570 million.

So far the pirates have not succeeded in seizing such a prize, but not for want of trying. In November 2005, the Bahamian-registered *Seabourn Spirit* came under pirate attack 100 nautical miles (185 km) off the coast of Somalia, en route to Mombasa in Kenya on a 16-day cruise out of Alexandria in Egypt. The 10,000-ton liner offered the height of luxury, with huge suites, marble bathrooms and more than one crew member to each passenger on board. Most of the passengers were American – a plum prize for any pirate. At 5.30 in the morning, passengers were woken to the sound of gunfire as two skiffs came up to the liner and opened fire as their occupants tried to board. Although firing RPGs and guns at the ship – some of which found their target – the pirates were repelled by use of a high-pressure water hose and an LRAD (Long Range Acoustic Device), combined with the captain taking evasive action. No pirate succeeded in boarding the ship and only one member of the security team was injured. With all cruise ships now carrying on-board security, the chances of a successful pirate capture of a cruise ship must be remote.

Next on the pirates' hit list are oil tankers, and with these they have had many successes. Tankers are a favourite for pirates. Lumbering through the oceans, and with a low freeboard when fully laden, they are easy to board and make vulnerable prey. Unlike faster container ships, they are not very manoeuvrable, taking a mile or more just to execute a turn. In fact, such vessels are little more than a huge oil tank with a propeller at the back. With a top speed of no more than 15 knots, and an optimum economical speed of 12.2

knots according to Lloyds List, there is no way they could outrun a pirate skiff.

Carrying a potentially flammable cargo, the risks of an on-board gunfight outweigh the value of armed security – and with a ship 1,000 feet (300 m) long, more than the typical security detail of four would be needed properly to protect them. The only really effective security is an escort vessel, but the costs of this are generally out of the question in a highly competitive market.

Above all, insurers would be keen to negotiate a quick release for these valuable vessels and their even more valuable cargos. Very large crude carriers (VLCCs) cost US$100–120 million to build, and can carry a cargo worth double that amount; the ransom value of its crew is also attractive to pirates. In addition, the losses continue to mount with each day the ship is out of operation.

Upon its seizure in November 2008, 450 nautical miles (830 km) off the coast of Kenya, the *Sirius Star* was headed for the US, full of Saudi Arabian crude oil worth some US$150 million. With a dead-weight tonnage of more than 300,000, at the time it was the largest vessel ever to be hijacked, and also the furthest out to sea that the pirates had struck. The supertanker was virtually brand new, having been launched just nine months earlier.

Negotiations started at US$25 million. By January 2009, a ransom of US$3 million was finally agreed upon, and the US Navy released an iconic photo showing a small package containing the ransom parachuting to the deck of the *Sirius Star* from a small aircraft. After splitting up the ransom and leaving the ship, five pirates drowned in rough seas, with one of their bodies reportedly washing ashore along with a plastic bag holding US$150,000. Karma, some may think.

As piracy has grown, and the perpetrators have realised the strength of their bargaining position, ransoms have continued to rise. The 2009 ransom paid for the *Sirius Star* was way surpassed by the US$9 million paid in 2010 for the Greek-owned *Maran*

Centaurus. That sum was itself just a small amount when compared to the value of the crude oil it was carrying – estimated at around US$150 million, not including the value of the ship herself. The vessel had been heading for the United States from Saudi Arabia with two million barrels of crude oil, and lacked any private guards to secure its cargo. The *Maran Centaurus* was hijacked almost 750 nautical miles (1,389 km) away from Somalia, where foreign navies had no presence.

A long stand-off ensued, with naval ships shadowing the hijacked ship closely while ransom demands were negotiated. In a curious twist, a group of rival pirates moved in to attack the ship just before the ransom was to be delivered, prompting the pirates on board to call the anti-piracy force for help – perhaps one of the more unusual calls for assistance that EUNAVFOR has had to deal with. A shoot-out between the two groups could have caused a catastrophic explosion: the ship's cargo is so flammable that smoking is forbidden other than in restricted areas. Even the burning of incense is considered a risk.

When helicopters from one of the nearby warships were sent to respond to the pirates' distress call, the approaching group of pirates appeared to have second thoughts and turned away from the *Maran Centaurus*. The ransom was successfully parachuted to the original pirates, who freed ship and crew, leaving it to continue on its way.

The actual amount of the *Maran Centaurus* ransom was a classic example of the disinformation surrounding ransom payments in general. The insurance world clearly wants to keep pirates' expectations of the sum they will be paid at the low end of the scale, to help with negotiations. After the ship was released, the tanker owners issued a statement that they '… will not be releasing any details of the talks which led to the release of the vessel, as they do not wish to provide any information which might in any way encourage further acts of this kind.'

The official amount stated to have been paid was around US$3 million. Reuters reported that US$5–7 million was paid. However, Ecoterra International, a Kenyan-based Somali group recognised as having good links with the pirates, stated that the cash payment had been US$7 million, with a further US$2 million transferred electronically through the banking system.

Only four months after payment of the ransom for the *Maran Centaurus*, that record was broken, with Somali pirates reportedly receiving a total of US$12.3 million in ransom money to release two ships. The consensus of reports is that a staggering US$9.5 million was paid for MV *Samho Dream*, a South Korean supertanker, and nearly $2.8 million for the Singapore flagged MV *Golden Blessing*.

Topping the charts in overall ransoms paid to date was the 2011 ransom paid for the release of the Greek-owned VLCC *Irene SL*; most reports confirm that this hijack achieved a ransom of US$13.5 million for the pirates. She had been taken while heading from Fujairah in the United Arab Emirates to the United States. The two million barrels of crude oil that she was carrying were the equivalent of one day's output of Kuwait, or one-fifth of the daily import volume of the USA. Interestingly, over the 58 days from February to April that she was held by the pirates, the price of crude oil for May delivery rose from US$90 to US$110 per barrel – a neat profit of around $40 million, for which I guess the shipowners never thanked the hijackers ... but which, even after the ransom was paid, left them with a nice bonus just shy of US$30 million!

Not all ransoms distributed are so high, but some of the stories surrounding hijacking incidents are intriguing.

Le Ponant was a sleek, modern, three-masted sailing vessel specialising in luxury cruises for up to 64 well-to-do passengers. Summers were spent in the Mediterranean, and winters in the Indian Ocean. Its clientele tended to be American or French, generally retired people. *Le Ponant* was headed for Yemen where it was to take on passengers for a cruise, but on entering the Gulf of Aden the ship was boarded by pirates armed with assault rifles who forced the crew to head for Somalia. Fortunately – or unfortunately for the pirates – no passengers were on board, just the 30 members of the crew.

This was one of the speediest ransom situations – within seven days, a €1.7 million ransom had been paid and the yacht and crew released unharmed. But there was a sting in the tail of this hostage story for the pirates.

Once the yacht had been freed, French commandos from a navy frigate that had been shadowing *Le Ponant* during the negotiations hunted down the pirates ashore, something that had not happened previously. In a helicopter pursuit, the commandos tracked the men through the Somalian desert, eventually intercepting a 4x4 vehicle as it left a village, finding US$200,000 and weapons on board.

The car's six Somali passengers were arrested, and *Le Ponant* crew members identified them as the pirates, although some crew subsequently said they were unsure of the hijackers' identities.

After four years awaiting trial in France, two were acquitted and a third – who was found guilty and received a four-year sentence – was granted immediate release due to the period he had already served on remand. The two men found not guilty were awarded compensation, which included €90,000 each in moral damages, together with €3,000 and €5,000 respectively for the loss of their salary as fishermen while in detention.

There are many nightmare scenarios involving pirates, but one of the worst occurred in September 2008 when a large group of around 50 Somalis calling themselves the Central Regional Coastguard captured the Ukrainian-operated ship *Faina*.

Faina's cargo was potentially the most volatile ever taken by pirates – a shipment of arms including anti-aircraft guns, grenade launchers, a wide array of ammunition, and 33 Russian made T-72 tanks.

The world press embarked on a frenzy of speculation: was the arms shipment actually legal or was it in contravention of an embargo on the sale of weapons to forces in Sudan? Would the pirates manage to land the cargo ashore, where it could contribute to further instability in both Somalia and the surrounding region? Who was actually responsible for the shipment? And if a ransom was paid, what price would be put on this cargo of weapons of war?

As the *Faina* headed towards the Somali coast it was closely shadowed by an American destroyer, soon joined by a Russian missile frigate and a number of other US warships from the anti-piracy coalition, all with one joint aim – to prevent the weapons getting ashore.

The pirates realised what a catch they had, starting the ransom negotiations according to some accounts in the region of $35 million. Only after a five-month stand-off was a final figure of $3.2 million agreed and paid for the return of ship, cargo and crew – an amount that one pirate told the international press was 'no huge amount ... but something to cover our expenses'.

No one will ever know the true story of the 11 Somali pirates who seized the Russian tanker MV *Moscow University* in 2010. The pirates took control of the ship some 190 nautical miles (350 km) off the Yemeni island of Socotra as it sailed for China, carrying crude oil worth US$50 million.

With the tanker's crew safely locked down below decks in the engine room, the Russian destroyer *Marshal Shaposhnikov* reached the scene and launched a rescue operation, opening fire on the pirates with its cannons. Under the cover of this fire, a helicopter from the ship landed on the tanker's deck with commandos on board, who quickly rescued the hijacked vessel.

One pirate was said to have been killed during the operation; photographs released to the press showed ten pirates lying face down, hands tied behind their back on the deck of the Russian ship. While it was initially believed that they would be taken back to Russia to face trial, they were unexpectedly released, with Russian officials saying there was insufficient legal basis to keep them in detention and that they would be too expensive to feed.

The official version of events is that the pirates were therefore cast adrift some 300 nautical miles from the Somali coast in an inflatable boat. Nothing was ever heard of them again, and sources in the Russian Ministry of Defence stated that they must have died at sea. The pirates' total disappearance, without even the inflatable having been found again in a heavily patrolled area, has raised speculation that they were never released but were simply executed by the Russian commandos, particularly in the light of Russian President Dmitri Medvedev's comments that 'We'll have to do what our forefathers did when they met the pirates'. There have been a number of apparently authentic videos appearing on YouTube showing the Russian Navy taking a somewhat robust line with pirates and their boats. Despite the Russian naval presence in the Gulf of Aden, I have been unable to find any record of Somali pirates being prosecuted in Russian courts...

In general, while the success rate of Somali pirate attacks has dropped dramatically thanks to improved safety measures and the use of armed guards on ships, those crews that do fall into pirate hands are likely to be held for much longer and treated more harshly in a bid to extract ever higher ransoms.

24

THE ANTI-PIRACY INDUSTRY

Protected only by barbed wire coiled around the deck railings, and a dummy security guard outside the bridge, the skipper of the *Maersk Weymouth*'s plea had been heartfelt: 'Just wire – only wire – there's nothing. If they would give us arms, it would be better – a machine gun, 50 calibre...' Things have moved on since we talked, and the Maersk fleet's anti-piracy defences are far more effective.

Going back to basics, the skill of the skipper in taking evasive manoeuvres and creating a large and confused wake that will swamp the pirate skiff is still the best technique for deterring attack. While ships with low freeboards such as heavily laden tankers, or ramped sterns such as trawlers, are easy to board, a high-sided wall of steel presented by a container ship that is swerving erratically and kicking up huge, choppy, unpredictable waves is an extremely formidable challenge to an attacker in a small boat. But no matter how able the captain, good seamanship alone is often not enough.

The maritime security industry has been quick to jump on the anti-piracy bandwagon. Futuristic pain rays, foul-smelling liquids, Doctor Evil-type sonic weapons, and even Britney Spears blasted at full volume – the range of ship protection devices ranges from inspired to quite bizarre. The tens of thousands of ships passing through the Gulf of Aden each year have proved to be a ready market for inventors and salesmen boasting the latest in ship security technology.

One option is simply to have weapons on board, but the problems of arming untrained ships' crews are overwhelming. There are practical issues such as upping the stakes; also, arming sailors could result in bloody on-board gunfights. On tankers, with their volatile cargos, the outcome could be truly disastrous. While some sailors would undoubtedly feel more comfortable if they were armed, how many would really want to double as unpaid security guards? How many indeed are trained to military standard to be ready for a firefight?

Legal issues also play a role. In many countries, any merchant ship entering territorial waters and harbours would immediately break the law if carrying weapons. If a crewman shot a 'suspected' pirate in the territorial waters of an African or Gulf state, would he face remand in jail until trial and imprisonment if convicted? What would be the insurance implications?

On-board armed professional security might be a compromise – ex-servicemen from around the world are keen to earn good salaries in exchange for largely enjoying a pleasant cruise. On-board armed security has certainly proved effective – to date, no ship carrying such personnel has yet been successfully pirated. The high expense, however, restricts most shipping companies from pursuing this option, their profits already shaved to the bone by rising fuel and insurance costs, alongside intense competition in a world in economic recession, where many ships are already laid up for lack of work. Costing US$1,500–2,500 per man per day, and with a minimum of four guards required to provide round-the-clock cover, few companies can afford this additional overhead.

Besides, there are considerable legal complexities surrounding not only the carrying of weapons on ships entering a nation's waters, but also if injuries or fatalities are caused at sea. Indeed, on the NATO website beneath the heading 'Fishing Activities – Possible Mix Up with Piracy', it warns: 'Fishing vessels may approach merchant ships to maximize fishing opportunities or to safeguard fishing nets which have been set. Furthermore fishermen in the region regularly carry small arms on board their vessels, so the visual identification of a small arm is not a positive indicator of pirates. It is not uncommon for fishing vessels to follow merchant and large vessels in order to capitalize on the often increased numbers of fish in the resultant wake.' It concludes with a guide to recognising dhows and skiffs.

The risks of armed on-board security are nowhere better illustrated than in the *Enrica Lexie* incident in 2012, which resulted in two innocent fishermen being killed, two Italian marines being charged with murder in the Indian courts, and a major diplomatic fallout between India and Italy.

The *Enrica Lexie*, a privately owned Italian-flagged tanker with a contingent of six jittery Italian marines on board, came across the unarmed Indian fishing boat *St Anthony* less than 21 nautical miles (40 km) off the coast of Kerala in southern India. The one-sided shoot-out that followed left two unarmed Indian fishermen dead.

The *St Anthony* is a vessel not capable of travelling at more than 8 knots, and was returning home from a fishing expedition. Its captain stated that although he had right of way, he hove to in order to let the tanker pass in line with normal maritime procedure. At that stage, they were fired upon from the tanker. There were no weapons of any type on board his boat – simply fishing nets.

The *Enrica Lexie* does not appear to have reported the incident to the Maritime Rescue Co-ordination Centre for around two and a half hours, travelling a further 40 nautical miles (75 km) on its route, and only filed the report after being contacted by the Indian Coastguard and asked to return to the port of Kochi. There, two of the marines were arrested for murder and remanded into custody by the Indian court.

The subsequent legal and diplomatic wrangling, when it is eventually finished, will be worthy of a book in itself. There have been legal arguments over which court, in which jurisdiction, and in which country, the trial should be held. Italy raised legal issues over the power of the Indian courts to force the attendance of witnesses from the Italian armed forces; the Italians also argued most strongly that the two accused marines, who had been bailed, should not be required to return to India, but eventually faced a humiliating climb down on this issue. Finally, the Italian government paid 150,000 euros in compensation to the families of each of the two deceased fishermen. Feelings over the episode run high in both countries...

What is most troubling over this scenario is that these were highly trained Italian marines, and not 'cowboy' private contractors.

Sadly, there are many tales of trigger-happy security guards firing upon innocent fishermen and their boats. Some of these are said to have occurred on the high seas, and have occasionally resulted in a fatality; most instances go unreported. The last thing that a commercial ship's captain wants is to become involved in red tape and possible criminal prosecutions that could arise if he broke off his voyage and pulled into harbour to report such an incident. His ship and crew could be impounded or held while investigations were carried out. A skipper might deem it far better to regard an innocent encounter as a pirate attack successfully thwarted – in a sort of 'hit and run' mentality.

I have even heard a tale concerning wealthy Russians, looking for the next thrill after big-game hunting, chartering a boat and going 'pirate hunting'. One of my sources, who works in the boat charter industry, told me that their technique was to cut engines in an area of pirate activity so that their boat appeared to be having engine problems, and then wait and see what came along...

Nonetheless, on-board security, combined with other sensible precautions, still remains the preferred choice of shipping companies that can afford the costs. For other options on the market, enter the combat zone of non-lethal deterrents, all aimed at preventing pirates from boarding their target ships. The maritime security industry is fully aware of the legal issues arising from carrying and shooting guns, and specifically markets many alternatives as 'non-lethal'. Some are designed to deter pirates from boarding the vessel; others to make life as difficult as possible for them if they succeed.

As the ultimate discouragement for some, and proclaimed with delight by the world's press, the greatest hits of Britney Spears have indeed been blasted at pirates, with resounding success in fending off attacks. While it makes a great story that the attackers hate all things Western, and that just the sound of Britney is enough to chase them off, the truth is rather more technical. The Long Range Acoustic Device (LRAD), developed by American Technical Corporation, has been used by police forces in many countries for crowd control, and even by Japanese whalers against the marine conservation campaign ship *Sea Shepherd*.

An LRAD focuses a blast of high-frequency noise to a volume of some 150 decibels – higher than the tolerance level of the average human. Thus, belting out Britney or indeed any high-pitch sounds would be equally effective beamed through it. It is a pain-inducing sound beam powerful enough to clear crowds of protesters, and certainly to deter Somali pirates – an LRAD was successfully used to foil the pirates in their attack on the *Seabourn Spirit*. It is not an infallible weapon, as simple ear plugs can lessen its impact; as it is directional, it is of limited use against more than one pirate skiff if different sides of the ship fall under simultaneous attack. Suggestions that playing Justin Bieber instead of Britney Spears should increase the LRAD's effectiveness have not been confirmed.

Another device that seems more at place in *Star Wars* than on a cumbersome merchant ship is the laser defence system devised by British-based BAE Systems. With an effective range of up to a mile, the 1-metre (3-foot) wide beam temporarily dazzles anyone who looks at it, literally hiding the vessel carrying it behind the blinding green glare of the laser. Used in conjunction with high-frequency surface radar that pinpoints the location of the small fast pirate skiffs, it aims to throw both their steering and gunfire off target. It can also be used against multiple targets, via a profound flickering that amplifies the 'dazzle effect'. Similar so-called laser dazzlers claim to be effective to a range of 4 km (2.5 miles) and cause mild disorientation and flash blindness at closer range.

Also in the realm of sci-fi weaponry is the 'Pain Ray'. Created by the US military, and officially termed the Active Denial System, it is 'a breakthrough non-lethal system that uses millimetre-wave electromagnetic energy to stop, deter and turn back an advancing adversary from relatively long range. It is expected to save countless lives by providing a way to stop individuals without causing injury, before a deadly confrontation develops.' To put it another way, it hurts but won't kill its target!

Unlikely but true – using golf balls to fight off pirates? Dubbed the 'Somali Stinger', the Buccaneer Launcher System is a small cannon that uses compressed air to fire projectiles hundreds of metres across the sea. It grabbed headlines on launch as it can fire a 'shell' packed with golf balls, which will travel up to 600 metres (2,000 feet) at up to 725 kph (450 mph) across the sea and bombard the pirate craft. The Stinger can also be used to rain a wide range of projectiles on to pirates, including smoke grenades, paint pellets, nets and ropes to entangle their propellers – and even ice (possibly for their post-attack gin and tonics?).

A similar product is the 'Less Lethal Launcher' – a confusing term: is the weapon lethal or not? The description that I found in *TASER® Conducted Electrical Weapons: Physiology, Pathology and Law* described it as a 'compressed-air powered semi-automatic launcher designed to fire nonlethal projectiles at nonlethal ranges'. Personally, when faced with pirates firing bursts of very lethal bullets from their Kalashnikovs coupled with the very lethal RPG rounds, I don't find this description reassuring!

There's still little that can beat the tried and tested water cannon. High-pressure hoses located around a ship provide a powerful wall of water that can be remotely operated, so that the crew using them are not exposed to the risks of gunfire. Used extremely successfully for decades in riot control, these have been easily adapted to shipboard use. Not only is the accurately aimed water jet enough to knock a man off his feet and cause injury, but the high volume of water delivered in mere seconds can be enough to swamp a boat and hinder its manoeuvrability.

Described by Captain Ralph Pundt of the International Maritime Security Network as a 'skunk on steroids', an adaptation of the water cannon technique involves showering approaching pirates with slick, foul-smelling green liquid that stinks and burns. The burning sensation and terrible stench allegedly forces pirates to jump into the water, thus obstructing a possible pirate raid!

Another variation on that theme, a Japanese invention, is the Anti-Piracy Curtain. This is an extremely low-tech idea – simply to hang multiple hoses over the sides and pump high-pressure sea water through them. Without being operated from a fixed point like fire hoses, these twist around fast and unpredictably with a force easily capable of painfully whipping a man and a ladder into the sea, where he would be alongside the fast-moving ship and in danger of being sucked into the propellers; the high volume of water would also fill a pirate skiff rapidly. Painted bright yellow so they are visible from afar, these violently gyrating, high-powered snake-hoses are certainly deterrent enough to make potential boarders think twice.

Flares are regularly used to chase off attacks – all ships carry them legitimately, although they are hard to aim accurately from a moving ship at a small fast-moving skiff. If all else fails, crews under attack can resort to the old-fashioned Molotov cocktail. No harbour master can quibble with a ship that has a few empty bottles as well as petrol for its outboard engines. Provided one had the courage to lob it accurately over the side, it might just be the final deterrent.

The Chinese crew of the MV *Zhen Hua 4* used empty beer bottles filled with petrol and ignited by a flaming rag in their battle to keep pirates from boarding, combined with using the fire hose and hurling any objects they could find at the attacking pirates. When the Somalis succeeded in boarding the ship, the crew retreated to their living quarters and continued the fight from there. BBC World News published an interview with the captain after his crew's most unusual battle with the Somalis.

'We were locked inside and the door was very thick. They were shouting "Open the door". So we climbed further up and used everything to threaten them, bottles, petrol. We used the high pressure water cannon to shoot at them. Eventually they retreated, they couldn't fight any more, there was smoke, there was fire.'

Captain Peng said that before they left the ship, the Somalis made an unusual request – for shoes, as they were barefoot and the deck was covered with broken glass. The crew threw down shoes. Then the Somalis returned, asking for fuel for their speedboats. By now helicopters had arrived at the scene from approaching warships and started firing on the pirates.

If the pirates have managed to scale the side of the ship, they can be greeted by electric fences delivering a 9,000-volt jolt running the whole length of the deck, which can be used as an addition to coiled barbed wire.

Particularly for smaller boats and yachts, a pleasant 'welcome aboard' for pirates might be the Mobility Denial System – an oil-slick-in-a-can, a combination of 'drilling mud additive, flocculent and water' that renders surfaces as slippery as wet ice for up to 12 hours. It was formerly known as 'Non-Lethal Slippery Foam'.

The claymore mine is a vicious and highly effective ambush weapon. With a killing range of around 50 metres (165 feet), when activated the mine fires hundreds of steel balls over an arc of 60 degrees. It has been used in many combat zones with horrific consequences, the best known being by American forces during the Vietnam conflict. For shipowners reviewing anti-piracy protection comes the non-lethal version: the M5 Modular Crowd Control Munition (MCCM). Creating a mighty bang and flash, this weapon is principally marketed for use in crowd control, firing 600 hard rubber balls with an effective range of 5–15 metres (16–50 feet). The marketing blurb claims, 'It will stop, confuse, disorient and/or temporarily incapacitate area targets or personnel at close range.' The obvious drawback here is that to be effective, the pirates will already need to be on the ship; whether it will make them change their minds and return to their skiffs, or simply infuriate them enough to take retribution on the crew... Well, I wouldn't want to be the one to test the theory. The reality is that once pirates have boarded the ship, it is probably game over so far as resistance is concerned, and the best the crew can do is take shelter.

It became an established feature of every James Bond film that before his mission Q would present Bond with the latest bizarre gadgetry he had created for him. As I explored the colourful world of anti-piracy devices, it often felt that Q's imaginative genius was behind many of them. The world's inventors have certainly left no stone unturned in their efforts to thwart handfuls of men in small boats.

25

KEEPING THE SHIPS SAFE

Jim Hills was sitting by the log fire in his cottage in a small Cornish harbourside village – as far as could be imagined from the hot and hectic world of the pirate alley where he earns his living. The late afternoon sun was slanting through the windows, but even though it was April here, it had rained earlier and there was a cold northerly wind; the fire cheered the room and took the edge off the chill. Off the Somali shores, the sun would have set after another relentless day of extreme dry heat and strong winds at sea.

His four-day-old son Felix lay fast asleep, cradled to his chest. Jim had just come in from surfing and his wife had made it very clear that it was his turn to look after Felix while she caught up on some sleep.

Jim's a tall fit guy who was five years in the Marines and two in the SAS. He's the sort of man who runs ultra-marathons, who paddled a paddle board home one night rather than take a taxi – which involved a 50-km (30-mile) trip around Britain's dangerous and most southerly headland – and who freedives on shipwrecks: in his own words, 'nothing too mental'. He now carries the grand title of Maritime Security Liaison Officer – 'Well, it sounds better than Tesco's security guard with a gun!' He is one of the army of expensive on-board guards who protect shipping passing in and out of the Gulf of Aden. Having learned of some of the problems that this job can entail, I wanted to hear at first hand how it actually worked.

'Our company requires a military background and a criminal records check, as well as psychological assessment and weapons training. We usually operate as a four-man team. It's the old military thing – if one goes down wounded, there's one to pull him out to safety and two to keep fighting. In theory, there's two of us on duty and two off, but it's mega-boring staring out at an empty sea for six hours at a time, so if the captain agrees we will sometimes do three-hour shifts with one on and three off.'

With every country having different laws about individuals carrying weapons in their jurisdiction, how do people like Jim get weapons on board the ships they're escorting?

'Inside a country's 12-mile limit, our weapons are bonded to comply with that nation's laws. Various countries have agreed to have armouries in their ports. I guess everyone from the shipping agent up to the government gets a slice of the action – one reason why it works out so expensive. Sometimes they get just too greedy and we move weapons elsewhere. We've also got a couple of floating armouries in international waters – gunboats in effect – where we can pick up and discard weapons. Before these arrangements, it was so sketchy getting armed that we would pick up AK-47s in Djibouti and ditch them overboard at the end of a trip.'

It is a very real problem that on-board security teams have to face. Understandably sensitive over armed on-board security since the *St Anthony* incident, the Indian Navy intercepted the privately run, anti-piracy ship MV *Seaman Guard Ohio* in October 2013, and detained the entire crew for allegedly entering territorial waters of India without authorisation, purchasing subsidised fuel, and possessing illegal arms. During the proceedings, the ship was repeatedly referred to as a floating armoury, exactly the sort of vessel that Jim Hills had described to me. In March 2014, most of the crew were released on bail, but only after some five months in jail, under conditions that reportedly led one crew member to attempt suicide. Only in October 2014 were charges dropped, a year after the ship had been seized, save for a penalty for using subsidised diesel fuel.

In the early days, the entire maritime security industry was still very unregulated – there are even tales of security guards armed with crossbows and catapults! Cowboys still operate in the field – one ship may employ a trained security team on board, the next merely some guy with a shotgun. By contrast, Jim Hill's company uses top-grade weapons. These will include a couple of Steyr Scouts, a sniper's rifle also popular as a civilian hunting rifle. On land, it is accurate to 1,000 metres (3,280 feet); on the deck of a moving ship, it is still accurate to 400–500 metres (1,300–1,640 feet). The team will also use older but still ever popular semi-automatic FN Fal assault rifles – 762 calibre with clout! The guards' priority must be to keep any attacking skiff at a distance, as pirate RPGs are effective at 1,000 metres (3,280 feet), although extremely difficult to aim accurately from a small, bobbing skiff, which is why pirates try to get as close as possible before firing.

Like most professional security guards, Jim is a self-employed subcontractor. Rates of pay depend on the region the ship is transiting. He is usually flown into Cairo and from there to Suez to meet his ship. Usually it is a cargo vessel, but it could just as easily be a large fishing vessel or a cruise ship.

'We won't know where they are going. It could be a straight transit through to Muscat or Sri Lanka. The profitable jobs are when we are attached to a ship that is working the high-risk areas – we could be on board for weeks, with the bank account notching up.'

The security teams are always welcome on board. 'Ninety per cent of the crews seem to be Filipinos. They are terrified of the pirates – so many seem to know a friend or family member who has been taken. Often the ship's captain will throw a barbecue for us at the end of the contract just to say thanks...'

The security team works under the direct command of the ship's captain, but many skippers defer to their expertise. Jim is all for safety rather than confrontation.

'I always make sure that we have at least 4 miles (7 km) between us and any boat – though in the crowded Bab el-Mandeb Strait that's impossible, and skiffs will suddenly dart at you from among the radar clutter.'

The Bab el-Mandeb Strait is the choke point for all shipping entering or leaving the Gulf of Aden. Just 32 km (20 miles) wide, not only does every vessel with business in the Gulf, the Red Sea and Suez have to pass through, but it is also the shortest point for all trade between the Horn of Africa and Djibouti on the southern side to Yemen and Oman in the north. Every type of vessel large and small, with cargoes ranging from livestock to human trafficking, crosses here. It has been a pirate's favourite, although their successes in this region have been all but stamped out by the blanket naval policing.

'Other than there – a 4-mile minimum. I'm there for the money, not for medals. I'm not interested in letting pirates get close enough that we end up with a firefight on board. And I know for sure, if we were taken, we armed guards can expect to be chopped up and fed to the fishes...'

Isn't he concerned that if there were a firefight and a Somali were killed, that he could spend months languishing in an African prison awaiting trial?

'What are termed "Rules of Engagement" in the military, we call "Rules of the Use of Force". Out at sea, we have the right to use reasonable force – maybe lethal – for self-defence. But our first tactic is to avoid coming within a 4-mile range of another vessel if at all possible.

If a vessel is approaching, we will first use a parachute rocket flare. That will alert the boat to the fact we are on board, and seeing our team in blue uniform with body armour is usually enough of a deterrent. Sometimes it might be a skiff approaching from astern, or a mother ship trying to position skiffs ahead of us.

If they still approach, we will show our weapons and fire warning shots. Most incidents are resolved at that stage – when they see that there is armed security on board willing to use weapons, they will back off.'

Jim has his own views about the decrease in reported pirate incidents. He reckons the problem has not gone away, but simply changed its form.

'In the early days, the pirates would initiate the use of weapons. They would come steaming in on their skiffs, RPGs aimed and firing from 600 metres (1,970 feet), AK-47s brandishing. That would be a contact. Now they are more careful. A skiff may approach looking perfectly innocent, no weapons visible, as if they show their weapons they know we will use ours.

So they are checking out whether the ship has security on board. It's like a covert drive-by, with their weapons under a tarp. They know that the worst that will happen is a warning flare so they can come in close with no fear. And if there is security, then they will break off and look for an easier target. It's like a slow-motion courtship; the incident can take between 30 and 40 minutes as they inch closer to see how far they can get and assess the strength of on-board gun power before backing off.

Unless we see their weapons and use our own, then there is no incident to report, so the numbers of reports appear to be declining. But we know they are pirates – if they were fishing, there would be two or three in a skiff – not five or six wearing knock-off Adidas tops and cheap sunglasses!'

On-board security work has been good to Jim. He got in on the boom early and in two and a half years his earnings have helped him buy a second house in the village that he rents out, but he sees the bubble bursting. Pay has been cut by 30 per cent, and while a lot of the experienced guys are looking to get out, there are always others to take their place. There's a lot of competition out there and prices are being pulled down by use of people from around the world who don't have the right background and training.

The shipping companies have to calculate the economics of carrying armed guards through these pirate waters. No ship travelling at over 20 knots has been boarded by pirates. On the other hand, 20 knots is far above the economic level of fuel consumption, and with ships burning around 200 tons of fuel a day the sums have to be done: faster equals safer but with high fuel consumption; slower equals greater economy but at higher risk. If vessels can travel slowly and the fuel savings more than offset the cost of security, then the equation is weighted towards armed security.

This financial balancing act means that quality security firms are often replaced with cheaper ones that are not necessarily as competent. Indian and Sri Lankan guards have become popular, although Jim doubts that their training matches up to that of the Royal Marines and SAS. All it takes is one successful pirate raid and the whole game changes again.

'With a trained security team on board, it is impossible for pirates to get aboard. Simple as that – impossible. But with cutbacks to save shipowners money, poorer quality guards with less training and experience – well, it's only a matter of time before the pirates take a ship, maybe with a bloody gunfight on deck too, with collateral injuries to crew. And a gunfight on a ship carrying a volatile cargo doesn't bear thinking about – it's the nightmare scenario.'

I caught up with Jim again shortly before this book went to print. He told me he was just back from a five-week transit of the High Risk Area. He reported that like his recent trips, it had been 'Really quiet again. I think that we are now on board solely for insurance purposes.'

While armed security teams may well be economically viable for larger ships, it's the smaller vessels running charters in the area that suffer the most. Without a defence presence, they are taking grave risks and often are not even permitted to leave harbour; but the cost per day of armed security pushes their overheads to a level that most potential passengers can no longer afford to pay. Although at the time that Francis Roucou and his boat were taken by pirates, armed on-board security was still a thing of the future...

26

THE SKIPPER AND THE PIRATES

An urgent hammering on the cabin door woke Francis Roucou from a restless sleep just before midnight.

'Captain, Captain, are you awake? Captain, those motherfuckers are boarding the ship.'

The 115-foot-long (35-metre) *Indian Ocean Explorer* was a great old ship that had started life almost 60 years before as a North Sea survey vessel. She had spent the last ten years operating among some of the remotest islands and atolls in the Indian Ocean, taking scuba divers and fly-fishermen to these far-flung destinations.

I knew her, Captain Francis, and all the crew extremely well. As an underwater film-maker, I'd spent a considerable time aboard her diving and filming those islands, particularly at Aldabra, a UNESCO World Heritage Site just a couple of hundred sea miles north of Madagascar. Despite being the planet's largest raised coral atoll, 34 km (21 miles) long and almost 15 km (9 miles) wide, it is uninhabited save for a handful of scientists at the research station.

Uninhabited but not empty – Aldabra has the world's largest population of giant tortoises – over 100,000 of them, and the lagoon and surrounding reef are teeming with life. Jacques Cousteau made a film there in 1954 and I was one of the few film-makers who had produced a documentary there since then.

Aldabra is actually closer to Somalia than to the Seychelles principal island Mahé, lying just 590 nautical miles (1,090 km) from Kismaayo, the nearest point of Somalia, and 895 nautical miles (1,660 km) from Hobyo.

Francis told me his story.

'I felt physically sick as I viewed two skiffs on the ship's starboard side and the men who were scrambling up like a swarm of spiders. Some were clothed in shorts with no shirts on, others in sleeveless T-shirts, and all were boarding the ship. I felt powerless. A group of them carrying AK-47s raced up towards the wheelhouse.

They were dangerous-looking people, dark-skinned and smelling of salt, rank sweat and the metal of the guns they carried. Some were thin and small, others tall and hefty, mostly with ruffled and matted hair. One of them took aim. I steeled myself not to flinch as he fired two shots at my feet, missing my toes by inches.

One of them brandished his gun. "Down, down, down!" he screamed. I decided not to let them see my fear. I needed to make clear to them this was my ship. I refused to obey...

"Is this tourism ship?" one of them asked.'

Francis could only feel relief that his passengers had just disembarked to take a plane from the dirt strip on Assumption Island in the Seychelles – a mix of wealthy fly-fishermen from South Africa, Canada and the United States who between them would have been a real catch for the pirates.

'"Where are we going?" I asked, expecting the inevitable answer, Somalia. But it was not to be, at least not yet. I was surprised when they said we were going to meet up with their mother boat.

"Is it very big?" I asked.

"No, no, very very very small," one of them answered.

I was surprised when they took out a portable GPS and showed me a reading indicating the mother ship 15 km (9 miles) west from our current position. I later learned that this was their usual procedure, so whether the attack succeeded or failed they could rendezvous again. About a mile from the position of the mother ship, they told me to switch all the lights on, a signal that it was safe to approach. When it did, it was an amazing sight.

A sole man stood at the helm of what in its previous life would have been a small inshore artisanal open fishing boat. The tiller was nothing but a big stick that he was manoeuvring with his left hand, while in his right hand he was holding two ropes that seemed to control the engine. He was holding a torch between his teeth.

"You came all the way from Somalia in that boat?" I asked in amazement.

"Yes, why?" replied a pirate who I had found was called Awali, as if people went capturing cruise ships in this joke of a boat every day. They probably did! I was consumed by a sudden impotent rage; we had been captured by a band of desperadoes using sticks as tillers, torches for lights, in a boat hardly big enough to sit in.'

The pirates ordered Francis to head for the Somali coast, and en route he had the opportunity to witness their attack strategies. Picking up a large container ship on the *Indian Ocean Explorer*'s radar, the pirates prepared to seize the ship. One of the skiffs was pulled alongside, petrol jerry cans were filled and loaded, the engines were started, and a handmade ladder adjusted on board. By then the vessel was clearly visible – a Maersk container ship – and with half a dozen pirates on board armed with AK-47s, the skiff headed for it at full speed.

The skiff zigzagged towards the ship, cutting diagonally across the waves, rather than taking them head on. It looked ridiculously tiny. It seemed that it would take the ship by surprise, until black smoke started belching from the ship's funnel; they had spotted the skiff and were increasing speed. By changing course, the huge ship kicked up a wake that threatened to swamp the tiny skiff. The attack failed, and the Maersk ship disappeared into the night.

As the *Indian Ocean Explorer* drew closer to the Somali coast, Francis managed a conversation with one of his captors, who spoke a little English.

'Why do you hijack ships?'

'Somalian is hungry. We need food.'

'Why don't you work then?'

'There is no work. Before, our grandparents went to sea to fish. They had no lights on their small fishing boats. Then all the big ships came at night, crushed them and they didn't come back. Now we, the younger people, we can't go fishing as there's no fish and we are scared of the big ships.'

'Which ships?' Francis asked in amazement, beginning for the first time to grasp the dynamics of the situation.

'European ships, Japanese ships, all sorts of ships...'

'So, why don't you fix lights on your ships now.'

'No, we want revenge on the Europeans who fished in our water and killed our grandparents.'

First landfall in Somalia at the port of Baraawe was like a nightmare. Al Shabab were attacking the town, carrying out random atrocities. The town was home to nine of the eleven pirates, and they were getting messages about family and friends being slaughtered in the fight. Francis was told to sail the *Indian Ocean Explorer* further north towards Hobyo.

Meanwhile, a negotiator named Abdi had come aboard, and in between his bouts of seasickness, ransom negotiations had already started. A number of things rapidly became clear to Francis and the crew.

With the pirates demanding a US$4 million ransom, it was going to be a long drawn-out process – there would be no quick release. The French owner of the ship seemed to have washed his hands of the whole situation. The pirates' moods fluctuated wildly. While some were kind towards the crew, others were threatening and violent. On occasions, Francis was slapped hard across the face and threatened with a pistol.

Anchored some 4 km (2 miles) offshore at Ras Assuad, about 80 km (50 miles) south of Hobyo, life for the crew slid into a pattern of excruciating boredom.

'I'd wake – another day ... What will it bring? When will we get some good news – that day, that week, that year? I never gave up hope.'

Early optimism about a release date was gone. The inevitable answer to the question, 'Are you going to release us?' was always, 'Tomorrow, if Allah says.'

The pirates who had captured them were replaced by guards from the shore who spent their days chewing *khat*.

'They got it every day fresh from Kenya. They would chew it all day to prevent them sleeping at night. They said it gave them energy. They would drink something very sweet with it – cola plus extra sugar or black tea with several spoons of sugar.'

From *Indian Ocean Explorer*, Francis and the crew could observe the pirates' daily routine.

'The mother ship would come and collect three 200-litre (44-gallon) drums of fresh water before they left to go hunting for ships. I counted 15 drums of diesel and about 40 jerry cans of petrol that they took for the skiffs. They would leave the beach at around 3 to 4pm and cruise along the coast before breaking into the open sea at dusk, to avoid being spotted by the military ships nearby. I secretly hoped they would get blown up and never come back...'

At one stage, Francis and one other crew member, Patrick, were taken ashore for 11 days, sleeping under trees and moving regularly from place to place.

'What I saw of the country was bush – small desert trees, red soil, flat. An endless brown landscape.' But the pirates seemed nervous, moving them around so they wouldn't be taken by other pirate groups.

One unpleasant experience for any captive is seeing their possessions ransacked by the pirates who have no concept of personal property. For a boat captain who has loved and cared for his ship for many years, maintaining her in pristine condition to meet the demanding expectations of tourists who have paid a great deal for the time they spend on board, to see one's vessel being thoughtlessly trashed is heartbreaking.

This pillaging led to one almost humorous incident during this trip ashore: as Francis and his colleague Patrick were being moved from one location to another, they were passing through Harardhere when Patrick spotted someone in the street wearing an *Indian Ocean Explorer* T-shirt; then another; and another... They spent the rest of that trip trying to see how many of their T-shirts and caps, taken from the ship, that they could spot among the crowd.

Apart from this short trip ashore, the reason for which he never learned, Francis spent the whole 88 days of his hostage experience aboard the *Indian Ocean Explorer*.

As the ransom negotiations became more fraught, the guards' behaviour towards Francis and his crew became increasingly unpredictable.

'They became suspicious about everything. They decided that the smoke detectors in the cabins were secret cameras, and the government were spying on them. They began to think of us as the source of all their hardships. They fought among themselves over the rations and would make us hide stashes of milk powder and cigarettes for them. But when others came, demanding to know where the booty was hidden, we had no choice but to tell them – we didn't want the gun muzzles in our faces for too long.

On one occasion, I heard shouting and found George, a crew member who they particularly picked on, in the crew toilets with pirates pointing guns at him and shouting. The toilet was flooded and they were accusing him of trying to sabotage the ship.

'It's you people who don't know how to use the toilets properly,' I shouted at them, blind with fury. "See here, dirty feet on the seats. You broke it yourself." I pointed out angrily that squatting with their feet on the seats meant that they leaned on the water pipe, and the pressure had broken it. I think they realised the fault was theirs, but one of them still fired a shot in the air near my head to remind me of my place.'

In another episode, three furious pirates herded the crew out on deck for some perceived infringement. Francis was convinced that this was the end: 'They lined us up against the setting sun. We were all convinced we were going to be shot. I thought wildly that prisoners are always shot at sunset in action movies. I will never see my wife and children again.' Fortunately, the shouting had roused another pirate called Asset, who had generally been reasonable to deal with. After an angry confrontation between him and the others, the crew were allowed to return to the cabin.

At one stage, the pirates even tried to recruit Francis.

'They wanted me to work with them. Their first suggestion was to use *Indian Ocean Explorer* as a mother ship. Then they said that when I was released, I could call them and tell them about shipping movements.'

Francis still finds it hard to express the emotions he felt when finally released. His departure from Somalia wasn't to be his last dealings with his captors.

'The first day that I landed after my release, I got a call from Asset. He asked, "How are you? Are you in Seychelles? Are you okay? I'm very happy for you." He last rang for a chat about two years ago. It was a friendly conversation – how are you, how are you doing... He did help me, help us, a lot.'

Francis was also called on to use his experience to help other hostages, something that led to another encounter.

'After I was released, I was a part of the team negotiating to free Rolly Tambara, and I heard the voice of Abdi who had been our negotiator. He had no idea that I was one of the people listening in on the phone conversation. He came into the frame during Rolly and Marc Songoire's negotiations for their release. It was bizarre. It was also weird to be on the other side of negotiations, trying to free other hostages. It was felt that my experience could assist. I hope that it did; then at least maybe something good would have come out of the ordeal that I and the crew went through.'

I was later to speak with Rolly Tambara myself, one of the two hostages mentioned by Francis.

'I would listen to Rolly talking to us – I could imagine what he was thinking – that tenuous connection with the world that he really wanted to see. I could hear the pirates' negotiator saying things and I just knew that he was lying. I was there. I'd been there. I know those people.'

After his release, Francis learned of the fate of the *Indian Ocean Explorer*, a ship that as skipper he had loved.

'The ship was set on fire because nobody would pay the pirates a ransom for it, and it was too big for them to use as a mother ship.'

Francis quickly returned to sea after his return home and still skippers vessels in the area where he, his crew, and the *Indian Ocean Explorer* were captured.

27

SHOPPING FOR PIRATES

Back in Seychelles, I'd spent my Saturday morning in the town's market doing some shopping for pirates. I felt that I had the best chance of a true insight from either Maalin Daud Olat or Balbal (Abdirahaman Nur Roble) and the price of a vest and a book was a bargain!

The concrete counters of the fish market were covered with every species that could be caught locally: bright red snapper, rainbow-tinted parrotfish, long-tentacled octopus, a large ray being chopped into steaks, a couple of small sad baby shark... Around the rubber-booted feet of the fishmongers, white egrets picked up scraps.

The fruit and vegetable section was vibrant with produce of every colour. The jostling crowd were just as vibrant – a Rastafarian fruit salesman haggling with a tiny wizened lady; large broad-hipped mothers dragging gaggles of children through the throng; pairs of young attractive girls more engrossed in texting on their mobiles than on the spectacle around them; a jet-black, finely muscled youth pushing through with a box of small sweet yellow bananas to restock his mother's stall; a Creole melting pot of ages, colours, and races, interspersed with the occasional camera-toting tourist from a cruise ship in their grossly inappropriate Hawaiian-style shirts and brilliant yellow shorts, fresh from the ship's boutique. The whole market crowd was alive with colours, and a mixture of pungent smells and delicate fragrances.

The shops I needed ranged around the perimeter of the market. A cool dingy general store that could not have changed in 50 years, where I stocked up with Mahé Kings – no Marlboro – and, after trying four clothes shops, I eventually found a plain white vest. But what sort of book do you buy for a Somali pirate serving a ten-year sentence in an African hilltop prison?

Anything too complex and it would not be any help to someone with just basic education and a minimal grasp of English; anything too childish could be perceived as an insult; anything with too much local information could be used to formulate an escape plan... Then I found it. In the section for 11–12-year-olds, the perfect book: *The Treasure Map* by Jan Burchett and Sara Vogler – a tale of Sam Silver, time-travelling, treasure-hunting, swashbuckling undercover pirate. This marvel featured largish print and pencil-drawn pictures. I wondered if the irony would be lost on Maalin.

On my return to the prison on Monday, despite the gift of the vest and another ten Mahé Kings, Balbal didn't help me much more. He told me that he had asked around the Somali wing, but been unable to track down any pirates.

'I cannot help you more as I have never talked to pirates. They go to sea and get ships – that is what I have heard. I understand that pirates have lots of money, they marry and get the most beautiful ladies in Somalia.'

But you have two wives already – so are you a pirate?

'Ah yes, but my wives, they are not beautiful...'

He then went back to his favourite theme, that the court had accepted what they were told by the Dutch Navy without any other evidence.

My only other hope was Maalin. He had stressed to me throughout that he was innocent, but he had admitted that he knew how pirates work, and seemed willing to help me. I'd spent another part of my weekend tracking down the judgement in his trial on the internet.

Before passing sentence, the judge had summarised the case.

The purse-seiner *Draco* is a huge modern fishing vessel. Built in 2006, she is 260 feet long (80 metres) and designed to harvest the rich tuna fishery of the Indian Ocean. *Draco* had just put out nets to start fishing when one of the security officers sighted a blue skiff approaching from the rear at a very high speed of about 27 knots. Since the nets had already been lowered into the water, *Draco* was incapable of manoeuvring. Being on the high seas, where no such boat would be expected, the crew were scared and thought that the occupants of the skiff had come to take their vessel.

Witnesses were able to see six to eight persons on board the blue skiff, which continued to move towards *Draco* despite flares and warning shots being fired at it. One of the people on board the skiff was standing with a bazooka on his shoulder, pointed at the *Draco*.

Undeterred by the flares and warning shots, the skiff continued to close the distance between the two vessels. The security chief Roman Vasilier intensified the fire; this eventually repulsed the skiff, which turned and sped away. In total, Vasilier had fired 171 rounds.

The blue skiff joined a white whaler – an open boat – that had been holding off about 6 nautical miles (11 km) away. Meanwhile, in response to *Draco*'s distress call, a nearby warship, *Canarias*, had launched a helicopter that was speeding to the scene.

The helicopter crew witnessed people quickly loading fuel cans from the white whaler on to the blue skiff, which then sped off. The helicopter fired several times ahead of both boats to stop them leaving until the warship arrived – altogether 127 rounds. The helicopter crew also saw the occupants of the vessels passing weapons from one vessel to the other, and the persons on the blue skiff throwing weapons overboard. The warship eventually arrived and arrested the Somalis.

In court, none of the Somalis gave evidence, but when interviewed by the police said they were Somali immigrants who had paid sums ranging between US$400 and US$800 to the boatowner to transport them to South Africa, where they would look for work. One month into the voyage, they ran out of water and decided to send one of the boats to approach *Draco* and ask for fresh water. They had not been in possession of weapons and certainly did not throw any in the water. They were not fishermen but migrants – they just had a small line aboard to catch fish for their own consumption.

Not quite the story that Maalin had told me. However, I wasn't there to challenge him about the court case. That would get me nowhere. It was clear that he wasn't the innocent and wrongly convicted man that he claimed to be, but I would play the game and go along with the fiction that whatever he knew of pirates and their ways he had learned from others.

He seemed genuinely pleased with the book and even laughed at my pirate quip. He pocketed the Mahé Kings with a nod, and then started talking. This wasn't going to be him answering questions – he knew what he was going to tell me.

'No one ever forces a pirate to go to sea. You look for pirates if you want a job with them. I have never seen a 16-year-old pirate, because you want someone good with a gun, experienced, someone who can climb on to a ship. People who are able to take a ship. Many more want to go out to sea than actually get asked.

There are different companies, so you go to the head of a company as he is the one who will employ people. He will know what he is looking for – captain, engineer. He will often work with the same captains – the same company will use the same captain and often many of the same crew. The head of the company will take you as engineer, to be on the skiff, as cook, as general crew, but the final decision who goes on the skiffs is the captain's. He makes these decisions.'

Company. I'd never heard the business organisation behind piracy described in such terms. Everyone knows that the pirates now receive financial backing from businessmen and investors outside Somalia, but to the pirates it is clearly a very rigid business organisation – like applying for a job at McDonalds.

'Before you go to sea, you are told what share you will get, what percentage, and you sign an agreement. You sign for everything – fuel, boat, guns, food, ammunition. It all comes out of the final reckoning. You know what you will get if you capture a ship. Guns are owned by the company and you sign that you rent the gun for $1,000 that will be deducted from the ransom, but if you have your own gun you don't rent from the company.

There are some complex calculations to be done, which is why an accountant or bookkeeper of sorts will get involved if a ship is taken, as from then on so many expenses are notched up: food, wages, fuel, payments to local elders and officials – even *khat* for the guards.'

Then came a question I never dreamed I would be asked by a Somali pirate – had I seen the movie *Captain Phillips*? When I told him that I had, his response was equally surprising.

'I love that movie. We have it in here.' Apparently there was a DVD player that was for prisoners' use. 'But it's not done like that now – it was years back, but not now. There are not crowds, everyone going to beach... The captain pointing at people, "I will take you, you, and you."' Maalan mimics a captain pointing to select his crew as is done on the film. 'The plan has already been made. The boss will know who he wants. Boss knows who is good and who is not.

It's done in private, there's more planning, everyone will already be signed up before we go to the beach. Then we drive to the beach and leave at night, usually a quiet beach, not one that the navy watch like Hobyo. And we leave at night, so we can be way offshore by sunrise.

We don't have things like radar. We don't need a compass – we know where Somalia is from the sun. Somalia is always to the west. But we sometimes have a compass, sometimes binoculars – one guy once had GPS...'

Interesting that within minutes it had slipped from 'they' to 'we'. I was now at last getting the information for which I had spent days visiting the prison.

'We are told what to do with the crew – just to take them, sometimes to threaten them as soon as we get aboard to get ransom as quickly as possible.

The skipper gets bigger money than the rest. The boss – the investor – automatically gets most of the money. Different people guard the ship from those who actually captured it, and they get lower percentage. Guards can be anyone – kids with guns, older men, men who just would be no use, no help taking a ship, men trying to prove themselves to the boss so they can be selected to go on a mission to sea...'

He pauses and I remember what the ex-hostage Francis Roucou had told me, that the pirates who held him had tried to recruit him to supply information about shipping movements. Did this happen?

'I have never been told that there is information about a specific ship that will be in a particular place at a particular time – you just go out to capture any ship at all that you can find.'

He paused again, and it seemed my cue to ask questions. Did many pirates just get lost at sea?

'Many do go missing and are never seen again – over 100 that I know of. Their mothers will come up to you on the beach and ask "Have you seen my son, he's been missing for five years." They never give up hoping. The families usually find out fairly soon if their men – husbands, sons – have been captured. But many just disappear. Maybe their boat sinks, maybe their engine breaks down and they drift till they die of hunger or thirst, maybe they get run down by ships or just shot and killed.'

And is there a reward for first on board – a bonus?

'Yes, but it's usually not money – maybe a brand new Land Cruiser. And if it's a really good ship, a valuable one with a big ransom, the skipper of the attacking skiff and the overall captain will get one too.

When the pirates get the money, it goes quickly... Within a few days they go back to sea again. They don't know how to use money. When the ransom is paid, they already know their share. The accountant then deducts all they owe the company. All they signed for on their agreement, what they have borrowed while waiting for the ransom plus the company charges interest on that, things like their *khat* bill! Once they have it, then they will give something to all their family and friends, to the clan chief and elders. Then the young ones party, go crazy, like to be the big man, waste their share, buy clothes, sunglasses, maybe cars if it was a big enough ransom... Soon it is all gone.

Some of the older ones will be more sensible, maybe buy a house, some camels or goats.'

And then for some reason Maalan returned to the first subject he had raised with me. 'No one aged 10 or 12 is a pirate.'

So what are you telling me? That the professionals don't want kids aboard, that those here are innocent, that those here are not 10 or 12 or 15 as they claim but are actually older, or even that young boys are taken as a decoy to make the crew look more innocent?

He obviously had a meaning but would not explain – as if he had said enough. He just shook his head and repeated, 'No one aged 10 or 12 is a pirate.'

He leaned back, and everything in his body language told me that the insights were over. Maalin then had a question for me: 'What is the world saying about us? What do they think of us?' I explained...

As he was leaving, he turned at the door. If I would come back again the following day, there was someone whom he might persuade to talk with me, a real pirate. I should bring no camera, and I could not write his name.

28

WHO IS REALLY PROFITING?

It seemed astonishing to me that the simple Somali prisoners to whom I had been speaking over past days were wreaking such havoc. The cost of piracy to the world economy was estimated as peaking at around US$12 billion in 2010 (some estimates placed this figure as high as $18 billion), dropping to in the region of US$6 billion in 2012, and US$3.2 billion in 2013.

Yet of all statistics produced to show the costs of piracy, the most revealing statistic is that, of this amount, only 0.5 per cent is going to the pirates themselves. Who is actually benefiting from the piracy phenomenon, and where is the other 99.5 per cent going?

The working papers produced annually by the One Earth Future Foundation, entitled 'Oceans Beyond Piracy', give an intriguing snapshot of the costs of piracy, and how they are covered.

Their 2012 figures break down as follows:

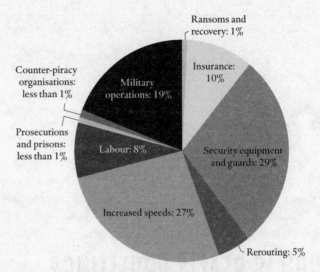

Breakdown of the costs of Somali piracy in 2012

The overall breakdown is that 21 per cent of the costs are being borne by governments, and 79 per cent directly by the industry. Either way it is perhaps academic – the ultimate cost is passed on to the public, whether through taxes or increased costs of goods.

Over the years that the Foundation has published these reports, the percentages and totals have varied; 2012 saw a marked decrease in piracy incidents compared to 2011, 2013 an even greater fall, and various items such as security costs and increased speeds have all fluctuated. This 2012 snapshot gives an idea of how the costs of piracy accrue.

The two principal types of piracy insurance are war risk and kidnap and ransom – known in the industry as K&R. Despite the relatively contained and regionalised focus of pirate activity, war risk insurance is charged to shipping throughout the Indian Ocean. The insurance industry would argue in its defence that insurance costs have actually fallen from previous years, as they allow premium reductions if there is armed on-board security. From any viewpoint,

Somali piracy has been a profitable phenomenon for insurers, and those professionals related to them.

Intriguingly, of the figure of US$63.5 million given for the cost of ransoms, only one half of that – US$31.75 million – is estimated to have gone to the pirates. The remaining 50 per cent went to the logistical costs of physically paying ransoms, recovering vessels, any damage to those vessels – and of course the fees for lawyers, consultants and negotiators. Not a bad business to be in!

A shipowner with a small fleet of specialist cruisers operating in the High Risk Area commented that he felt the real pirates were the insurance companies. How could they justify increased premiums ten times the actual cost of piracy to them – and indeed 20 times the actual amount being paid each year to pirates. It's a very fair question!

The security industry has also massively profited from piracy. Of the estimated cost of between US$1.6 and US$2 billion spent in that year on security equipment and guards, the lion's share went to the companies providing on-board armed security, with between US$1.15 and US$1.53 billion spent on armed guards alone in 2012.

To date, no ship has been successfully hijacked that was travelling at over 18 knots, and BMP4 advises that ships capable of proceeding in excess of 18 knots are strongly recommended to do so. Fuel, however, is the greatest expense in international ocean shipping, and increased speed means higher fuel costs – Oceans Beyond Piracy estimates that shipping companies spent an extra US$1.53 billion on fuel costs in 2012 associated with steaming at faster than optimal speeds in order to prevent pirate attacks. Large container ships that normally consume 100 tons of fuel per day would double that consumption at just over 20 knots, and nearly quadruple it at 25.

Rerouting vessels is one option that shipping companies always factor in to their calculations. Some hug the western Indian coastline, keeping as far as they can from the areas of pirate activity, even though that involves substantial and costly detours from the most direct route. Another option is to avoid the Suez shortcut, and instead take the old sailing route around the Cape of Good Hope. It is not the most attractive option; there is extra time involved, meaning that the ship can transport fewer cargoes in any year and so earn less money for the owner; additional fuel is burned in taking the 4,000-km (2,500-mile) diversion; and ships must risk the unpredictable and often dangerous weather off the southern tip of Africa. There were many good reasons why the Suez Canal was built! Nonetheless, some shipowners choose that option rather than risk the hazards, the extra fuel burned to maintain a higher than economic speed, and the extra insurance costs of the pirate alley off Somalia.

The 2013 figures are shown here:

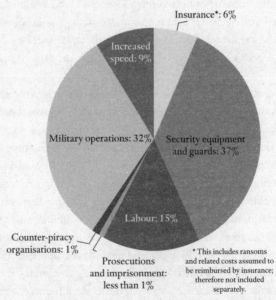

Breakdown of the costs of Somali piracy in 2013

The 2013 figures from Oceans Beyond Piracy show interesting trends. In that year, the cost to the world economy of Somali piracy had halved to an estimated $3–3.2 billion. That works out at 139 million US dollars per pirate attack. The proportions of expenditure had also significantly altered.

With shipowners reverting to their previous routes, the cost of rerouting totally disappeared from the equation, and the cost of increased speeds dropped by 76 per cent or, in hard cash, $1.16 billion.

The expense of on-board security equipment and guards increased to 37 per cent of overall costs but dropped in real terms to around $1–1.2 billion. Insurance costs have also dropped both proportionately and in real terms; much of this reduction can be attributed to the huge decrease in ransoms paid in 2013.

Increased labour costs are also substantial – a figure just under US$500 million, which includes the cost of hazard pay for all crews operating in the area, as well as the cost of paying seafarers while a vessel is being held hostage. Crew wages in both situations double under most maritime union agreements.

Compared to other outlay, the expenses of the legal process of prosecuting and imprisoning pirates is minimal. What is not small is the cost of the sustained military naval operations to contain the pirates – just over US$1 billion.

With just 0.5 per cent of the total cost of piracy actually reaching the pirates itself, this is still not a pittance. Oceans Beyond Piracy estimated that US$31.75 million in ransoms were paid to Somali pirates in 2012, and US$21.6 million in 2013. This represents a huge decline in ransoms paid from 2011, when US$159.62 million was paid to them.

These figures need to be put into Somali context. The fledgling administration of the semi-autonomous region of Puntland, which has historically been the base of the pirates, has an annual budget of just US$41.1 million, 70 per cent of which comes from taxes on the import and export of livestock. Thus, even in a bad year for the pirates, they are bringing into the region an amount almost the equivalent of the state's budget.

In an area of such instability, profits of this size have naturally attracted businessmen – speculators who can front the cash. Putting a few tens of thousands of dollars into a piracy venture that could net ten million dollars is a far surer investment than doing the lottery!

Writers, journalists and academics have tried to analyse the financial structure of current pirate operations. Mainly it is all informed speculation – the Mr Bigs of the piracy world do not exactly file corporate accounts and tax returns. Every deal is different. The general consensus remains that of any ransom received, it will be split between various team members and financiers in pre-agreed proportions.

The pirates will already have their split of the take worked out. The captain will get more than the crew, and the stories of bonuses for the first man on board – cash, a four-wheel-drive vehicle – had been confirmed to me by Maalin. It takes a certain desperate courage to try to hook a metal ladder on to the side of a cargo ship that is executing evasive manoeuvres in a choppy sea, then to make that leap of faith from one's skiff, hoping to grab the ladder and scale the sheer steel wall, often under a blast from the jets of high-pressure hoses. For any unlucky pirate who doesn't make it, his last moments of life will be terror in the undertow sucking him towards the huge thrashing propellers of the ship.

If a ship is successfully taken, expenses really start to mount for the criminal enterprise. While some ransom negotiations are concluded in a couple of months, many last for a year or more. In that time, the hostages and ship must not only be guarded around the clock to prevent escape, but also against other bands of pirates who may want to take the prize. The guards will usually not be the pirates who took the ship, but lower-ranking group members, wannabe pirates proving themselves, or others just not having what it takes to actually hijack a ship at sea. All groups have an accountant to keep an account of all expenditure, all the costs of the expedition, of any advances and loans made to group members. There will usually be a cook, and even his share will be agreed in advance. Food for everyone when the ship's supplies run out, fuel for running to and from shore and for the land-based vehicles. Bribes may also have to be paid to local chiefs to keep the ship in their area.

The negotiator is a key man who now gets involved, and he will be on a percentage of the ransom. The basic skill needed is a command of English, so the negotiators come from many walks of life, including students and expatriate Somalis who have returned to their homeland, maybe for this very task. Some negotiators will already have experienced negotiations; they could well be handling more than one at any time. When the final cash is delivered, first all the costs are deducted. The balance – or profit – is then available for distribution, with the financier usually claiming the lion's share.

With so many feeding at the trough, the average pirate's earnings from a hijacking may only be around US$20,000 – maybe less, maybe more depending on the size of the cake to be divided. In a nation where the average per capita income hovers around US$600 per head, this is the equivalent of over 30 years' earnings; little wonder then that no matter how many pirates are captured and imprisoned, or die at sea, there is always an endless source of new volunteers to take their place.

Profits transferred to investors through the *hawala* money transfer system and wire transfers leave Somalia and do no good for the local people. Likewise, pirates who acquire flash four-wheel-drive vehicles purchase them outside the country – Somalia is somewhat lacking in luxury car dealerships! Stories abound of Somali pirates investing their profits in property in neighbouring Kenya. Does piracy in any way inject money into the local economy?

Some studies believe it does, particularly one completed by Dr Anja Shortland of King's College London, formerly Brunel

University in the UK. She analysed development in the three main locations associated with piracy, comparing high-resolution satellite images of the coastal pirate towns of Eyl and Hobyo as well as the provincial capital Garowe before and after the explosion of piracy in 2008. Changes in settlement size, investment in large-scale buildings and improvements in local infrastructure were used as a measure. I am quoting some of Dr Shortland's conclusions (see http://www.chathamhouse.org/sites/files/chathamhouse/public/Research/Africa/0112pp_shortland.pdf for the full report).

'It is commonly asserted by local residents that pirates are living and spending money in Garowe – they are said to be easily identifiable by their flash cars, lavish weddings and expensive drug habits. The satellite images provide some evidence for this: in the 2002 image there are very few cars associated with residential buildings... In the 2009 image ... there are ... a significant number of houses in residential areas of town with a car parked within the perimeter walls. In most cases these are newly-built, not particularly large houses, with very noticeable security walls, often in small clusters of other new houses with cars. While the "home plus car" combination is evidence of new money rather than pirate money, it should be interpreted in combination with the pirates' own statements that they tend to buy "a house and a car" and local residents' common assertion that piracy and car ownership are linked.'

Dr Shortland concludes: 'Piracy has created direct employment and considerable multiplier effects in the [Puntland] economy even if a significant proportion of the proceeds is invested in foreign goods and some of it is channelled abroad. The distribution of the gains of piracy follows traditional patterns in Somalia, with redistribution through clan networks and employment generation in urban centres far from the coast.'

It all makes sense. A ship is captured and brought close to shore, and everyone in the region knows about it and hopes for a share of the action. Guards are needed and there are plenty of keen volunteers.

The crew and guards need to be fed for a year, maybe two, as well as the shore party. That's all good business for the locals, for those with cattle or goats to sell. There's always the chance to earn a dollar, helping load and unload the supply skiffs at the beach. There are errands to run, and there is cash to be made. Easy women arrive looking for easy money – prostitutes, both amateur and professional. The local *khat* dealers have a field day.

Dr Shortland's studies had focused on the Puntland region. However, the election of a new administration in 2009 in north-eastern Puntland saw a sharp decrease in pirate operations, as the provincial authorities launched a comprehensive anti-piracy campaign and established an official maritime police force. Since 2010, pirates have mainly operated from the Galmudug region to the south.

Another unexpected side effect of piracy off the coast of Somalia is that it appears to have had a positive impact on the problem of overfishing by foreign vessels. With foreign fishing fleets scared off from Somali waters, stocks have recovered in a way unprecedented in any regulated fishery anywhere else in the world. Somali waters at present, unfished for so long, are probably the planet's richest.

One might question whether piracy has done Somalia any harm? In a country plagued by horrific warfare in the south and rival warlords feuding throughout the rest of the territory, what true damage has been done by a couple of thousand rogues heading out to sea and, if fortunate, bringing back a prize? Some would even argue that the reduction in piracy is causing greater harm to Somalia. A July 2013 report from the UN Monitoring Group on Somalia and Eritrea stated that, 'With the decline of pirate activity generally, in northern Somalia a number of criminal networks are reverting to prior, familiar patterns of illicit behaviour, including armed protection of fishing activities and illegal fishing, arms trafficking, human trafficking and even trans-shipping of narcotics.'

However, any criminal gang with a disproportionate income and consequent influence over generally honest poor folk can never be good. The human cost of piracy extends into the communities of Somalia and impacts many Somalis on a personal level. Two case studies released in 2013 provided interesting insights into the link between sex trafficking and piracy. The joint World Bank, UNODC, and Interpol study 'Pirate Trails' describes how pirate networks pressured women into domestic and sexual service. The Department of State Office to Monitor and Combat Trafficking in Persons 2012 report specifically names the pirate towns of Eyl and Harardhere as locations for sex trafficking and the exploitation of Somali women and girls.

For genuine Somali fishermen, also, the pirates' activities have made going to sea more dangerous. The growing use of armed security increases the life-threatening risk for Somali fishermen, who may be mistaken for pirates by armed guards, firing shots before they can even determine whether the boat poses a threat or carries blameless men going about their everyday business. Furthermore, Somali fishermen may even encounter pirates themselves, with potentially dire results.

For Somalia, the pros and cons of piracy are subtle and complex, unsurprisingly so for a state in such disarray. However, for those taken hostage, it's all too straightforward.

29

ROLLY – THE 70-YEAR-OLD HOSTAGE

I hope Rolly Tambara wouldn't mind me saying that he resembled a tiny wizened hobbit – although hobbits are fat and that's something he certainly was not. 'When I was released, I was 47 kilos (7½ stone) – now I'm 55 (8½ stone),' he told me, as if to suggest that 55 kilos was an excessive weight.

Around 1.5 metres (4 feet 10 inches) tall, he had a mischievous face. The sort of granddad anyone would want to have – and that is what he is. How many grandkids?

He grinned. 'I have a lot of grandchildren – I have ... three, five, another two,' counting on fingers, 'seven, yes – nine: I have nine grandchildren.' Rolly's capture by the Somalis seems one of the most pointless and futile, and also one of the most heartless pirate actions that I came across. He was fishing with his lifelong friend Marc Songoire within sight of his home island. His boat was only 26 feet (8 metres) long, a small type of inshore fishing boat built in Seychelles, meant just for overnight trips. Both he and Marc were almost 70 years old when taken.

Why? Did the Somalis need to use his boat to tow theirs back to their home shores? That is what happened, although Rolly never found out whether the pirates' own main boat had engine problems. Were they planning on using his boat as a mother ship, to lull other prey into thinking it was simply an innocent local fishing boat? Or did the Somalis really think that two ageing fishermen in a vessel barely bigger than their own were a valuable catch? We will never know...

The traditional fishing dock lies across the water from the main fishing port, where the huge tuna boats disgorge the silver shoals they have annihilated. This is where the small boats moor, the local guys who fish the shallow fertile waters of the Seychelles Bank. They haul red snapper from the reef; drop their handlines among the schools of mackerel; spend weeks on small boats collecting sea cucumbers from the seabed. Their boats are small, their incomes little above subsistence level, but they would do nothing else. They are fishermen.

Rolly was held hostage for precisely one year from 5 November 2011, and returned home on the same date in 2012. Now approaching his mid-seventies, he told me his story. He would have preferred to speak in Creole, his native tongue, but in English, his second language, he explained to me without bitterness the year that was stolen from his life.

'I started fishing a long time ago, when I was 30 years old. Before that, I was a diver at Aldabra Island. I stayed a long time at Aldabra fishing, diving for lobster, green turtle, hawksbill turtle, before they were protected, when it was legal to dive there. And for the green snail, we were diving for that. I was there for about ten years. When I came back to Seychelles, I started fishing again, diving for lobsters.

When I was captured, I had my own boat with my daughter. No insurance, nothing. Here I would fish to sell in the market, then selling to Oceana Fisheries. Lobster sometimes, but red snapper mainly.

I got captured one night in October. About 10 in the evening. I had a light on – I didn't think about getting captured. I heard a noise on the back of my boat and I saw about six of them jump on board. They asked me about my passport. I said that I had no passport because I was in my own country. They said to me that if you have no passport, go to sleep and tomorrow morning we will release you. I did not sleep – just watched them all night as they went through everything on the boat – which wasn't much as we were only out for an overnight trip.

At five o'clock in the morning they told me, "Come – you are captain. Did you see any other boats, any ships?" I said no, I hadn't seen any. They said, "OK, we will release you." Then in the engine room he said, "Oh, you have GPS, start your engine." So I started the engine. The boat was so old I didn't even have an electric starter, just a starting handle to wind and turn the engine over. I started the engine and he said, "We go to Somalia." He showed me on the compass the heading to take – exactly 300 degrees – straight to Somalia.'

Rolly told me that all the Somalis had weapons. They put guns to his stomach and made him afraid, and hit him several times with a torch. They repeatedly demanded that he give them his passport, despite him repeatedly telling them he had no passport and didn't need one to fish in his own waters. There were around a dozen pirates and they had two small skiffs and a larger one.

'It took seven days to Somalia. They had a lot of fuel – their boat was full of fuel – I had nowhere near enough on mine but they kept filling up my fuel tank from the diesel they had aboard their big boat.

They caught me Saturday – we left Sunday morning and arrived the next Saturday – 709 miles (1,140 km). About six of the pirates were on my boat with me and Marc – the others stayed on their boat. They made me tow all three at the back of my little boat – their main boat and their two skiffs. Some days the weather was pretty rough and we had to go very slow towing all those boats, sometimes it was OK.

My friend cooked food. They would ask me questions – sometimes I answered, sometimes not.

We landed at Hobyo. They took us ashore the next morning, gave me clothes, took me to a house and told me to take a shower. They gave me one gallon (4½ litres) of water – I said that's not enough for a shower – they said it was plenty, it was fine. They took a mattress outside and said I must lie there, out on the sand. That was for daytime – at night they put me in the house downstairs. I wanted to cry. I stayed about four days without eating or drinking. I only started drinking and eating on the fifth day.

There was a lady, a good lady, she cooked for us. I thought she was an old lady because of all her clothes and her veil, but she wasn't an old lady, she was a young lady.' He laughed. 'Because when they bring me to the forest, after four months I saw her again and she was pregnant. I said to her – she cannot speak English – you are having a baby. But she was very good to us – she brought us clothes when we were in the forest; she brought us food. She was very, very good.

They kept us in the house for eight days then took us to the forest and we were in the forest all the time after that. The forest is only sand and plants. There are a lot of goats and camels. It was not dirty in the forest – much better than in the homes. The house was dirty – lot of flies and smell. The forest was better. They moved us around, maybe 10 days in one place, 20 days in another place. It seemed like every time they talked to Seychelles, every time they got a call, they would move us.

They would kick you in your back – get in the car. Very bad people. These weren't the same guys who caught us. Once we got to Somalia, the guys who captured us left us with their boss. I think the guys who caught me went fishing again – fishing for people. That's what I called it. I said to them, "You say that you are fishermen. You are not fishermen – you fish for people not for fishes."

They were all different. Some would be very good to you; others were very, very bad. Some of them would shout at you, "Send my money, I need my money. Tell your family to send our money – we need our money." I told them my family has no money. I am 69 years old. If I had money, I would not be at sea fishing – I would be at home with my wife and family. I had my 70th birthday over there.'

We were talking in the Fishermen's Association's office alongside the fishing quay. It was a small one-room place with just two desks. While we spoke, the association's secretary carried on with her work, and from time to time we were interrupted as fishermen entered to do a bit of business. All of them knew Rolly and all of them stopped for a quick chat. He was certainly very popular, and I had witnessed how strongly emotions had run in the country during the time that he and Marc were held hostage.

'After about four months, the boss took me to another place in the forest, gave me a phone and told me to talk to my family and tell them to send money. It was the first time I had spoken to them. The longer I was there, the more angry they got. "If your family has no money, your government will pay for it." Sometimes they let me talk to my family, but not in Creole – they made me talk in English so they would know what I was saying. I didn't know if there were negotiations – the police talked with me and asked how I was, said maybe one day I would be released, take care, be patient – but I didn't know if there was anything really happening to get us released.

They beat me a lot. One day they hung me upside down from a tree – tied my feet together and hung me – and they beat me and said, "Tell your family to send our money." They beat me with a stick. I was very, very sad – cried. I asked them why they were beating me and they said, "Because your son is a son of a bitch!" Then they took photos of me – I think to send to the government here – to make them send money maybe. In the end I was not afraid. "Shoot me if you want – my family has no money to give you. I'm 70 years old. I've had a good life."'

It was hard to imagine how anyone could treat this tiny, gently smiling grandfather in this way.

'Every day we did nothing. There was a guard with us all the time. They didn't want me and Marc to talk together – if they saw us sitting they would say, "You sleep – lie down." They made us lie down all day. If you want to take a piss, take a shit, they would follow you with a gun at your back. Always. Very, very bad.

When they put us in the car to move us around, they would tie your hands and feet together. Very painful – the roads are bad there – lots of bumps. They would drive very fast and you couldn't stop yourself from bouncing, being thrown about everywhere, it was very painful.

There was an American with us as well. Michael Scott Moore. He was captured in Somalia. I asked him why he came there and he told me he came to make a book. I think he's still there – he's been there two years by now.'

Michael Scott Moore is an American freelance journalist and writer who was kidnapped in January 2012 and who, when I spoke with Rolly, was still being held by his captors after more than two and a half years with minimal contact with the outside world. Rolly and Marc were among the very few non-Somalis he met with during his ordeal. Michael was eventually released in September 2014 after 977 days as a hostage.

'Most of the time, we didn't have any idea what was happening. Day after day after day – just told "Go to sleep" – by which they meant for us to lie down. Even if they saw you sitting they would say sleep.

After a few months in the forest, we were transferred to a Filipino fishing boat called *Naham 3*; it's a longliner.' (At time of writing, this remained the only ocean-going vessel being held by the Somalis, having been taken on 26 March 2012.) 'They kept Marc in the forest and took me and Michael to the boat – they split us up. Marc stayed in Hobyo. There were 28 crew on the *Naham 3*: five Filipinos, three Vietnamese, ten Chinese, five Indonesians, four Cambodians, and one Taiwanese. They are still being held. The pirates had killed the captain, shot him when they captured the boat – they were firing from their skiff at the bridge and shot him. His body was in the cold store.

We spent five months on board. The boat was kept anchored at Hobyo until the anchor broke, then went to another place. We met two other boats there – I forget the names. They said one sank, a Malaysian boat [the cargo vessel MV *Albedo*]. The other was released.'

In fact, after it lost its anchor, the *Naham 3* was tied alongside the *Albedo*, which had been held for almost three years until it sank in rough seas. Several crew members and pirates were drowned. I was soon to learn more about attempts to negotiate their release.

Rolly always referred to the *Albedo*'s crew members as 'the children', because they all looked so youthful to him!

'In the forest, they gave us boiled goat to eat every day – it's not good. But on board the ship, the children cooked. In Somalia there is a lot of fish. The place that the boat was anchored, the children fished off the boat and caught a lot of fish – red snapper – a lot, a lot, a lot. I said to the pirates, "Look, you have a lot of fish – why do you not fish for fish, instead of for people?"

The crew were very young – only around 19, most of them. I had a little friend among them who always talked with me, called me grandfather, brought me food. I learned to use chopsticks there!

When I was over there, I thought I would never see my family again as once I was on the boat I got to talk to no one back at home.

When I was on land, sometimes I got to talk to my son, but never when I was on board. I only started talking to him again September and was released in November.

The day I was released was very difficult. The pirates were fighting among each other. There was a lot of noise, a lot of shouting. They put me in one car and Marc in another. They took us to the airport at Galkyro. There was more shouting, arguing, waving guns – then they turned round and took us to the forest again. There was a fat guy in Galkyro – spoke very good English with an American accent – said he was the boss in Galkyro – assistant president, something like that. And then eventually we flew to Kenya, to Nairobi.'

After his return home, after being met by President Michel, and undergoing all the interviews, the parties, with every relative, friend and neighbour arriving at the house with small gifts of cakes, fish, or fruit-bat curry they had prepared for him; after all the prayers of thanksgiving in the churches; after being for the first time in his life a celebrity to whom everyone wanted to talk, this quiet unassuming grandfather wanted to be in one place only – back at sea, fishing. Rolly would spend his days on the fishing quay, talking to the fishermen preparing to head out to sea; meeting every boat that came in and discussing where they had fished and what they had caught; getting involved in odd jobs wherever he could – help with a lick of paint, some unloading; and chatting with the boys in the Fishermen's Bar on their return from a trip. Within a matter of weeks, he was back at sea again.

'They won't get Rolly again. I'm not worried or scared. I've been fishing with a friend – he's even older than me – he's 73. Now I'm going with another boat. I went back because I like fishing. I'm happy to fish. I'm not scared. Everybody's back fishing now and it's safe, but when I got captured, it was different. But I thought I'd be OK – I thought that captured was not for Rolly... I was wrong.'

I asked him his views on all that happened. I'd expected he'd be bitter. All he had to say was 'Somalia is a nice place, but the place I stayed in Hobyo is not nice – it's a dirty place. A lot of goats, a lot of camels, a lot of sheep; African sheep, not like European ones...'

30

THE FORGOTTEN HOSTAGES

It is a massive understatement to say that being held hostage is unpleasant. The weeks and months of uncertainty, lack of contact with family, inactivity, held at gunpoint by men whose behaviour is erratic and threatening, all add up to a horrific and traumatic experience that can only be fully understood by others who have lived through the ordeal.

At least crew on a modern supertanker, which together with its fully insured cargo is worth hundreds of millions of US dollars, can be reassured that people are working for their safe release and that there are funds available to pay the ransom. It is generally a matter of time, and the pirates will want to ensure their captives' safety and physical security as part of the negotiating package. These crew are A-list hostages.

Sadly, there are also B-list hostages – those who are captured on an uninsured and ageing vessel of little value, then abandoned by the shipowner, with no hope of ransom being raised. A motley crew of this type often hail from several Asian nations, working at minimum wage on a boat flying a flag of convenience. Pirates have become increasingly violent towards these hopeless hostages, who bear the brunt of their captors' anger and frustration. These are the forgotten hostages, with little prospect of early release, facing ill treatment and even death.

In an assessment by Oceans Beyond Piracy, hostages meeting at least two of the following criteria are at significantly higher risk of lasting injury or death than hostages who meet none of them. Some forgotten hostages fall into all four criteria:

1 They have been held for more than one year, leading to a greater likelihood of abuse or death as strains and anxiety increase among both pirates and hostages
2 They are held on land, where the risks are higher
3 No shipowner or insurance company is actively negotiating for the release of these hostages, meaning that tensions are rising with no clear resolution
4 The captured vessel was a sailing yacht or fishing boat, indicating that the hostages are unlikely to be covered by insurance offering ransom payouts

Today, around 40 per cent of the world's shipping tonnage operates under flags of convenience, and is registered in Panama, Liberia, and that well-known shipping nation, the Marshall Islands. In an always competitive market, this means that labour costs can be slashed without concerns about union rates; manning levels can be kept to a minimum; maintenance costs can be controlled without interference from regulatory authorities with high standards; and profits can be maintained. The true ownership of the vessels can be concealed behind a smokescreen of shell companies in many different countries, making prosecution of owners virtually impossible.

Despite being a failed state almost to the catastrophic level of Somalia, Liberia still manages to maintain the world's second-largest shipping registry – in fact, formerly one of the only legitimate sources of income for the despotic regime of President Charles Taylor, now serving a 30-year sentence for war crimes. The continued success of Liberia's shipping registry during the 14-year civil war was probably due to the registry being based in Virginia, close to Washington, DC, and run and operated from offices around the world.

For lowly paid crews taken on an aged ship operating under a flag of convenience, the misfortune of falling into the hands of pirates may create a nightmare scenario. With a vessel of little worth, the owner will not be troubled to negotiate for its return. Similarly, no ransoms will be forthcoming for expendable crew who are easily replaced in the labour markets of Philippines, Burma and Indonesia. While Western governments may go to extreme lengths to secure the release of their nationals, including the use of special forces if necessary, the downtrodden crews of these tramp vessels can hope for no such attention.

Meanwhile, the pirates' increasing frustration with fruitless ransom negotiations for Third-World crews, coupled with spiralling costs for guarding them, has led to reports of brutality against hostages who seem worthless: a desperate hope that acts of violence might trigger some payment?

In the spring of 2010, the MV *Iceberg 1,* a cargo vessel that had seen better days, set sail from Aden, at the start of a voyage to deliver electrical equipment to England. Only 10 nautical miles (18 km) out to sea, the *Iceberg 1* suffered a fate all too predictable for slow-going cargo craft in the Gulf of Aden: along with her 24-member crew, she was seized by Somalis and one of the longest pirate hijackings in modern maritime history had begun.

Registered in Dubai and flying a Panamanian flag, the ship was a typical mongrel of the sea. The Emirates-based owners had neglected to obtain insurance to cover payment of a ransom. The multinational crew, made up of eight Yemenis, six Indians, four Ghanaians, two

Sudanese, two Pakistanis and one Filipino were thus abandoned by the owners, who also ignored pleas from the sailors' families even to pay wages in absentia.

Over the course of nearly three years in captivity, the crew suffered intense psychological and physical abuse. It was the classic stand-off position. The pirates had taken a ship that they believed would bring them a ransom, but none was forthcoming, and started to appear increasingly unlikely. Frustrated with the absence of any progress, the pirates took their anger out on their captives.

The crew were locked in a sweltering and dark hold and rarely even allowed on deck. They were constantly watched by armed Somali guards. Limited to one meal of dirty rice per day, and with so little fresh water that some took to drinking salt water, their health deteriorated alarmingly. They lived under constant threat of violence from their captors, who at one point even said they were planning selling the crew's kidneys to cover their expenses. Punishments included throwing crewmen overboard and shooting at them, whipping them with electric cable, and hanging them upside down for long periods.

So violent were the beatings that one crewman lost the sight in an eye and another had an ear cut off. In an interview with the *Daily Telegraph* after their release, one crewman said of their captors: 'The pirates were just cowboys, bush people and criminals from all over Somalia. They drank whisky, took drugs, and often fought each other.'

In September 2011, the dilapidated and crippled ship was driven ashore by the sea on to a remote Somali beach, its final resting place. There it lay, the hostages still aboard, until they were finally rescued, not by any of the state-of-the-art warships patrolling the region, but by the Puntland Maritime Police Force (PMPF) after a lengthy shoot-out lasting almost two weeks, in which three pirates were killed. Those released had spent 1,000 days as captives. The ship had been held for so long that the two Sudanese found themselves citizens of the new state of South Sudan – a country that had not even existed when they were taken hostage.

With ransoms becoming increasingly difficult to extort in such situations, the pirates developed a new negotiating strategy. In order to squeeze every last dollar and cent for their hostages, they started releasing just part of the crew, demanding further payments for the remainder.

The MV *Orna* is a good example of this. Owned in Dubai, managed in Sweden, operating under a Panamanian registration, crewed by 18 Syrians and one Sri Lankan, carrying a cargo of coal from South Africa to India, and seized 400 nautical miles (740 km) north-east of Seychelles, this elderly bulk carrier had none of the value to warrant a speedy release. It was a mongrel ship that no one really seemed interested in.

Taken in December 2010, she was only released in October 2012 after a reported ransom payment of as little as US$600,000. During the period that the ship was held, just about everything that could go wrong did go wrong. She was reported as being used as a pirate mother ship for a time; the bridge and accommodation were destroyed by an on-board cooking fire; one Syrian crewman was murdered and another injured after ransom payments were delayed. This latter incident was believed to be the first time Somali pirates had killed a hostage as a tactic to speed up ransom payments.

At one stage, the captain was reported as claiming the owner had abandoned them, stating: 'We are being treated like wild beasts in the jungle. We do not have any fresh water, no toilets, and not enough food.' There were also reports of the ship being fought over by two gangs of pirates. When after 22 months the ship was finally released – having to be towed away as it could not sail under its own power – only 13 of the 19 crew were released; the remainder were held captive on land and only finally released three months later.

One of those final seafarers from MV *Orna*, released in January 2013, described his abuse at the hands of pirates: 'We were starved and tortured. The pirates would remove all our clothes, hit us with sticks covered with thorns and kick us. They would tie us up with thick rope, almost stopping our blood circulating. The nights were cold and the days were scorching hot. We were made to stare into the glare for hours.'

The MV *Orna* was not the only ransom situation that resulted in a partial release of the crew. The Malaysian-flagged container ship MV *Albedo* was hijacked in November 2010 west of the Maldives, over 900 nautical miles (1,500 km) from the Somali coast. On this occasion, there was no one at all to finance the release of the final hostages retained by the pirates.

The *Albedo* was a rust bucket of a ship with little more than scrap value, and with no insurance cover – together with an owner who either couldn't help or didn't care. The 22 crew members faced an ordeal that seemed to have no end. It was the classic polyglot crew in these situations, coming from Pakistan, Bangladesh, Iran, India and Sri Lanka.

Frustrated that there was no apparent prospect of ransom, the pirates became increasingly violent towards their hostages. After a particularly heated phone conversation with the shipowner, the pirates shot dead a young Indian crewman to raise the pressure. Captain Jawaid Khan then became the prime target of the pirates' anger and frustration – at one point, he was trussed up with rope and lowered into the sea as his captors sprayed bullets around him.

Eventually, the shipowner simply disappeared and his company went out of business, leaving the crew to their fate. After almost two years, the captain and the six Pakistani crew were released for a US$1.2 million ransom raised in a nationwide effort by Pakistani families, businessmen and charity groups. The remaining 15 crewmen continued to be held on board.

Once released, the full extent of the crew's treatment by the pirates became known.

Chief Officer Mujtaba said the pirates repeatedly hit them with pipes and with the butt of their AK-47 assault rifles. They also used pliers to rip out the webbing between men's fingers. Other torture tactics included keeping sailors in solitary confinement inside containers for days without food.

'These men are not human. When they hit us, they would not stop. They hit us on the head. They tortured us a lot. They would lock all of us into the small empty swimming pool. We couldn't sit or sleep. We had to stand. For three days they didn't give us any food or let us go to the toilet.'

For the remaining 15 sailors left on board – seven Bangladeshis, six Sri Lankans, an Indian and an Iranian – there was no prospect of release, and conditions became even harsher. Eventually the leaking ship simply sank in a storm off the Somali coast, killing four hostages and several pirates. There were now just 11 hostages ... of whom a pirate spokesman said, 'If their governments and people do nothing, they will surely die. We will start killing one by one.'

The surviving crew of the *Albedo* were held on shore within Somalia – forgotten hostages, with no company or country to pay for their ransom. After almost 1,300 days in captivity, the remaining 11 crewmen were finally repatriated to their home countries. Their salvation had come from an unexpected source – Colonel John Steed of the Hostage Support Programme (HSP) run by the United Nations Office on Drugs and Crime (UNODC) Maritime Crime Programme. I was subsequently able to track down Colonel Steed to hear his version of how he had managed to negotiate the seamen's release.

When the Panama-flagged MT *Asphalt Venture* was released after payment of a US$3.6 million ransom in 2011, the issue of partial release of hostages took a further twist: the pirates released most of the crew but kept hold of seven Indian seamen in retaliation for the arrest of Somali pirates by the Indian Navy.

NBC News quoted a pirate identified only as Ahmed as saying: 'We have received $3.6 million early this morning for the release of the tanker. The ship has just sailed away but we have taken some of its Indian crew back because the Indian government is currently holding our men. We need the Indian government to free our men so that we can release their citizens.'

This was a very different situation, and was the first time hostages had been used in this way – as political pawns – rather than to elicit ransom payment. The pirates were refusing further dealings with the shipowner, and now wanted to make their demands direct to government representatives. India has been a major player in the war against piracy – particularly as the menace has reached closer to its coastline. Indian warships have escorted merchant ships as part of international anti-piracy operations since 2008. The remaining seven Indian seamen were only released in October 2014 after over four years in captivity, extremely lengthy negotiations, and what the Maritime Piracy Humanitarian Response Programme (MPHRP) reports as 'a modest payment to cover the logistical and transport costs of the group holding the men'.

When the last four crew of the *Prantalay 12* were released late February 2015, they were the longest-serving hostages in modern pirate history. This Thai-owned/Taiwanese-flagged fishing boat was one of three sister ships hijacked in April 2010, some 1,200 nautical miles (2,220 km) from the Somali coastline. While the other two vessels were subsequently released, *Prantalay 12* and its crew were not so fortunate. Until sinking in July 2011 the boat was used as a pirate base; six crew members died while in pirate captivity; and though 14 crew were released in 2011 these remaining four men were kept back in the hope of additional ransom being paid. Until John Steed opened negotiations for their release late 2014, nothing whatsoever had been heard from them for over two years.

31

A MAN ON A MISSION

Was anyone doing anything about those forgotten hostages, abandoned by their employers and governments? I tracked down one man who is.

John Steed has devoted the last few years to helping these unfortunate souls. A man with an impressive background, he spent nearly 40 years in the British Army, the last ten based mainly in Africa, including Sudan. Mr Steed received an MBE in 2004, and after retiring from the Army in 2012 at the rank of Colonel, took up a post as the UN's Chief of Counter Piracy and Maritime Security. He is now a Senior Adviser to the United Nations Office on Drugs and Crime, and head of the Hostage Support Programme.

John's initial involvement with hostage release negotiations started while he was still in the army, both working with the UK High Commission and as military adviser to the UN's top man in Somalia. He dealt with a number of cases but primarily that of the British yachting couple Paul and Rachel Chandler, who were released by the pirates in November 2010 after 388 days of captivity. John's work only became a properly funded programme once he had left the army.

'The shipowners and insurance companies are doing absolutely nothing to help these guys. It's left to organisations like us to try and help the crews.'

In fact, to say he 'leads' the programme is perhaps too grand – along with his colleague Leo Hoy-Carrasco, he *is* the programme! When we spoke by Skype, John was talking from his bedroom in Nairobi, on the walls of which I could see various maps and charts of the Somali region.

'There's just the two of us. We use my room at home and have another little temporary office as well in the UN compound; but mainly we work from my office here in my house.'

To date, the two men have assisted in bringing 112 hostage crew home, including those of the MVs *Iceberg 1* and *Orna*.

The day we talked was the end of a very busy and successful week for John. The remaining crew of the MV *Albedo* were newly released, and he had literally just got back home after his flight to a dirt runway in Central Somalia in the small plane that had brought them home.

'It has been a long story. We've been living with the *Albedo* for nearly a year now. We first got directly involved in June or July 2013. She had been taken in November 2010 but now there were clear indications that she was taking on water, she was listing, and she was going to sink. The navies – particularly EUNAVFOR – were telling us she was getting lower in the water. As she got closer to the point of actually sinking, we engaged directly with the pirates, trying to convince them that on humanitarian grounds – although they were getting nowhere with the owner – that they ought at least put the crew in a lifeboat so that we could get a naval ship in to rescue them, purely as a safety of life at sea issue.

They ignored us and then the ship sank. Tied astern of the *Albedo* was the *Naham 3*, a Taiwanese fishing vessel that had been pirated in

March 2012. When the *Albedo* sank, we were still in communication with the pirates. The sinking must have been a terrifying experience – it happened in a storm at night. A lot of the crew couldn't swim; the pirates had most of the lifejackets; and everybody was having to jump into the water. Persuading men who can't swim, in the dark, in a storm, to jump overboard into the sea took quite a lot. Some of them didn't have lifejackets so they were clutching big water containers and literally jumped into the sea holding tight to those.

Four of the crew didn't go overboard – four of them went down with the ship. They were all Sri Lankans, they wouldn't jump into the sea, and sadly they lost their lives, although we officially list them as missing as we don't have bodies and so can't officially prove that they are dead.

Naham 3 was still tied astern of the sunken *Albedo*; this ship's engine hadn't run in 12 months so they couldn't manoeuvre. But one of the *Naham 3*'s crew, a very brave Vietnamese guy, jumped into the water and saved the lives of people who were struggling to get close to the *Naham 3* and got them out. The crew of the pirated *Naham 3* literally saved the lives of the surviving 11 crew from the *Albedo*.

We think six pirates died when she sank as well – they didn't make it either. So you ended up now with everybody on the *Naham 3*. And we are still negotiating, pointing out to the pirates that the cable joining *Naham 3* to the sunken *Albedo* isn't in great shape, so that's going to give way soon and then *Naham 3* is going to be wrecked ashore, possibly with more loss of life.

Eventually, the crew of the *Albedo* were taken ashore. By this stage, the owner can't be contacted, his Malaysian shipping company seems to have gone to ground. We ended up acting as the sort of intermediary between the crew, the international community and the pirates trying to resolve this situation, because there was nobody else to do it.

The final release of the *Albedo* crew this week – yes, there's always more than meets the eye. We were negotiating with the pirates from the time the ship sank and the crew went ashore, trying to persuade them to let the crew go on a humanitarian basis, but it was quite obvious that you can't negotiate with nothing in your pocket. These guys expect money, that's the only thing they expect and that's the only thing that's going to work. That's a pretty difficult situation for the UN; it's not a role the UN would take on. So in the absence of an owner or insurers we tried to find a coalition of donors, investors, charities, call them what you like, who might put up the sort of money that would bring the release about. In our minds, the payment of ransom and the sort of thing the pirates were looking for was out of the question, but maybe some monies could be fronted that would facilitate a release.'

It has to be understood that in situations such as this, when there is no owner or insurance company involved, the situation becomes increasingly entrenched. The pirates themselves have run up considerable expenses feeding and guarding the hostages for a long period. The guys on the ground find themselves deeply in debt both to locals and to the financiers of the operation. As the situation is a stalemate, there is increasing violence to the crew – torture, killings even; the pirates see this as a way of maybe breaking the stalemate. In an ever worsening situation, a number of agencies have come up with a compromise solution; not the payment of a ridiculous ransom, but a compensation payment to the pirates to cover their expenses so they can walk away from the situation. The pirates' 'expenses' formula is a solution that has worked in other cases where no ransom cash has been available. It will be a fraction of what the pirates would have wanted, but it will hopefully persuade them to give up on a bad business prospect, and allow the crew to go home.

It takes a great deal of negotiation to reach that point, to persuade pirates that there is no pot of gold at the end of this particular hijacking, no matter how cruelly they treat their hostages. The *Albedo* was one such situation. John had to find someone who would help pay those expenses.

'We had a response from Maritime Piracy, Humanitarian Response Programme (MPHRP), it's a UK-based charity that receives donations from the shipping industry. They offered to front up some money if we could negotiate this compensation type of release. In our discussions with the pirates, it was clear that they wanted a lot more than the charity had available, so we looked around for other donors.

A donor came forward who offered us US\$600,000, which together with the money from MPHRP gave us enough to make a deal with the pirates for what was required. Negotiating with the pirates for money was something that the UN could not do, so we handed the negotiations over to a lawyer in London appointed by the charity, who in turn appointed a kidnap and ransom negotiator who worked pro bono as they decided they were doing this for charity.

Long and short of the story – the additional money didn't come through, we ended up without the extra \$600,000. We were down to the couple of hundred thousand that the charity had offered. So we started negotiating all over again and eventually made a deal with the pirates and the local community for the release of the crew for a smaller compensation fee.

There was still a problem; we had been talking to only part of the pirate gang, not the whole gang. It was clear that those we had negotiated with were going to have some difficulty getting the crew away as more of the local investors felt they should be paid too. We had to wait for the right moment, the right conditions, which eventually came along.

The crew managed to escape out of a window into the darkness. We had arranged somebody to be waiting for them, local militia across the valley, who then transferred them to contacts from the regional government whom we paid to send a secure convoy to pick up the crew. The next day they handed them over to us.'

So how did it feel to finally secure the release of these 11 men who had been through a living uncertain hell over the last three years?

'A rollercoaster of emotions... Huge relief because we have had so many ups and downs. When the ship sank and we couldn't get them off; when we tried to find money and that all went sour; several false alarms and failed attempts to get the crew out; then the long period of waiting when they had to try and escape.

Euphoric – absolute huge sense of relief when we got them out. When we landed our plane in a desert airstrip in central Somalia and we were met by our friends from the government whom I knew very well – a lot of this is done on personal relationships and I know a lot of these guys in Somalia really well – the crew members said that was when they really believed that they were free. When they saw me and my colleague Leo getting out of the plane, that's when they knew that they were going home.

They had medicals in Nairobi and stress counselling because a lot of them had been tortured. They are just wonderful people. The Pakistani crew had been released on payment of a ransom some time ago, four guys had died, so of the remainder the Iranian bosun was the only officer. There was fabulous leadership from him; he really kept the crew together. Even during the escape they agreed to work together – if one got captured they would all give up, nobody would try and escape on their own, leaving the others behind.'

The only way that John can achieve such success is through a nonstop dialogue with the pirates, bringing them to realise that in certain cases there will never be a ransom paid.

'The basis of our negotiations is that there is no value in any ships now – for all the remaining hostages it's just about individuals on their own. There's no insurance, no shipowner behind them – there's just very poor families who can't hope to raise the sort of money that the pirates are expecting. So we have been conditioning the pirates to understand that there is no money and there is only a compensation payment for their expenses. That's the only thing that they can get.

Every day they hang on to the crew is costing them more money. Food, guards and so on. And the investors in all these negotiations expect a return on their money. Just a little bit of compensation for their "services" over the past years isn't going to generate the sort of money that they want. So it makes it difficult to get them to accept a really low fee.'

Winning the pirates' confidence is a matter of many tiny steps. One major step forward in the *Albedo* negotiations had been that some months prior to release, the pirates had allowed doctors to visit the crew members – the first time that this had ever happened in a Somali hostage situation.

'We achieved it because the doctor who we used is from the same clan as the pirates and therefore he is safe and acceptable to them. So he goes in and does an assessment and then delivers them the medicine they need. That's a huge morale boost to guys who have been kept for over three years. And it also builds up some trust with the pirates. On this programme we're not trying to screw them, we're not trying to arrest them – all we want is the hostages safely released.

And following on from that, we've also provided a doctor recently to other crews, where we are trying to warm up the negotiations: to the crews of the *Naham 3* and also the *Prantalay 12*.'

Building that relationship with the pirates is essential to John's success.

'When the *Albedo* sank, I was between jobs with the UN so was just doing this for free, from my bedroom at home. At the height of the negotiations, just after the ship had sunk and when the crew got taken ashore, I was hospitalised for a few weeks. The pirates that we were negotiating with immediately started sending messages about "How's Mister John doing?", "We are very worried about Mister John". My colleague was saying – never mind Mr John – what about these poor hostages? Let them go and Mr John will be fine if you do that.

But it's just the nature of dealing with Somalis – they can be quite funny at times.'

There are still more hostages being held by the pirates whom John and Leo are working to help.

'There are now three cases – 38 guys left. There are the 26 or 27 on the *Naham 3*, and we are talking to the negotiator right now. We are also talking to the negotiator for the Thais from *Prantalay 12* – we have been involved in that case for quite a long time. The original 14 Burmese who were released from that crew, that was our first success, the first guys that we got home.

And there are potentially ten other hostages taken by Al Shabab and others, some of whom are held by pirate groups because the pirate groups are very good at doing the negotiations. Michael Scott Moore – we've been trying to get spectacles from his mother to him through our contacts to replace those that were damaged when he was taken.' I had increasingly been discovering that the more I investigated the tangled web of Somali piracy, the more links were coming to light. Michael was the American journalist with whom Rolly Tambara had shared his captivity, and was eventually freed in September 2014.

'There are still unscrupulous shipowners out there who force their captains to cut corners, to travel without escorts or protection in the High Risk Area, and some who will still even do it without crew insurance or insurance for their ships. They are just putting people's lives at risk deliberately.

The maritime industry collectively could do more, the insurance industry, the shipping industry. The insurance industry particularly is making a lot of money in premiums from ships travelling in the High Risk Area. And yet we have just 38 guys now left, that's all, just a small handful, and it would take very little cash to get these back home; but with a very few exceptions, the shipping industry could do a hell of a lot more. Maybe they don't want to be seen to be doing it, but under the table they could do it very easily.'

It is a very valid point. Many countries have schemes funded by insurance companies that mean if someone is injured in a road traffic accident with an uninsured driver, the scheme will pay up despite the absence of insurance for that specific driver. With the shipping industry and their insurers still making massive profits, why are they not doing something to help these forgotten hostages?

John's constant contact with the pirates has given him considerable insights into their organisation, funding, and rumoured links with the militant Al Shabab organisation. He is uncompromising in his assessments.

'Each of the pirate gangs is individually clan-based, on one of the sub-clans. It's a criminal enterprise, nothing to do with illegal fishing or toxic waste dumping, or all the other excuses that people give for this. This is a bunch of kingpins who send young Somalis to sea with no real thought for their safety, and make huge money out of it. It's business, and they don't give a damn about Somali politics or Al Shabab or anything else. They are purely in it for the money.

But in the early stages, when they were operating well south of Mogadishu, south of Kismayo, in order to get down to the Mozambique Channel to operate, the pirates needed to have the co-operation of people, and in some cases those people were Al Shabab. Particularly south of Kismayo, paying a tribute to Al Shabab was essential in order to conduct their operations.

More recently, as Al Shabab have been under more military pressure, we believe there has also been some co-operation between pirate groups and Al Shabab. They are sort of operating in the same areas of Central Somalia. We've seen evidence where Al Shabab and other criminal elements have taken hostages and then they have been handed over to pirates for negotiation, because the pirate gangs are much better equipped for international negotiations – they know how to do it. Michael Scott Moore is quite a good case in point.

But philosophically, doctrinally, there is no real connection between pirates and Al Shabab; it's just a matter of convenience, and Al Shabab are particularly short of money at the moment so they have found a revenue stream from the piracy gangs in this way.

The pirates are also paying the local community who provide the guards, who provide the food, the *khat* and so on... And I'm sure some of them have Al Shabab connections. It's not a doctrinal thing – it's a marriage of convenience.'

I asked John if he thought the funding for pirate operations now came from outside Somalia.

'Clearly some of the kingpins are outside Somalia and a lot of the negotiators back in the old days could have been absolutely anywhere. The negotiator for the *Albedo* was in Mogadishu, not with the pirate gang itself. But the key investors tend to be Somalis – business people who have assets and resources outside Somalia, and this is where they place their profits. In the old days when these big ransoms were being paid, a percentage of the money was being paid to the investors on the ground for the guards, the attack teams, the local expenses. But the bulk of it they would launder in other countries, particularly Kenya and Dubai, through legitimate businesses such as building, which were part of their bigger financial empire.'

And the future?

'The shipping industry has been much better of late; it got wise as it was costing them money. The fact that piracy is down is that shipowners are implementing Best Management Practices and putting armed guards on their ships. The navies are presently making it difficult for the pirates to succeed and guards on the ships are making it impossible for the pirates to get on board. But the key thing is that the conditions that allow piracy to succeed – a ready supply of ships and an ungoverned space in central Somalia where there is no security – those conditions have not changed and they are not going to change any time soon. So if the naval presence started to reduce or the shipping industry started to cut corners, then we are going to have more ships taken again.

The solution is onshore, as everybody keeps saying. You need an element of security, but you also have to offer the people along the coast in the coastal communities an alternative. And that's what we are trying to do by developing a Somali maritime strategy, where they can make best use of their maritime resources – improve conditions in the coastal areas and offer an alternative. With organisations like UNFAO [Food and Agriculture Organization of the United Nations] redeveloping the Somali fishing industry, their tuna industry...'

And finally I wanted to know why he had given up such a high-powered job or the chance of a pleasant retirement to spend his time in stressful situations dealing with unpredictable and demanding Somali pirates, and with the lives and freedom of complete strangers as his responsibility.

'Why do I do it? I don't know! I was military attaché out here when this thing first started, we had British hostages and that's how I got involved. I guess partly because I come from a small fishing village in Cornwall, I have a lot of sympathy for the hostages. And if I don't do it, who else is going to do it? So me and my colleague Leo work for not a lot of money, but because it's the right thing to do. We did it even when we weren't being paid to do it, because there is nobody else doing it...'

In researching this book I had encountered all sorts of people, but none who impressed me more than John Steed. He has 100 per cent committed himself to being the sole lifeline that exists for these hostages who would otherwise be without hope. Our homes in Cornwall are less than 8 km (5 miles) apart; I look forward to meeting the man in the flesh next time he is home.

32

THE PIRATE CAPTAIN

'They are just another harvest of the sea – big fish to be taken.'

We'd already shaken hands, several packs of Mahé Kings had been exchanged, and we had agreed terms. No photographs, no names, but he would tell me the part of my story that I was still missing – what it is like as a pirate to capture a ship. Maalin had come through as promised, and at last had arranged for me to talk to a man who would fill in the missing piece of my investigation.

Over the past few days at Montagne Posée Prison in Seychelles, I'd spoken with around a dozen 'pirates', although not a single one had admitted that to me. Even those whose legal process was complete had still been sticking to their version of innocence. The best quote had been from Balbal: 'There are no pirates here... I've never met a pirate'! But at last I had someone who would tell the final part of the story.

The Captain – he was happy that I call him that – was physically different to the other Somalis I had met. He was easily 1.8 metres

(6 feet) tall, and well proportioned – and the most striking thing about him was his goatee beard. Now a salt-and-pepper grey, I had seen it once before, dyed a surprising shade of bright green; that had been in his arrest pictures in one of the newspaper archives I had studied. Overall, he had a distinguished bearing and a friendly smile, although I could see that quickly disappearing if he was not getting his way. An aura emanated from him of a man in control, even though he was serving a long prison term. I could imagine casual violence coming easily to him. Of all those that I interviewed, even the evil-looking Mohamed with no other name, or the aggressive Ahmed Abdi Barre, he was the Somali I would least like as my captor.

We got right to the point. I asked him to tell me what it was like to attack and capture a ship.

'You will almost always be coming from behind – usually catching up with a ship that is travelling away from you. These are not ships of war with huge crews keeping lookout, and the few men on the bridge will usually just be looking ahead, not behind. Many cargo ships do not even have windows at the rear of the bridge so they are often unaware that we are there until we are actually climbing on board, and by then it is too late for them.

As you get closer to the ship, if you run inside the wake it will have flattened the water behind, making it easier to catch up. At the last minute, you have to go through the wake of the ship. It's big and bouncy but a good boat driver can handle that; he won't take the ship's wake head-on but diagonally, so our skiff just slides over the wake. It's a rough ride but if you are gaining on the ship, then as long as the skiff's engine is good, you will get through the wake and can get in the smoother water.

Once you get alongside, if you get on the correct side of it, the ship will shelter you from any waves if the sea is rough – the sea will be much flatter there. The ship is a big steel wall protecting you from the waves. From there, it is easier to hook the ladders on to the ship's rail. There is less movement too if the boat tries to swerve to escape you.

And coming alongside at the back means you can shoot at the bridge – on most cargo ships the captain is at the back of the ship. You can scare them, shoot at the windows, maybe make them stop or hide so they don't come on deck to try and stop us getting on board.

You have a moving wall of steel next to you, sometimes choppy seas, and behind you is a huge propeller churning up the water. But you don't think about it, here is more money than you will ever have in your life... If you are the type who gets scared, you would not have been selected for the mission. This is the moment of the most excitement.

The boat driver must be good – he must know what he is doing – we have to get right alongside the ship to be able to hook the ladder over the side – sometimes the skiff hits the ship and bounces off. Both boats are travelling fast.

If we get alongside, the crew usually hide – if we shoot at them, they always hide. If they have guns on board and fire back at us, then we will not try and board – it is too dangerous – we will leave that ship and look for another. No, the ship has too much advantage and we don't want to die. Many ships have water hoses. If you get hit by them, it will knock you off your feet and fill the skiff with water. The boat driver must keep clear of them.

But some ships still don't even have hoses. Some just stop and give up if we fire the RPG at the bridge. Then it is easy...

When the ladder is hooked on, then the boat driver must get close enough again for us to jump from the skiff to the ladder. It's hard to keep the skiff alongside all the time. But when you make that leap and are climbing the ladder you know you have won – the ship is yours. That's the best excitement you can know; far better than taking a woman.'

He may have been speaking of a moment of climactic excitement, but the Captain's voice showed no emotion; perhaps because he would not know either of those pleasures for around two decades.

'Most of us have never been on anything bigger than a small skiff or fishing boat. These are giants. The first time you get on a deck, it is huge. But we have been told where the captain is and where the controls are and the crew and we head for there. Doors and lots of steps inside with lots of other doors, but ignore those and get to the bridge and the captain.

Everything is new the first time you board a ship. The smells of diesel, the noise of the ship, its movement under you, the steel deck, pipes everywhere, it's like another world for us.

You must get to the bridge as fast as you can. Do not let them use the radio. Do not let them call the warships. Do not let them talk to anybody. And we do not to talk to the warships. Though sometimes people do but that is stupid – that is just bragging, boasting, trying to be the big man. That is not our job. That is for the negotiator. Our job is to get the ship back to the coast.'

Clearly, the pirate teams were well briefed before heading out to sea.

'Firing our guns is usually enough to get the crew to obey us. You don't want to harm them as they are valuable in the negotiations. Unless they do something stupid and try and resist us, disobey us, try and call for help. Then we will hurt them.' Again, spoken so totally without emotion – my instinct told me that this man was not one to mess with.

'It is a feeling of power – of exhilaration – I control this ship – I am a rich man – the captain must obey me now. The power and excitement as I get him to turn a big ship towards Somalia. I know I can ignore the navy ships and their helicopters and planes, as they don't attack if we have hostages.

On a container ship, there are huge towers of containers – all worth money. The biggest money is oil tankers – they pay big ransoms and pay quickly. I have never captured an oil tanker. If I had, I would not be here; I would be home with my wives, my family, my animals.

The big fishing trawlers from Spain and France used to be easy to take. They would have to stop to put out their nets, and you don't even need a ladder – you can just walk up the back where they slide the nets into the sea. But not now – they all have armed guards.

When we get to shore, our work is done and we hand over to the guards who will keep the ship safe from the navy and from other pirates who might try and take it over. The locals do well too when a ransom is paid. When a ship is there, a big ship, they know that a ransom will be paid. So they let the pirates owe them money, the guards too. The *khat* dealers, everyone. They charge a lot more because they are not getting paid at first and may have to wait a long time, but when the ransom is paid everyone gets paid. Everyone does well, not just the pirates.'

Things were going well. Time for more detail.

'So, tell me about the ships you have taken.'

A flash of anger – I had clearly overstepped an invisible line.

'I have taken many ships.' And collecting the cigarettes from the table, he stood up, spoke briefly to the interpreter, and walked out of the door. Interview ended.

Only after the door had closed did the interpreter explain my mistake. So far, our conversation had all been in general terms. Once I started asking specifics, about ships for which he had not been captured or prosecuted, the Captain had decided that I was some sort of policeman, and there was no way that he or any other Somali in the prison would now speak further to me.

As I walked down the stairs for the last time, stepping over the dog which for the first time seemed to be showing signs of life, lethargically scratching itself, I felt I had got what I came for.

Balbal had been wrong; there was at least one pirate in the prison.

33

THE UN AMBASSADOR TELLING IT AS IT IS

Famously outspoken, Ambassador Ronny Jumeau is one of the true characters of the United Nations political scene. He was Seychelles Permanent Representative to the UN at the height of the piracy crisis, and addressed the UN Security Council on the matter when it was discussing piracy off the coast of Somalia in August 2010.

He was also on the Contact Group on Piracy off the Coast of Somalia (CGPS) which was created in January 2009 following a UN Security Council resolution.

He is currently Seychelles' New York-based roving Ambassador for Climate Change and Small Island Developing State Issues, dealing with such key issues as oceans, biodiversity and the environment, sustainable development, and renewable energy.

I was fortunate to catch him during one of his rare visits home to Seychelles. I'd suggested that we meet at his office, but ever keen to get out of town, Ronny came down to the beach by taxi, and we sat on the terrace of the tiny cottage I was renting. A heavy rainstorm hammered down on the corrugated roof, at times making it hard for us to speak; when that happened we would just sit in silence till it passed, watching the rain clouds roll across the ocean, and finally a rainbow break through, arching from horizon to horizon. My first question was one that I had been trying to find an answer to without success.

Why has there been no real UN intervention in Somalia, when the UN seems prepared to seek resolution in most situations? There has been minor UN intervention and food aid, but not on a scale that could really change things on the ground.

'Somalia is too messy. Who do you talk to in Somalia? The people holed up in Mogadishu hardly control Mogadishu. And how do you talk to Somaliland and Puntland without conveying a certain amount of legitimacy? It's very complex. You have the Federal Transitional Government which is based in Mogadishu, which for some time couldn't even control Mogadishu. You have breakaway states – Somaliland, Puntland – who control their areas better than the central government controls Mogadishu. The UN recognises the central government, so how do you talk to these others without ... sending the message that it's OK to break away? Especially when west of them, you have the example of South Sudan and Sudan.

So, in Somalia who do you talk to? It's a lawless country – I repeat – who do you talk to. There's no starting point – the UN has to have some sort of legitimate government to support, to invite them in under international law – otherwise it becomes an invasion, an illegitimate intervention. You need some sort of authority who says, "I need help, can you come in and assist me." Somalia is a country with borders, on paper at least it has a government, but until that government tells you "I need your help," there's not much that the UN can do.

And then when you say to them I want to go here, I want to deliver food there, they say, "I can't get you there." So, can I go talk to the rebels? And if I do that, does that mean I am recognising the rebels as another government? There are all these complexities, which is why the UN as a military force has kept out of Somalia.

We had a meeting here in Seychelles to discuss the repatriation of convicted pirates to serve out their sentences in Somalia and invited the Ministers of Justice of the Federal Government in Mogadishu, of Somaliland and Puntland, and it was the first time that they had even sat in the same room together! If the Mogadishu government had not attended we could not have spoken with the others – it was their presence that legitimised the meeting.'

I'd never before heard as a reason for the UN not intervening in a country that it was just in too much of a mess! They had sent peacekeeping forces into such hotspots as the Balkans, Central African Republic, Rwanda, Haiti, and the Democratic Republic of Congo. But Ronny's insight made sense. In all those countries, there had been a government structure and the UN role had generally been to act as a peacekeeper or to monitor the situation, not to rebuild a whole nation state from the ground up.

Like many with whom I had spoken, Ronny felt that the international community could have done far more and far sooner.

'If piracy had been a global scourge, the world would have acted far more quickly, but it was limited to the Indian Ocean, it was Somalia. They weren't interested in Somalia ... hadn't been for the last 20 years or more. But they may be interested now. If Sudan has oil, if Uganda has oil, if Kenya has oil, Tanzania has found offshore oil and gas, Mozambique has potentially more gas than Qatar, then it's almost certain that Somalia has oil and/or gas... *Then* the world will sort out Somalia – they will find that they can do all sorts of things that they couldn't do before. I'm cynical about this, but I know how it works... I've read that they think that the mother lode of oil may be in Somalia itself.

Piracy helped concentrate minds, because now they were hitting foreign interests directly, by taking ships or cargo or people. Now we had powerful interests in other countries, shipowners, fishing companies, traders, the commercial sector, who if their ships weren't taken wouldn't have cared about Somalia. If the Somalis want to tear themselves to pieces, that's their concern – until you take my ship, until you take my cargo, my crew...

Then suddenly, you have insurance companies coming in, you have bankers coming in, you have traders coming in, and saying to their own governments – you have got to solve this problem, because this is hitting our revenue. And that bit always works. It doesn't matter if they are starving over there, at least they are not starving on our doorstep. The commercial interests don't care, until they take a ship.

So Mister so and so tycoon picks up a phone and says, "What the bloody hell is happening, they are taking our ships now..."

During his term at the UN, Ronny had been able to observe exactly how the world reacted to the piracy threat. But eventually, it was tiny Seychelles that led the way in legislating to combat the problem.

'People, for political reasons, hid behind the fact that there wasn't any international law on piracy – until Seychelles came along and embarrassed them. If a warship picked up pirates in international waters, what were they going to do? They were taking them back to the beaches of Somalia, because it was just too complicated legally. They were getting away with it! They were being given a telling off, a finger-wagging, put back on the beach and they were back out on the next boat.

So you know what Seychelles did? We just changed the law. We made our law applicable to the situation.

This nonsense from so many countries, "We can't try piracy in our courts." If you don't want your seamen taken hostage, go to the legislature and change the law! So this is what we did – we changed the law. It was just political will. It was just that the threat was so big to us, we had to do something, to send a message and say don't mess with us. Seychelles is the second most impacted country by piracy after Somalia itself. No other economy was affected like us.

We had to do something to protect ourselves, and it just happened to benefit the whole international community. Something had to be done and we did it – we felt we had to do what was necessary. We led the world, we changed our laws, and said – look, if you capture pirates, bring them here, we will give them a fair trial, legal representation, and if they are found guilty we will give them sentences that will deter others.

We got serious about piracy when no one else would. We are the smallest country in Africa, the smallest in the region, we looked not for excuses but for solutions – how do we solve this problem. It was simply political will, and a very practical look at the issue. We didn't agonise over it – does it fall within international law? Fine, then let's do it. And suddenly everyone starts queueing up to dump the pirates they capture here, for us to deal with. They claim that back home they can't do it – but if we could do it, if we could change our laws to meet the 21st-century problem that piracy poses, then why can't these other countries?

Some Western countries – they say, well if we have them in our courts, our prisons, then they are going to claim asylum and we will then have to house them and support them at cost to our taxpayers – well, just don't give them asylum! They are pirates! They are convicted pirates! They shouldn't qualify for asylum!!'

Ronny's voice goes theatrically high as he ponders the ridiculousness of the situation...

'You convict them of a crime in your courts. Do you then take foreign criminals into your asylum programme?'

I had to agree with him; because of the stupidity of the European Human Rights Laws, we probably would be legally obliged to grant asylum, or keep the pirate sitting in a nice house on state benefits for many years while legally aided lawyers argued his case through the appeals processes, all at public expense.

'I think Seychelles played a big role. We said OK NATO, OK EU, OK USA, we are taking these pirates off your hands and jailing them at such a rate that around a quarter of our prison population are pirates. That's way too many. Either we stop taking the pirates from your navies, and you will have to find somewhere else to try them, or you help me get rid of the ones that have been convicted. In other words, can we send them home to serve their time in prisons in Somalia? By that stage, the UN were already building jails in Somaliland and Puntland, so by that act alone, they were conveying a certain degree of legitimacy to the governments there.

Much of the progress that's been made has been through the UN. Take the courts, even if the British are sending prosecutors to help us prosecute the suspected pirates, it's still all through UNODOC. If the UN hadn't built jails in Puntland and Somaliland, we would have reached the stage when we would have stopped taking pirates off the hands of foreign navies and trying them. So it wasn't a British thing, or a NATO thing, it was a UN thing, which means you can engage the Chinese, the Russians, the Indians. It's not a Western thing, a NATO thing, this is Africa. We worked a lot through UNODC, and the fund that they have set up against piracy, that's under the UN.

And of course the UN has been active on the ground through all the humanitarian work. That has been massive, and without it who knows how many tens of thousands more may have died.'

I wanted Ronny's take on the origins of piracy – the image of latter-day sea-going Robin Hoods, stealing from the rich who were despoiling their seas.

'The Somalis have always used that argument and there was a certain amount of truth in it, but what people don't know is that Somalia never had an EEZ (Exclusive Economic Zone), never demarcated their EEZ. I don't think they have even done it up to now. So when they say you are taking fish from my waters, where are your waters? Apart from your territorial 12-mile limit, of course.

I think a lot of foreign fishing boats were probably fishing too close to the Somali shore, without licences, but then they didn't have a government authority to go to in any case to get a licence! And they couldn't get a licence because Somalia didn't have an EEZ. That's the part that's not told. It's more complex. How can you be unlicensed if there is no authority to grant a licence to you?

But even if that was their argument, maybe they would have a degree of legitimacy seizing ships illegally fishing or dumping in their territorial waters – but not 1,000 miles (1,610 km) away, in someone else's waters or the open ocean! There is no justification either morally or politically for that. And once you start taking *our* fishermen fishing in *our* waters, then *we* have every right to stop you.'

Ronny was becoming quite impassioned now, banging his hand on the table for emphasis. It was clear that whatever wrongs may have been done to the Somalis, he had no truck with them taking it out on the Seychelles people.

'First of all, get your own act in order. You can't accuse someone of trespassing until you define where your boundary is. And we go round in circles – to set up an EEZ, to set up those boundaries, you need an authority, a government, a maritime administration to talk to.

I think piracy was an indication that not enough was being done on the ground in Somalia. But in time, it became clear that piracy was being orchestrated from abroad, from foreign capitals, by people in the diaspora and other people – and that's when the Somalis lost any sympathy.

The answer to piracy lies in Somalia. What makes you want to take a boat and go out to sea and risk your life like that? Somalia is not the only state with problems, but apart from West Africa and the Malacca Straits, which has been an age-old problem, why don't we see this elsewhere? Why don't we see poor people in South Africa doing it – there's a lot of shipping going to Durban and around the

Cape. There have been terrible problems in Mozambique – why didn't they do it?'

I knew Ronny had a meeting with the President scheduled soon, so pressed on to the final point I wanted to discuss: the future.

'Piracy has been contained for now. So some people say there is no need for the massive expense of keeping warships off the Somali coast. But if you pull out and don't solve the problem on land, the pirates are going to come back. Now we have contained it, and showed them they can't solve their poverty issues, their survival issues, by taking ships any more, maybe there are other ways.

We recently had a delegation of fisheries officials from all regions of Somalia here in Seychelles. Together with the UNFAO (Food and Agriculture Organization of the United Nations), we are looking at the possibility of Seychelles using its know-how and experience in industrial fisheries to help Somalia set up an industrial fishing industry. We are the smallest country in the region, but we have the most developed tuna fishery. And they are looking at the possibility of Seychellois going to Somalia to train them on the ground, bringing Somalis to the Seychelles Fishing Authority to be trained, advising them how to set up an EEZ and then license boats to fish in their EEZ. Their port infrastructure is not yet ready to trans-ship fish, but fish caught in Somali waters could be trans-shipped in Seychelles until their ports are up and running.

It is in our interests to get the guys who were pirates to become fishermen. And this is the irony now – the smallest country in Africa – it's not the Kenyans who are going to help set up their fishing industry, not the Tanzanians, not even the Mauritians – it's the Seychellois who are the most advanced in industrial fishing. What a story it's going to be when this plays out.

It's an example to the whole world. Not only is Seychelles the smallest country in Africa, the last time I checked, Seychelles was among the dozen smallest countries in the world, both in size of land and in size of population. And we are offering to do in Somalia what the international community should have been doing a long time ago. If things go well according to the discussions we are now having, the smallest country in Africa is going to help solve one of the most intractable problems they have ever had.'

Ronny's taxi had been waiting at my gate for several minutes so it was time for him to go. But he left on an optimistic note. Yes, wouldn't it be a great story if Africa's smallest nation could help sort out Somalia's problems, when the combined might of the planet's naval forces had failed.

34

NO HAPPY ENDINGS

Written two thousand years ago, the New Testament Bible told of the four horsemen of the Apocalypse. All four have ridden across Somalia's scorched red earth over the past 20 years – conquest, war, famine and death. But there have been additional riders – degradation of the ocean, toxic waste poisoning, drought, exodus, and in the mass refugee camps loss of hope.

Out of all this arose piracy. For its victims, it was and remains a fearful plague. The ordeal of freed hostages will haunt many of them for the rest of their lives. Some hostages still await deliverance, enduring dreadful conditions; a number of others never survived being taken by the pirates.

Among international politicians, some naively now claim that the problem of piracy is resolved. In 2013 and 2014, there were no successful attacks on merchant ships by pirates in the region. The cost of piracy to the global economy fell yet again. Surely all is now well, or at least on the way there?

Statistics are hard to collate, deriving from multiple sources including international agencies, governments and navies; but the most respected source of information is the annual Oceans Beyond Piracy report.

While agreeing that there were no merchant ships pirated in 2013, they report hijacks on regional shipping of four smaller vessels – two dhows and two fishing boats, with 60 crew between them, in that year. They have also gathered reports of 23 actual attacks on shipping and 145 suspicious approaches, many of which were ended by warning shots from on-board security.

More than one-third of those suspicious approaches were to tankers, which of course with their low freeboards when fully laden are easy to board and make extremely valuable prizes.

Only 18 days into 2014 came the first pirate attack on an oil tanker in the Gulf of Aden. The attack was beaten off by the on-board security team, and the EUNAVFOR ships diverted to the scene subsequently arrested five suspected pirates on board a dhow that they had seized several days before and since then used as a mother ship.

A further unsuccessful pirate attack the following month evidenced that vigilance could not be relaxed. As Lieutenant Commander Jacqui Sherriff had said to me when I visited EUNAVFOR HQ, 'We have to be lucky every time – the pirates only have to get lucky once.'

The cost of Somali piracy to the world economy has also plummeted. Oceans Beyond Piracy estimated it peaked in 2010 at US$12 billion, falling in 2012 to around US$6 billion, and in 2013 to US$3 billion.

Much of the reduction is due to the shipping industry reverting to previous practices. With the security curtain of the world's navies and the consequent reduction in pirate activity, shipowners have been able to review their own economics in this largely safer climate.

They have reconsidered the cost of on-board security and now use cheaper teams from nations such as the Philippines; routes have returned to tracking closer to the Somali coast, reducing the expense of detours; average speeds have dropped back to optimum economic speeds giving massive savings on fuel costs; and the cost of insurance has fallen substantially from its scandalous peak.

Although costs have plummeted, that still amounts to US$3 billion in one year. If even a proportion of that were invested in the future of Somalia, what a difference it might make.

Human costs have also remained high. Another Oceans Beyond Piracy report in 2012 tallied up the deaths and found that 35 hostages lost their lives as a result of pirate activity in 2011. These tragedies resulted from attacks, malnutrition, or simply getting caught in the crossfire. Also during that year, 111 Somali pirates died in clashes. In total, 1,206 people were held hostage by pirates in 2011, of whom 57 per cent reported mistreatment, including physical abuse and employment as human shields. Pirate gangs still hold a number of hostages, captive now for years rather than months.

The pirates also received ransom monies in 2013 – an estimated US$21.6 million, down from US$31.75 million in 2012 and considerably less than the 2011 peak, when they hit the jackpot with US$159.62 million in ransom fees.

Much of the figure from 2013 came from the ransom of two ships that had been captured during the previous year. The Panama-flagged chemical tanker MT *Royal Grace* and the Greek-owned oil tanker MT *Smyrni* were both released in the same week: the *Royal Grace* with its crew of 20 had been held for a year, and the *Smyrni* with 26 men for ten months. The Smyrni had been taken while in transit with a cargo of crude oil, valued at US$130 million.

It was interesting to read the Reuters news report of the latter ship's release, as quoted by Oceanus Live. The shipowners themselves had declined to comment on the amount of ransom paid;

Reuters, however, included a statement not from the shipowners but from a chief pirate:

'"We took $9.5 million in ransom money and got off from the crude tanker on Friday night," Isse Abdulahi, who is understood to be one of four pirates who financed the hijacking operation, told Reuters by telephone.'

It reads almost like an announcement of annual trading figures from the CEO of an international corporation – a named pirate financier telling the world his results.

The dry statistics may offer some complacency; but they should not. Somali pirates currently hold no large cargo vessels, but there are still many high-risk hostages who remain in their grasp – and the hunters still lie in wait out there on the high seas.

When I produced my documentary for *National Geographic* in 2012, the narration over the opening sequence was: 'For the first time in our planet's history, the navies of every superpower are united in battle with a common enemy – a couple of thousand ragtag barefoot Somalis in small boats. And it's a battle that is increasingly recognised as unwinnable.'

If I wrote that opening narration today, I would have to amend it – the navies are winning the day-to-day battles and piracy is indeed being contained and restricted, but the war is far from won. The question is, how long can the world continue to fund this costly naval presence off Somalia? Certainly not indefinitely.

The pirates are still there, as are the financiers and business interests that profit from their attacks. The analogy of a fizzy drink in a bottle is still the most apt. Remove the lid – take away the enormous co-ordinated international naval presence – and piracy will froth out of the bottle once again.

Whatever else it has achieved, piracy has focused the minds of the world on Somalia, because over the previous two decades the world had simply looked the other way. Apart from the work of the aid agencies, Somalia had been left to its own devices. In fact, if the phenomenon of piracy had not arisen, the world would probably still be ignoring Somalia.

The European Union Center of North Carolina is funded by the EU with a declared mission statement to advance knowledge and understanding of the EU and its member countries. In their EU Briefings of July 2011 they conceded that: 'For the EU and US, Somalia would not be a cause for active concern were it not for the growth of the piracy industry, which is having a substantial impact on shipping traffic moving through the Gulf of Aden and the Indian Ocean near Somalia.'

Western financial interests were threatened, and at last Somalia became a priority issue. All parties concerned recognise that the long-term solution to piracy in the region lies not on the ocean but on land.

To keep down the costs of fighting piracy – the expense of maintaining fleets of warships, the additional overheads to the shipping industry – the world has been forced to focus on this troubled nation. Potential mother lodes of oil and gas, which cynics might say have been the only reason for Western nations' previous interventions in Asia and Africa – have aroused keen interest. Exploratory rigs are already drilling off the Southern Somali coast and in other locations, but a well-regulated nation is essential if exploitation becomes economically realistic, and highly desirable in light of the world's need for new sources of fossil fuels.

In 2012, after countless transitional governments, Somalia's first formal parliament in more than 20 years was sworn in, although due to fear of attack by Al Shabab, this took place not in Mogadishu's parliament building but at the city's heavily fortified airport, which adjoins the base for 17,000 African Union troops. The world is placing great hope in this administration as the first step towards a more stable and united Somalia, but in truth there is a mountain to climb.

This mountain includes recouping territory from Al Shabab, which still remains a huge threat to the very physical safety of the government – as shown in their attack on the parliament building in Mogadishu in May 2014. Opening the assault with a car bomb and suicide bomb, members of Al Shabab fought their way into the building itself, and were only repulsed after a gun battle lasting for several hours, resulting in nearly 20 fatalities. This incident was preceded by a February strike on the presidential palace in Mogadishu that left at least 17 people dead, and followed by a further raid on the palace in July. Al Shabab have also extended their deadly tentacles into neighbouring Kenya, where it has been responsible for random lethal attacks.

Even now, the question of who controls Somalia is very pertinent. Other than the breakaway regions of Puntland and Somaliland, a map of Somalia would show numerous and fluctuating areas of influence. The Islamists control the majority of the land area; regions close to the Ethiopian border are pro-government, backed by Ethiopian support; the government itself controls the small Mogadishu enclave and a region close to the Kenyan border, propped up by African Union forces. Only in the region close to the Puntland border do pro-government administrations survive without external assistance. It's an ever-changing patchwork and hardly a united nation.

The anticipated immense reserves of oil and gas could be the saving of Somalia. If confirmed, it seems likely that the world's industrial nations, with their ever-increasing demands for fuel resources and with existing supplies slowly drying up or threatened by political instability, would suddenly find the commitment to help Somalia function – at whatever the cost.

As Ronny Jumeau pointed out, Somalia is also sitting on a second gold mine if it could get organised enough to exploit it – its coastal waters have been described by Peter Lehr, Lecturer in Terrorism Studies at the University of St Andrews, as 'an El Dorado for fishing fleets of many nations.' A 2006 study published in the journal *Science* predicted that at the current rate of commercial fishing, by 2050 the planet's oceans would be virtually devoid of commercial fishing stocks. While in most other parts of the region many species have been exploited to the extent that fisheries have collapsed, thanks to the no-go zone created by piracy Somalia's seas still offer rich fisheries for shark, tuna, lobster, sardines and mackerel.

If Somalia's fishery were protected and properly exploited, alongside the establishment of an Economic Exclusion Zone, appropriately controlled by a non-corrupt licensing agency, then instead of Somalia losing US$300 million each year to illegal fishing, the EUNAVFOR briefing that I attended estimated that Somalia could earn US$475 million per annum from fishing licences.

Would it not be a happy ending if, as Ambassador Ronny Jumeau predicted, the smallest country in Africa that, after Somalia, was most heavily affected by piracy – Seychelles – could help Somalia turn the situation around and establish their EEZ and industrial fishery. Great oaks from little acorns grow...

For all this to happen there must be a stable administration in place, governing a confident, well-run nation. If despite all the odds the government in Mogadishu does succeed, even as a united federation of three Somali states, there is hope. Is it naive optimism to believe that Somalia might become one united country? Might it be more realistic to recognise the three main components as independent states and deal with them as such – for the world finally to acknowledge the progress made by Somaliland and to a lesser extent Puntland? International recognition as independent countries would give them instant access to many forms of constructive international aid that as just regional governments they are currently denied.

Until the failed state of Somalia is once more ruled by a strong government, and poverty, lawlessness and desperation are no longer the driving force, the unique 21st-century phenomenon of Somali piracy will remain a constant and dangerous threat to seafarers in the western Indian Ocean.

Until then, there will always be young men willing to risk their lives in small boats.

APPENDIX 1

SEYCHELLES POLICE

Memorandum of Interview before formal charge

Name of Officer recording memorandum
  of interview:

Rank: D/C No:

Name of Witness: Rank: No:

Name of Interpreter:

CB No:

Statement of: Abdirahaman Nur

Surname: Roble   Other Names:
                                   Abdirahaman Nur

Clan: Hawye   Sub Clan: Abgal

Address: Mogadishu   Tel No:

Occupation: Watchman   Religion: Muslim

Nationality: Somalian

Date and place of birth: 19 years old, Jowhar

Dated: 06 September
  2012, Time 13:38hrs   Place of caution:
                                   Mont Fleuri Station

(Rule II: You are not obliged to say anything unless you wish to do so, but what you say may be put into writing and given in evidence.)

I, Abdirahaman Nur Roble wish to make a statement. I want Detective Constable Timothy Hoarau to write down the answers I give. I have been told that I need not say anything unless I wish to do so and whatever I say may be given in evidence.

Memorandum of Interview recorded with the assistance of Mr Abdullahi Yerrow Salat who acts as interpreter by translating questions asked in English to Somalian and translating answers given in Somalian to English which are recorded in writing.

Prisoner informed of Constitutional Rights: YES.

Q1. Do you understand these rights?
A. Yes.

Q2. You have been arrested on suspicion of having committed an act of Piracy on the 11th of August 2012 by the Dutch Navy Ship HNLMS ROTTERDAM?
A. They did not arrest me, I surrendered to the ship.

Q3. In which part of Somalia are you staying and with whom?
A. I have one wife named Darajo Osman who lives in Galkayo in Mudug region, and I have another wife who lives with my mother in Mogadishu and her name is Raho Abdirahman.

Q4. For how long have you been in that profession?
A. I have been a watchman for seven months.

Q5. Is that your first job? Do you like it?
A. No, my first job was a welder.

Q6. Who recruited you for this trip? Who is he?
A. Abdihrahman Gardheere. He is the owner of the skiff.

Q7. What was your port of departure?
A. Gesalay.

Q8. When was that?
A. Since one month ago.

Q9. What kind of boat did you leave in? What was the name of the boat? How many were you?
A. A small skiff. The skiff's name is *Leila Alawi*. There were six of us.

Q10. What was the purpose of the trip?
A. We went to sea to escort a fishing vessel and bring it ashore.

Q11. Who was the Captain?
A. All of us knew how to ride a boat.

Q12. What type of equipment did you have on the boat?
A. We had a satellite phone, a GPS device, food and drinking water.

Q13. What type of weapons did you have?
A. We had three AK-47s and an RPG.

Q14. You said you were going to escort the fishing vessel to port: where was the boat and who was the owner of the boat?

A. The boat was an Iranian vessel. I do not know the name and the owner of the boat.

Q15. Who told you to escort the boat?

A. The owner of the skiff, Mr Abdihrahman, and the one man named Bashir.

Q16. Who are those two persons?

A. They are two well-known businessmen in Somalia, Iran and Oman.

Q17. How did you end up on the Pakistani vessel *Burhan Noor*?

A. When we left Somalia, after five days we had an engine problem; we drift away by the waves until we met a Somalian boat escorting goats from Somalia to Oman. We asked them for assistance; they gave us food and water, and the captain told us that there is a Pakistani boat coming from Dubai – it will take us to Bosaso. Then a German warship approached us and told us to stand aside so they can search the Pakistani boat. As we were getting on one side, Dutch ship approached and told us we have to surrender. We surrender to the warship and left our weapons with the Pakistani captain.

Q18. Who fired the two shots to *Burhan Noor*?

A. None of us.

Q19. Where are your weapons?

A. The Pakistani captain throws it in the water.

Q20. What happened to the boat you were supposed to escort to Somalia?

A. We did not manage to see it.

Q21. How many Pakistanis were there on board the Pakistani vessel?

A. There were several of them.

Q22. There were reports saying that the Pakistani vessel was going to Oman but you forced the boat to divert to Somalia?

A. Those reports are not true.

Q23. Is there anything else you want to say?

A. Yes if there is justice in this world I want to sue the warship that detained me. I also left some clothes and cream that was given to me by the Pakistani captain. I want to contact my people in Somalia for me to speak to my wife as she is pregnant.

Statement was read over to me. I was invited to correct, alter or add anything, if I wish to do so. This statement is true; I made it voluntarily.

Signed: Abdirahaman Nur Roble

Transcript is quoted verbatim.

APPENDIX 2

EUNAVFOR Press Release
· 21 November 2014

EU Naval Force Somalia
www.eunavfor.eu

The Council of the European Union has extended the EU's counter-piracy Operation Atalanta by two more years, until 12 December 2016. The Operation's main focus is the protection of World Food Programme vessels delivering humanitarian aid to Somalia; and the deterrence, repression and disruption of piracy off the Somali coast. In addition, Operation Atalanta contributes to the monitoring of fishing activities off the coast of Somalia.

Despite the significant progress that has been achieved off the coast of Somalia since the operation was launched in 2008, it is widely recognised that the threat from piracy remains; the pirate business model is fractured but not broken. The Council of the European

Union has therefore added certain secondary tasks to the Operation's mandate. EU Naval Force will now contribute, within existing means and capabilities, more widely to the EU's comprehensive approach to Somalia, including in support of the EU Special Representative for the Horn of Africa. It will also be able to contribute to other relevant international community activities helping to address the root causes of piracy in Somalia.

In this respect, the operation could, for example, provide logistical support, expertise or training at sea for other EU actors, in particular the EU mission on regional maritime capacity building (EUCAP NESTOR). In addition, Operation Atalanta can also support the EU Training Mission (EUTM) Somalia.

'EU Operation Atalanta has considerably helped in reducing piracy off the Somali coast. We must maintain the pressure on pirates to help ensuring security in the Horn of Africa. This is in our mutual interest,' EU High Representative for Foreign Affairs and Security Policy Federica Mogherini said. 'The EU Naval Force will now also contribute to addressing the root causes of piracy,' she added.

The common costs of EU Naval Force for the two years 2015 and 2016 are estimated at €14.7 million. The operation is currently commanded by Major General Martin Smith MBE of the UK Royal Marines. Together with 21 EU member states, two non-EU countries currently contribute to Operation Atalanta.

APPENDIX 3

STATEMENT FROM MINISTER JEAN-PAUL ADAM
MINISTRY OF FOREIGN AFFAIRS, SEYCHELLES
JANUARY 2015

At the peak of the phenomenon of piracy off the coast of Somalia, the repercussions of this illicit activity sent tremors through the fabric of Seychellois society and had a grave impact on the socio-economic stability of the state. We were conscious of the fact that we needed a consolidated effort from international partners who offered greater resources to combat the scourge. Seychelles also stressed that the problem of piracy was global in a nature akin to the threat of terrorism.

The support of the international community in assisting Seychelles to fight piracy has been remarkable and we are presently reaping the benefits as the piracy business model has been broken. Seychelles has also emerged as a leader in finding innovative ways through its inter-ception, prosecution and legislation to break the piracy model. Seychelles has been at the frontline in the battle against Somali pirates, and has been instrumental in detaining and sharing evidence with international partners to incarcerate the main financiers of piracy.

It is important to reiterate that there is no place for complacency. We are better connected today than we ever where, in terms of our regional intelligence sharing practices and coordination, and have sent a strong message that no impunity will be tolerated for crimes of piracy.

However we are very conscious of the fact that we must continuously reinforce our maritime security framework. Piracy can easily re-emerge in the context of several areas of instability in the Indian Ocean and Horn of Africa.

The security capacity of the region, through initiatives such as the East Africa Standby Force, should also be reinforced as piracy evolves to incorporate new maritime security challenges including arms, narcotics and human trafficking. There is also the added dimension that terrorist groups use established sea routes for their own gain thus posing a severe security threat to humanity.

We must maintain the proactive relationship we have with all parties involved in helping to ensure no tolerance and no resurgence in piracy.

ACKNOWLEDGEMENTS

For being so generous with their time and sharing so much valuable insight, I'm grateful to President James Michel, Ambassador Ronny Jumeau, Minister Joel Morgan, Colonel (Retd.) John Steed MBE and Minister Jean-Paul Adam.

I'd also like to thank Francis Roucou both for his time and for permission to use extracts from his book *88 Days*.

Superintendent Maxime Tirant, Raymond St. Ange, Srdjana Janosevic and Beatty Houreau for their invaluable help to me in achieving access to interviewees.

Abdullahi Yerrow Salat for several shared days in Montagne Posée prison and his patient and extremely accurate translation skills.

Gilbert Victor, Rolly Tambara and Stephen Barbe for reliving and sharing their hostage experiences with me.

Judge Duncan Gasawaga, Tony Juliette and Michael Mulkerrins for their assistance with the legal aspect of the issue.

Captain and crew of the *Maersk Weymouth*, MV *Alakrana*, Seychelles Coastguard vessel *Topaz*, pilot and crew of the Seychelles Defence Force patrol aircraft, and Commander Enrique Cubeiro and crew of SPS *Patiño*, all of whom gave me access, insight and shared first-hand experiences.

Commander Jacqueline Sherriff MBE and Squadron Leader Geoff Fleming of EUNAVFOR.

Dr Anja Shortland for permission to quote her intriguing research paper.

Jim Hills – I owe you a couple of pints in The Ship!

Oceans Beyond Piracy, on whose highly authoritative annual reports I relied substantially.

Fionn Crow Howieson, who worked with me on the film *Pirates in Paradise* and for reading the first proofs.

Elizabeth Multon, for the original concept and guiding me through the process from initial proposal to final publication.

Clara Jump and Henry Lord from Bloomsbury.

Monica Byles for her careful and constructive editing.

And of course the Somali prisoners who agreed to speak to me.